NANDIPHA MNTAMBO

NKULE MABASO

Penny Siopis

robin rhode

SAM NHLENGETHWA

Same Mdluli

SANTU MOFOKENG

STEPHANÉ CONRADIE

STEPHEN HOBBS

SUE WILLIAMSON

NISI NKOSI

THANIA PETERSEN

THULI MLAMBO-JAME

USHA SEEJARIM

WAYNE BARKER

William Kentridge

ZANDER BLOM

COBI LABUSCAGNE

First published by Jacana Media (Pty) Ltd in 2019

10 Orange Street
Sunnyside
Auckland Park 2092
South Africa
+2711 628 3200
www.jacana.co.za

ISBN 978-1-4314-2912-7

Cover design and layout by Breinstorm Brand Architects
Editing by Efemia Chela
Proofreading by Megan Mance
Set in FreightMicro 9/12pt
Printed by Multiprint Litho
Job no. 003586

See a complete list of Jacana titles at www.jacana.co.za

EXPLORE! AWESOME SOUTH AFRICAN ARTISTS

by COBI LABUSCAGNE

Illustrated by LAUREN MULLIGAN

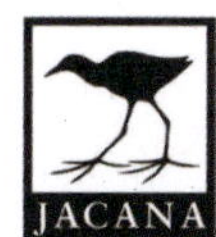

JACANA

The artists within these pages take the time to look at what is going on around them, who they are, what the world is like, then create artworks or exhibitions that can help us understand these things better. I am very grateful to all the artists who made time to speak to me about their work and their lives.

I hope that *Explore! Awesome South African Artists* introduces you to some of our great artists working today so you can go on and learn more about them. Enjoy this book and know that you can become an artist yourself if you really want to.

COBI LABUSCAGNE

CONTENTS

ANDREW TSHABANGU

Growing up in Soweto around the late 1970s Andrew Tshabangu followed his older brothers around. He loved going to the community centre with them, there were different activities at the centre. Through theatre, visual arts, poetry and music he got to understand why there was so much political violence in his township. At the centre, he listened to poets like Ingoapele Madingoane who was known for his acclaimed poem 'Africa My Beginning, Africa My End' and became aware of the political situation in the country.

When he finished school, Andrew wanted to study theatre, but his school, like many schools in black communities, did not prepare him well enough to be accepted by the Wits University drama school. He was denied and decided to go the Alexandra Art Centre to study photography, to make a portfolio so he could reapply. But as time went by, he met friends at the centre and they were interested in enlarging their scope of photography. They went to libraries, museum exhibition openings and encouraged each other to build their own portfolios. He tried to start working as a freelance photographer, but business was slow. Most of the available work went to white photographers at the time.

As a young photographer Andrew was aware of the stories that were being told in the media about black lives. He knew there were many other stories and lives that were very different from those images that were in the news day after day. He wanted to tell other South African stories of religion, schools, shebeens, grieving, public transportation and so on. He was, and still is, interested in the quieter stories of his community. He was influenced by the previous generation of documentary photographers, such as Peter Magubane, Ernest Cole, David Goldblatt, and other *Drum* photographers. But his mentor Santu Mofokeng encouraged him to have his own voice, and said to him, 'Who is Andrew Tshabangu, what does he want to say?' These conversations shaped him and were very valuable to him as he was developing his own voice as a photographer. His first solo exhibition was curated by Santu in the city of Bamako, in Mali. Like Santu, Andrew became more famous outside of South Africa before people started noticing him in his home country.

Andrew feels that, as South Africans, we are still far from each other. He believes that people were told that by now South Africa would be different for everyone. But it has not happened for the majority. For Andrew, that is still the South African story that belongs at the centre of the table.

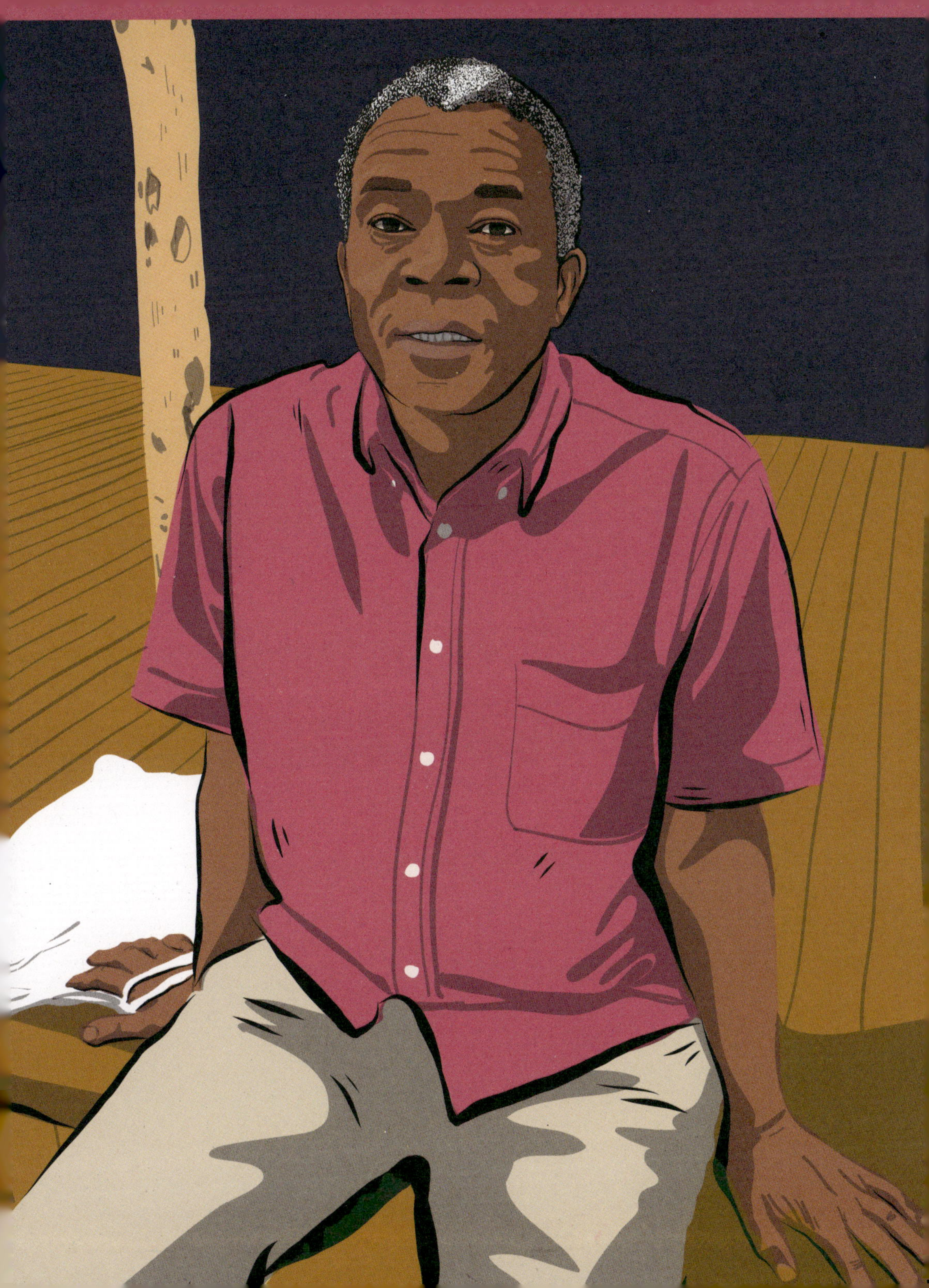

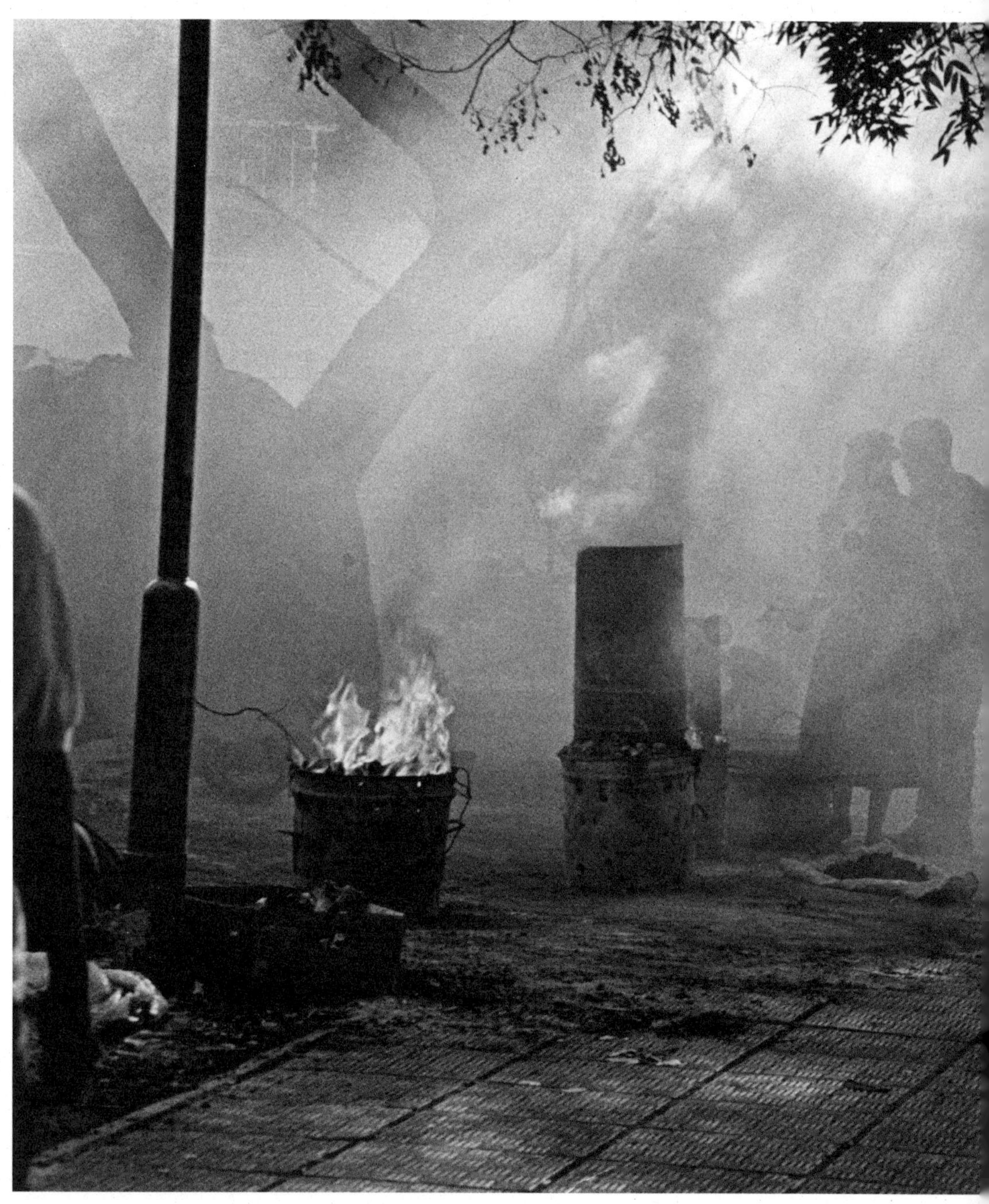

● *'Brazier – Joubert Park I' (City in Transition Series), 1994. Courtesy of the artist and Gallery MOMO.*

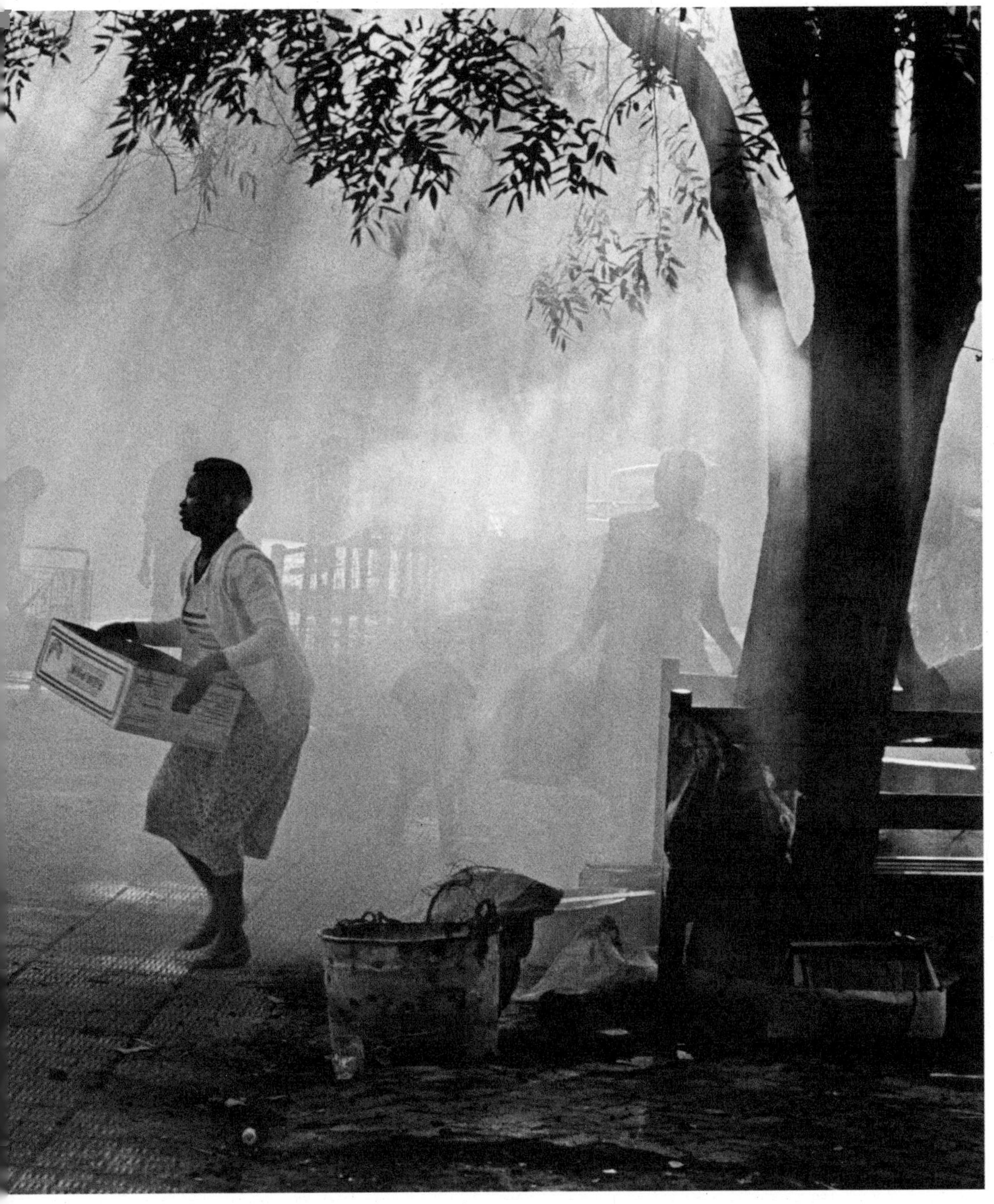

ATHI-PATRA RUGA

At home, with his family, Athi-Patra Ruga felt safe, understood and affirmed. That means that his parents loved him just the way he was and always encouraged him. Both his parents were political activists. His father was a sports journalist and a boxing agent, which was rare in the Transkei. He did a lot to open the borders for boxing and became a hero to Athi. His mother was a midwife. Athi was told by his parents that he was an amazing person and that he could be whoever he wanted to be. That made him feel good about himself.

But unfortunately, the world outside of his home was not that friendly and accepting. He went through a lot of very difficult experiences because of who he was. He knew from a young age that he was queer. In high school he tried to protect himself from the bullies in woodwork class by taking home economics instead. But his parents taught him: 'There is a moment when people define who you are, and then there is a moment when you define yourself.' This is another way of saying it is not about what happens to you, but how you react to it.

He started going to art school in the afternoons in high school and learnt everything he could about art. Then he got a scholarship to study fashion in Johannesburg and opened a fashion studio when we was 19.

Making art started with him parading around downtown Johannesburg in the strange-looking clothes that he made. A friend suggested filming and photographing these performances and so his art career was launched. When this happened he felt ready

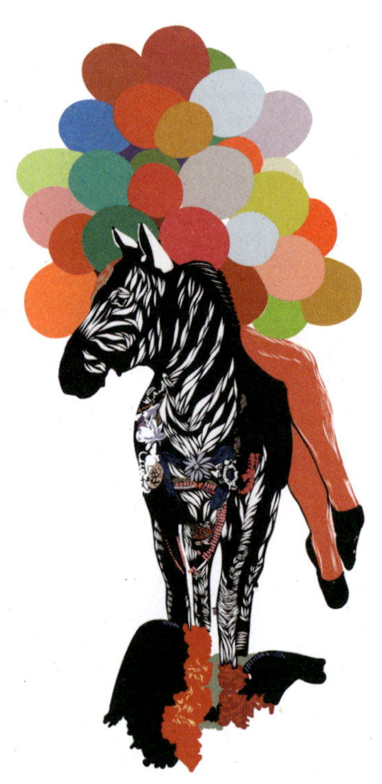

• Illustration from 'Night of Long Knives (I)', 2013. Photograph.

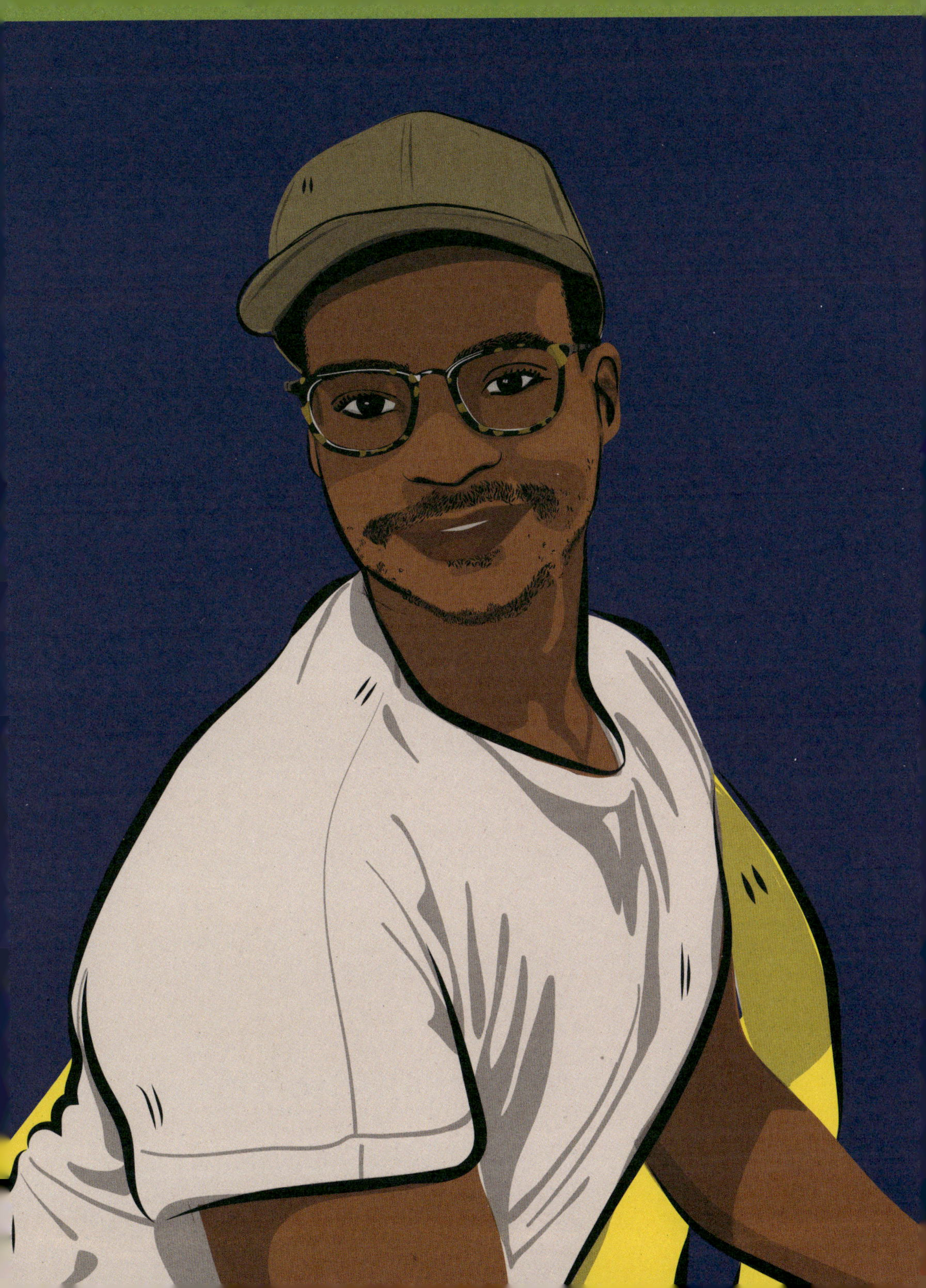

for the art world to start noticing him as he had long prepared himself with reading and making things.

When Athi makes his art he often has children in mind. He feels very connected to the youth of this country and he wants to create work that they understand. He wants young people to see that they can also tell their own stories, while being professional artists. He uses objects like balloons to symbolise different sides of your personality, or things that weigh you down in life. He also creates fantastical worlds in his art that feel safe and empowering. He works in many different mediums like sculpture, performance, photography and film. Through his art and his mentorships, he explains that you don't have to wait for others, you can make your own opportunities and fill the world with your own forms of knowledge.

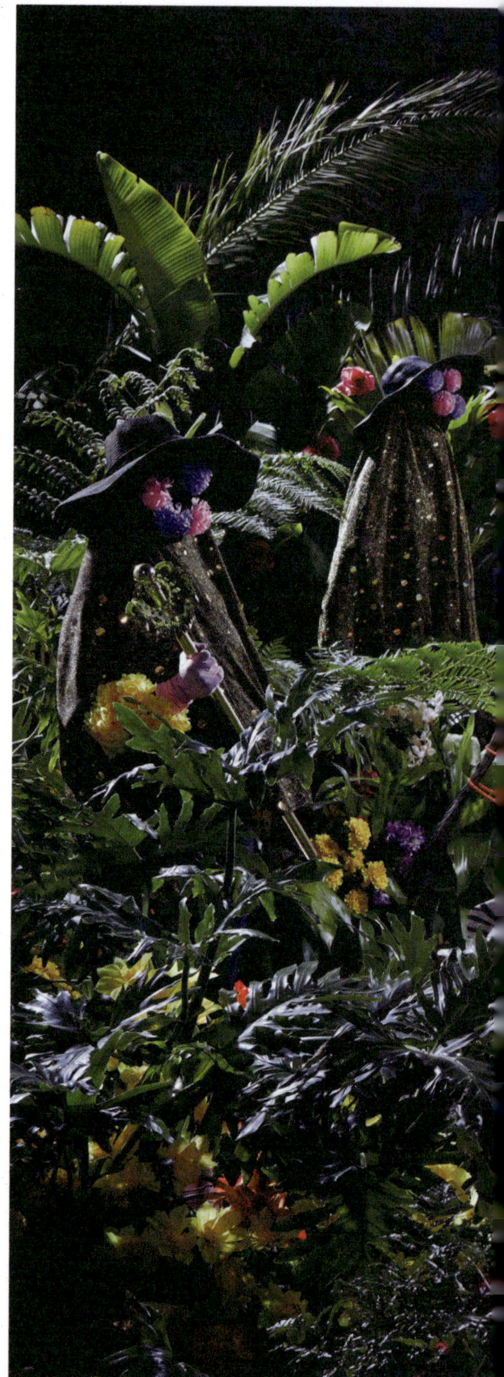

● *'Night of the long knives (I)', 2013. Archival inkjet print. Courtesy of the artist and WHATIFTHEWORLD.*

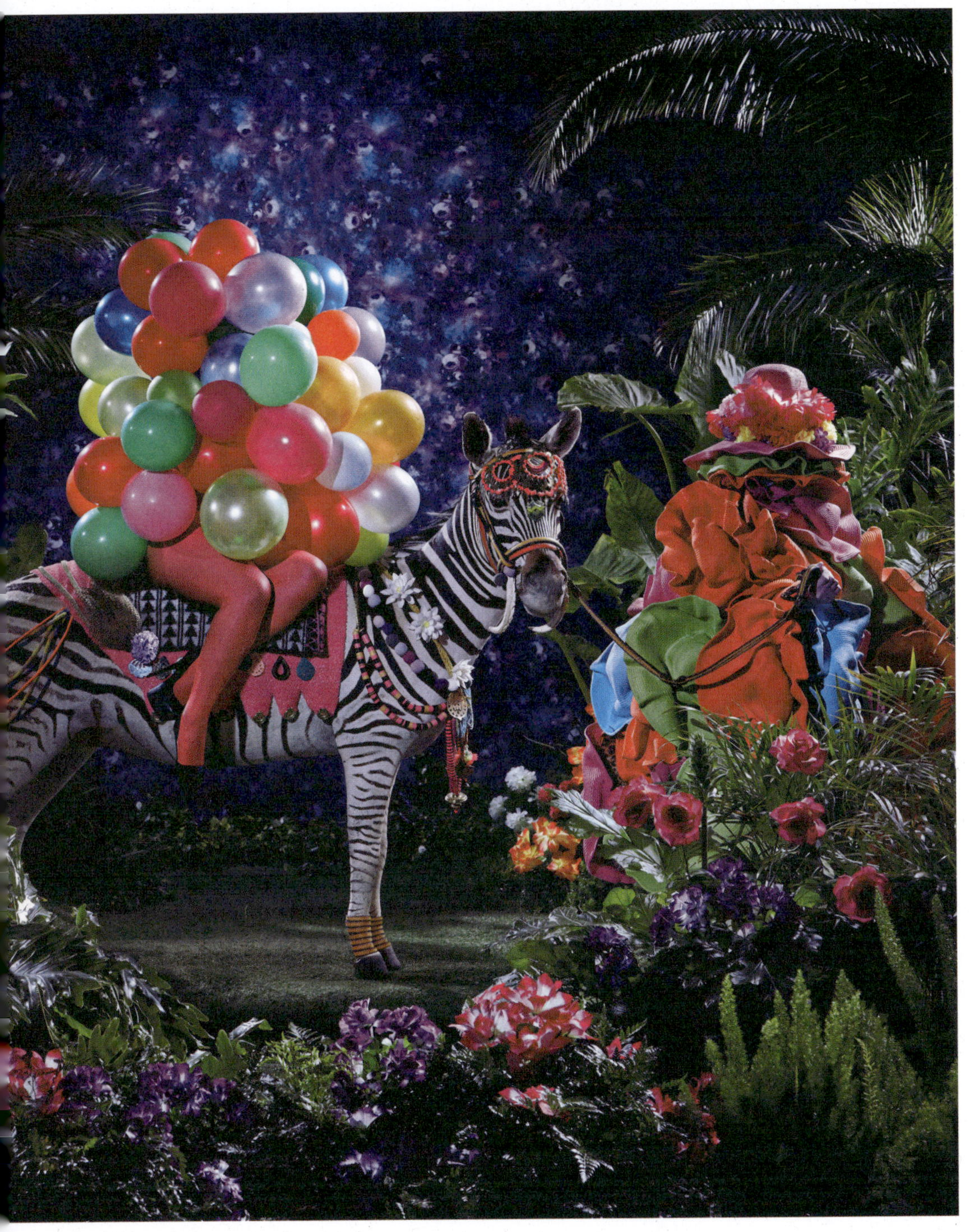

Because he was a clever child, Banele Khoza was told that he had to become a doctor. Where he grew up, becoming a doctor was the most prestigious thing that people could imagine. He was scared that if he was just himself, he might disappoint his parents and others in eSwatini. But Banele had a dream and so he moved to Pretoria to study to become an artist.

And it didn't take very long before he was quite a successful artist. Even when he was still a student, Banele had lots of followers on social media and that was how he started to find people who understood him and had the same feelings that he did. He started selling his work to close friends and staff members at school.

The most important moment was when he won two big art competitions. He tried for three years to win without getting anywhere. This did not bother him too much though, because he saw it as a way to get more people to see his work. Eventually he won and he got the opportunity to work in the big city of Paris for three months. Living and working as an artist in Paris was Banele's biggest dream for his future and he achieved this when he was just 23 years old!

Banele thinks many people like his work because his artworks are all about emotions that he feels every day. Art has become a 'friend' that doesn't judge him so that he can be completely honest with his thoughts and feelings. Talking about emotions and sharing them with others can sometimes be hard for people: Like feeling embarrassed because you said something silly to someone, or feeling sad when someone gossips about you. When people look at this art, and read about it, they can recognise: 'Yes I have felt that way before!'

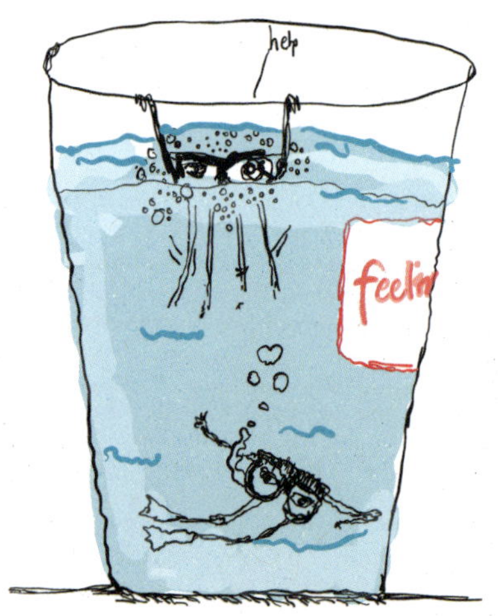

● Illustration of 'Pool of feelings', 2019. Digital drawing.

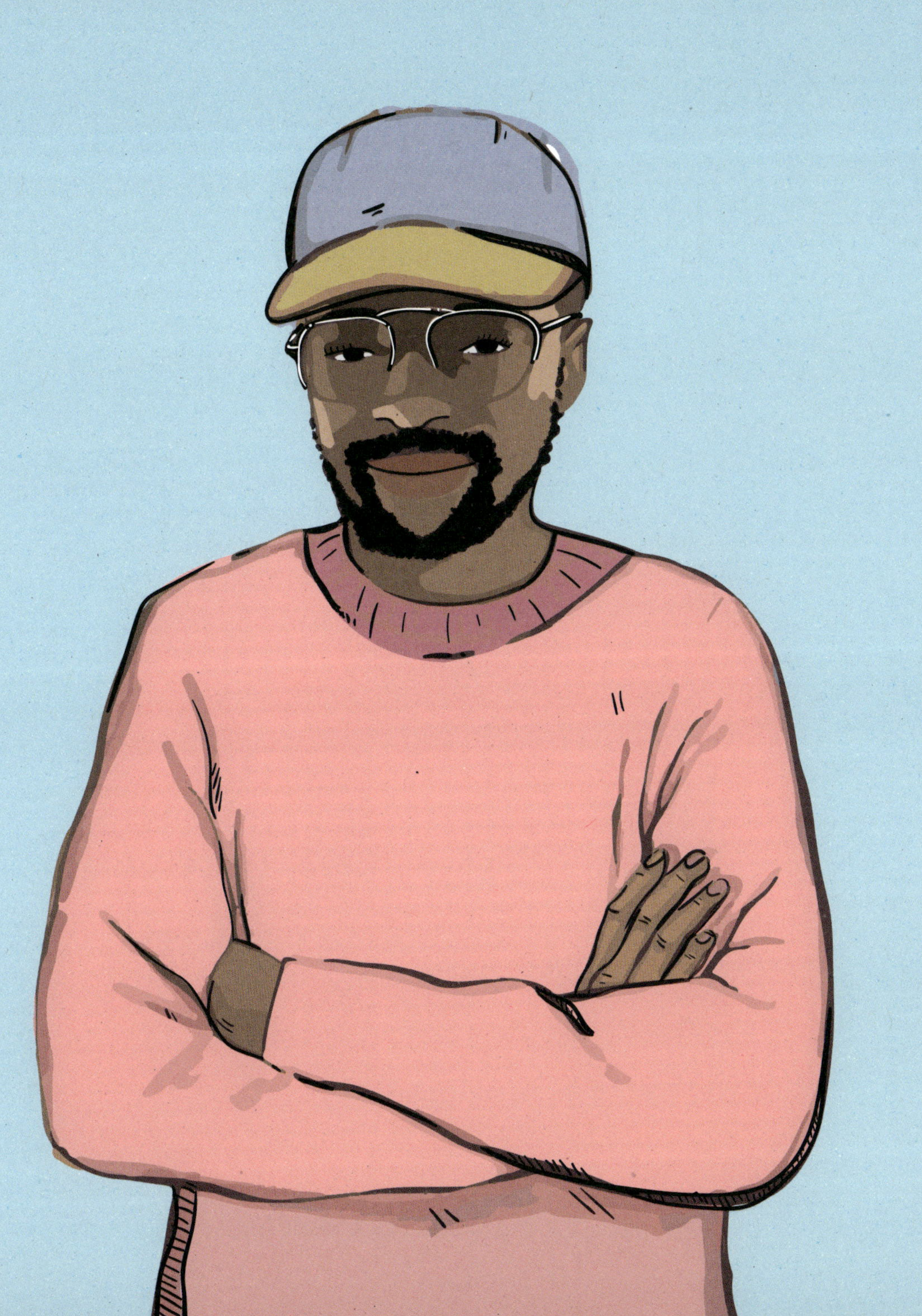

But Banele was worried that not enough people
thought that they could go into galleries because
they didn't understand what art was, or how they
should behave in a gallery. He was also worried
that he was successful while many of his friends
were not. So he created a gallery space that feels
nice and comfortable where anyone can come
and see and learn about art. When you go into
Banele's gallery space you get the same warm
and friendly feeling from the space that you get
from talking to Banele himself.

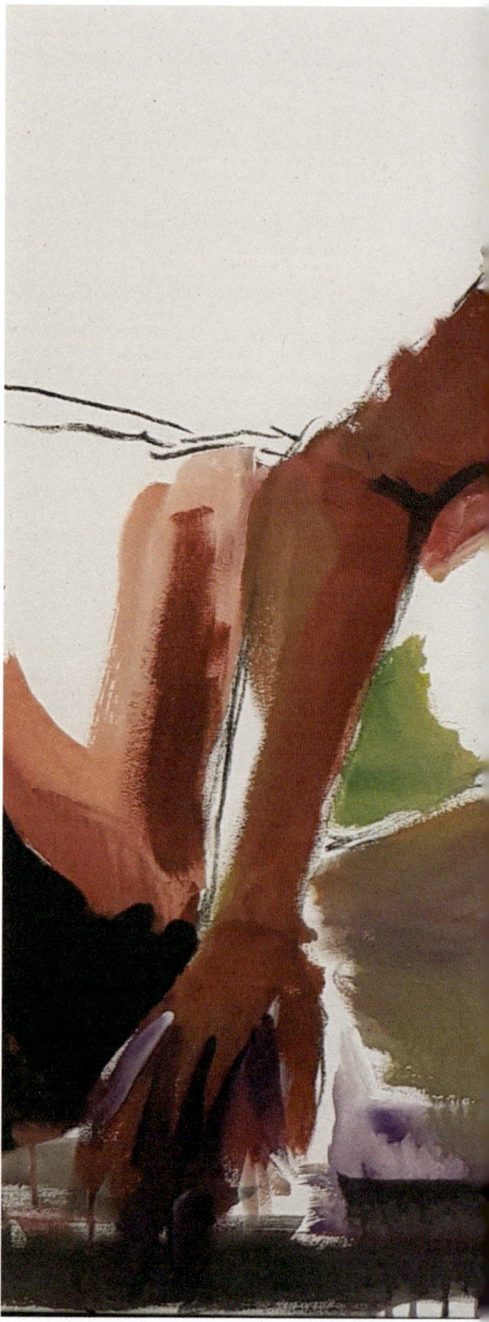

• *'Amidst', 2018. Acrylic on canvas.
Courtesy of the artist.*

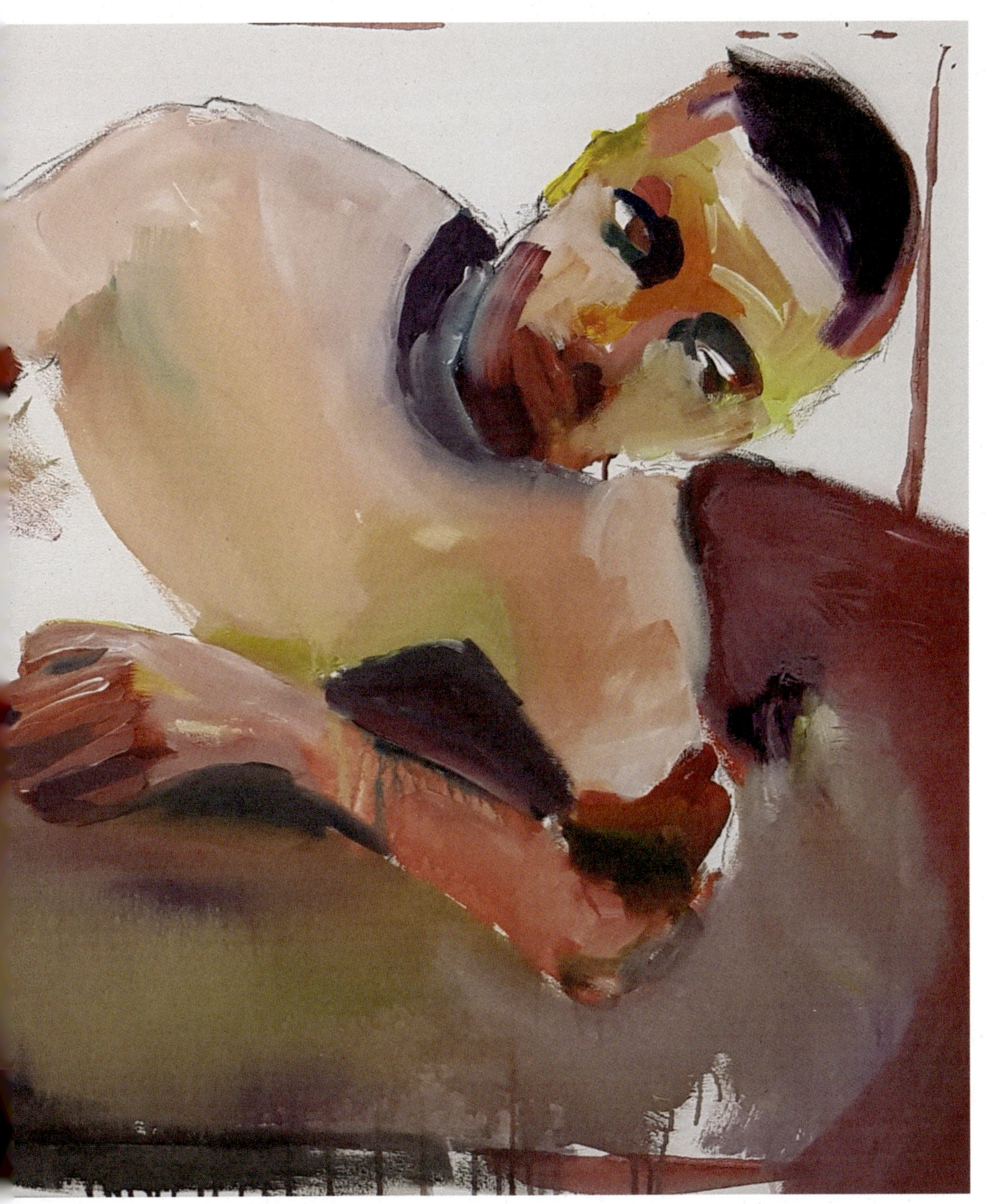

Berni Searle

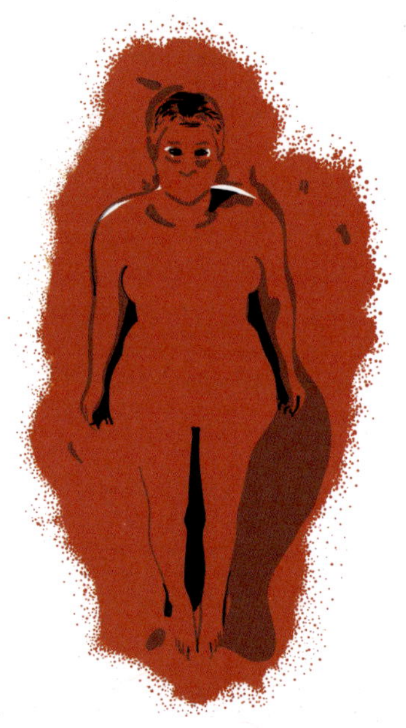

into her own imaginary world in her room. Sometimes she would make clay beads for jewellery, other times she would pick flowers and press them between the pages of books to use when decorating cards.

By the time she reached matric she knew she wanted to do something creative. When she applied for art school in Cape Town, she had never really drawn in her life and so didn't get in the first time around. There were not many non-white university art schools at the time. Berni spent a whole year at the Technikon studying the basics of colour and drawing, so that when she applied again a year later, she was much more ready. But things kept on being challenging for the first two years. It was also not so easy to fit in because art schools were mostly full of white people at that time.

Berni knew that she had grown up in a place, South Africa, at a time, during apartheid, when other people placed her in a category and tried to define who she was. She wanted to make art that resisted these categories and said: 'This is who I am. I want to present myself as I see myself and not as others would like me to be seen.'

Berni Searle was an only child until she was ten years old and during these early years she spent a lot of time playing by herself. She didn't mind it, the hours just disappeared as she turned the rocks in the garden into pet rocks and went

● *Illustration of 'Traces', 1999, from the 'Colour Me' series. Digital prints.*

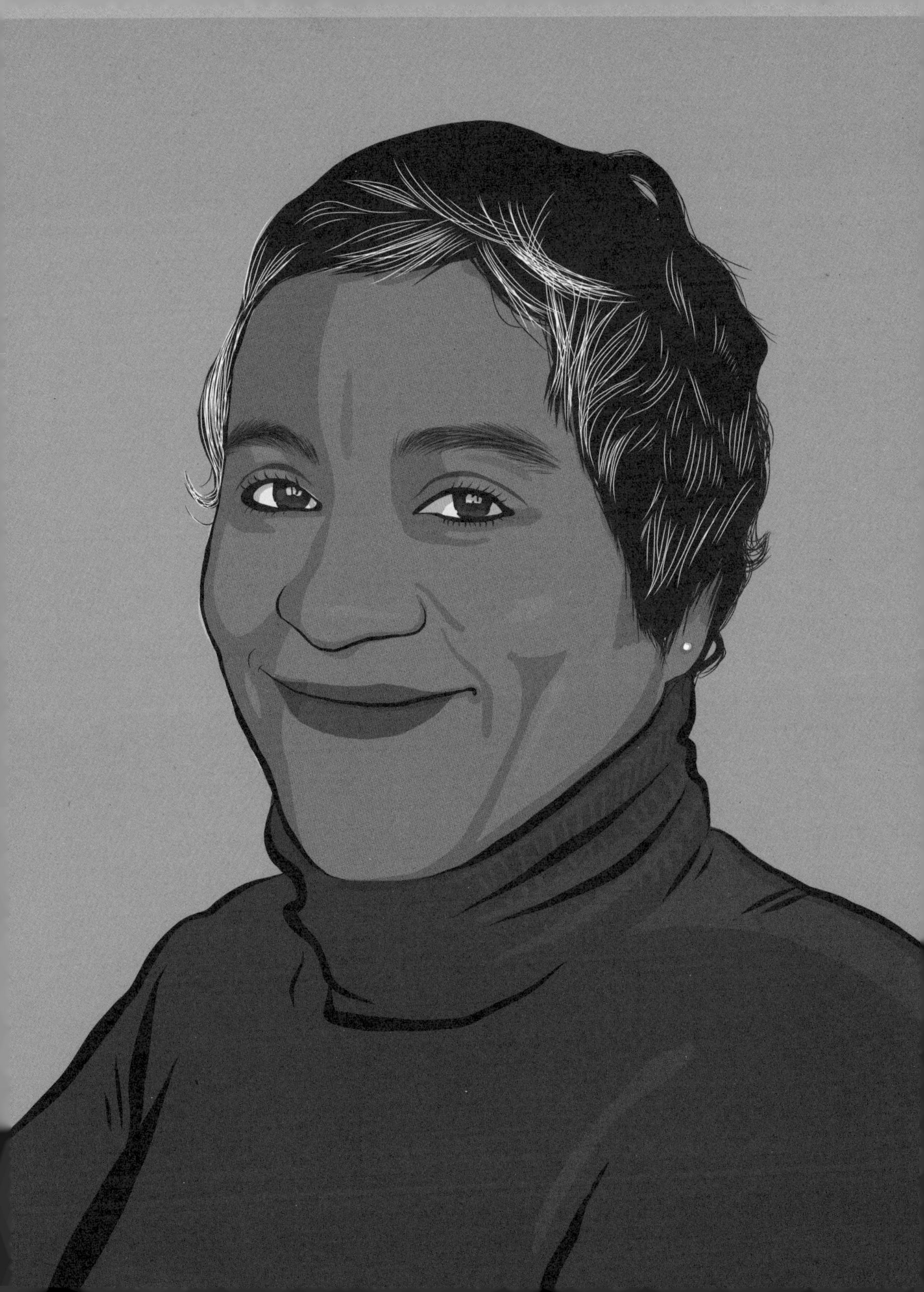

She started working in photography, video, performance and installation.

Berni turned to her own life and her family to try to understand her heritage and where she comes from. For example, her mother passed down to her how to cook with spices and make roti. This was passed down to her by her mother, and to her mother's mother by her great-grandfather who was a cook from Mauritius. She didn't eat curry and roti every day, but this way of cooking was something that connected her to where her family had come from. She also made artworks called 'Colour Me' where she covered her body in different spices, and she found a freedom in being able to challenge and play with her identity by creating herself in different colours: yellow, red, brown or white.

Berni believes art allows you to ask questions and to do this really magical thing of making something from nothing, something that was not there before you started and that comes into being through your imagination.

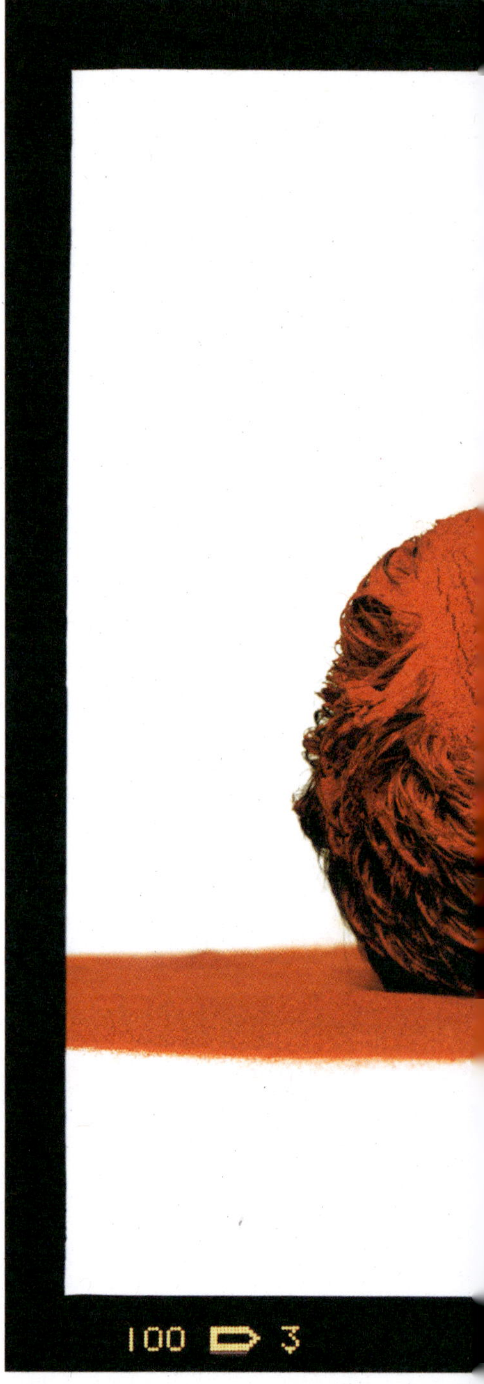

● *Untitled (red). From the 'Colour Me' series, 1998. Lightjet print. Courtesy of the artist and Stevenson, Cape Town and Johannesburg.*

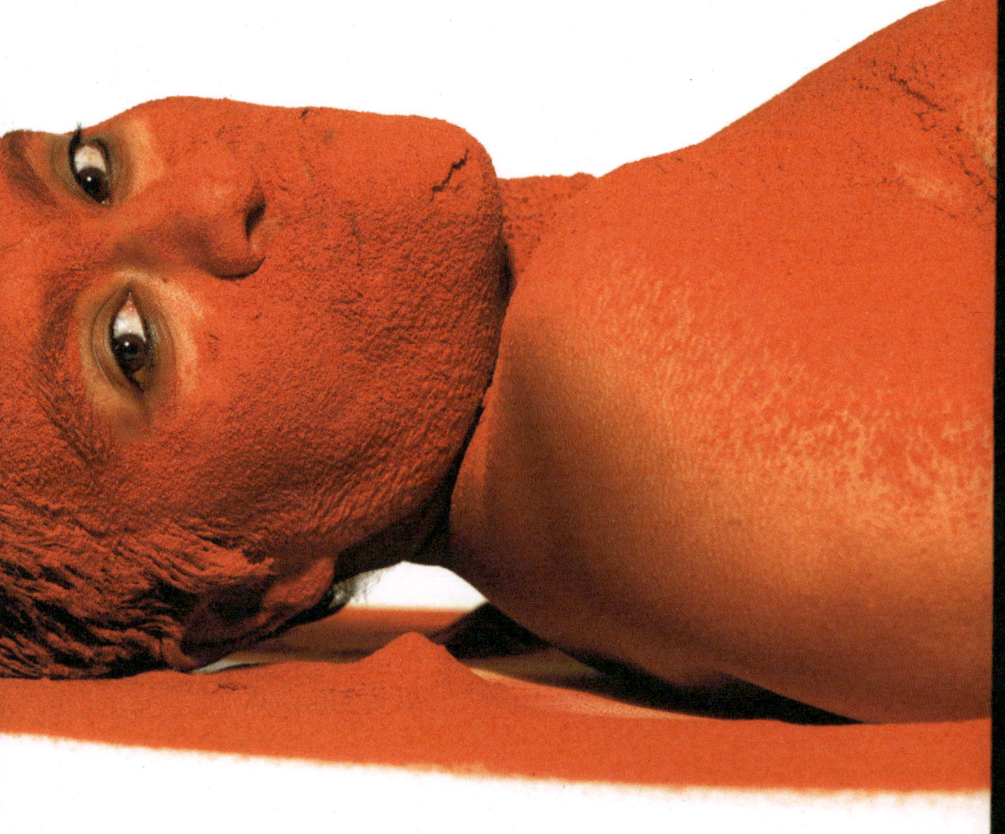

100 503
FUJI .00
100 4

BILLIE ZANGEWA

Once there was a girl who wanted to live in the big city of Johannesburg and make art. Billie Zangewa knew from a young age that she loved beautiful clothes and drawing. In the calm suburbs of Gaborone, Botswana she used to sit at the bookshops and page through international fashion magazines.

When it came time to go to university she told her family that art was the only thing she was interested in studying. Her parents were worried about how she would care for herself, but when she insisted, they gave in. Her parents wanted her to be happy.

It took her a really long time to be able to earn money as an artist. In the day, she worked at a clothing shop and at night she made bags to sell. One bag took her months to finish because she decorated it with tiny embroidery. Billie remembers thinking at the time, 'Wow this was not what I thought my life would be! I went to good schools, I did well at A-levels and here I am cleaning shop windows!'

One day her friend took her to a fabric shop to get some small pieces of fabric. Billie fell in love with these little blocks of colour. They reminded her of the little windows and buildings of the Johannesburg cityscape. She started sewing pieces of cloth onto larger pieces of cloth to make pictures and she has been doing that ever since!

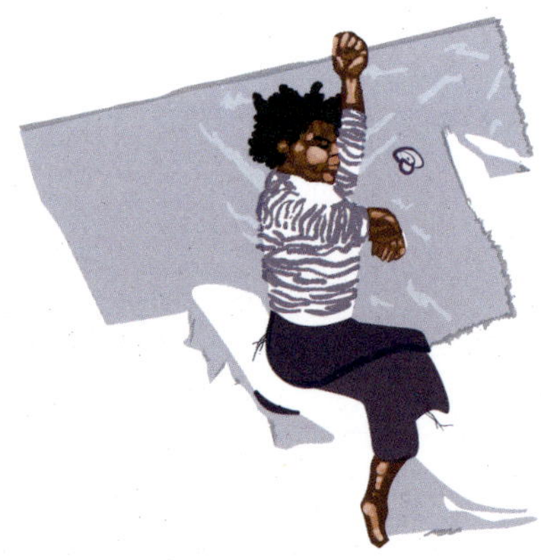

• Illustration of 'Temporary Reprieve', 2017. Silk tapestry.

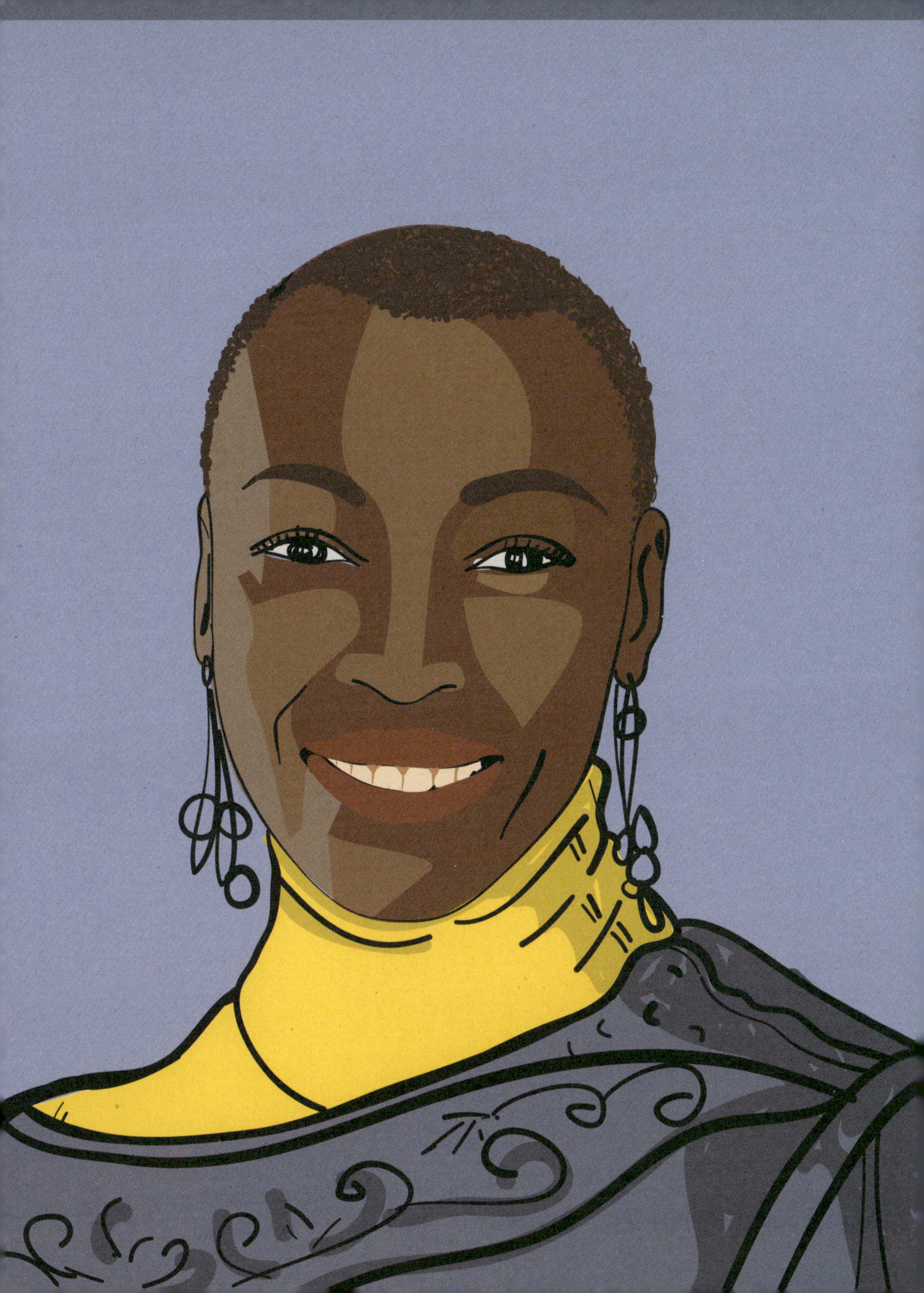

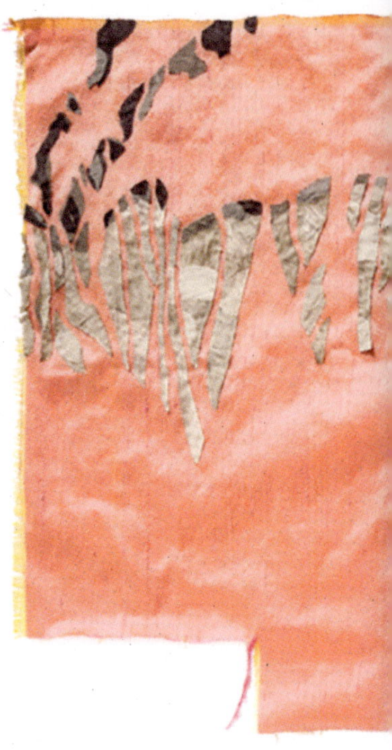

Moving to the city was very hard for her and she often thought that it is so much harder for women than for men. Billie likes to tell the stories of ordinary women. She feels that showing the world how a woman lives and all the little things she does around the house, like making tea, or having a nap, can teach people about the lives of women. In some of her pictures she has made herself into a superhero who can protect herself in this big city. She wants her son to know that women can look after themselves.

It still takes Billie very long to make each work. Now, if you want to buy her art, you have to put your name down on a list because there are so many people who love her work and want to buy it.

● 'Return to Paradise', 2017. Silk tapestry.
Courtesy of the artist and Blank Projects.

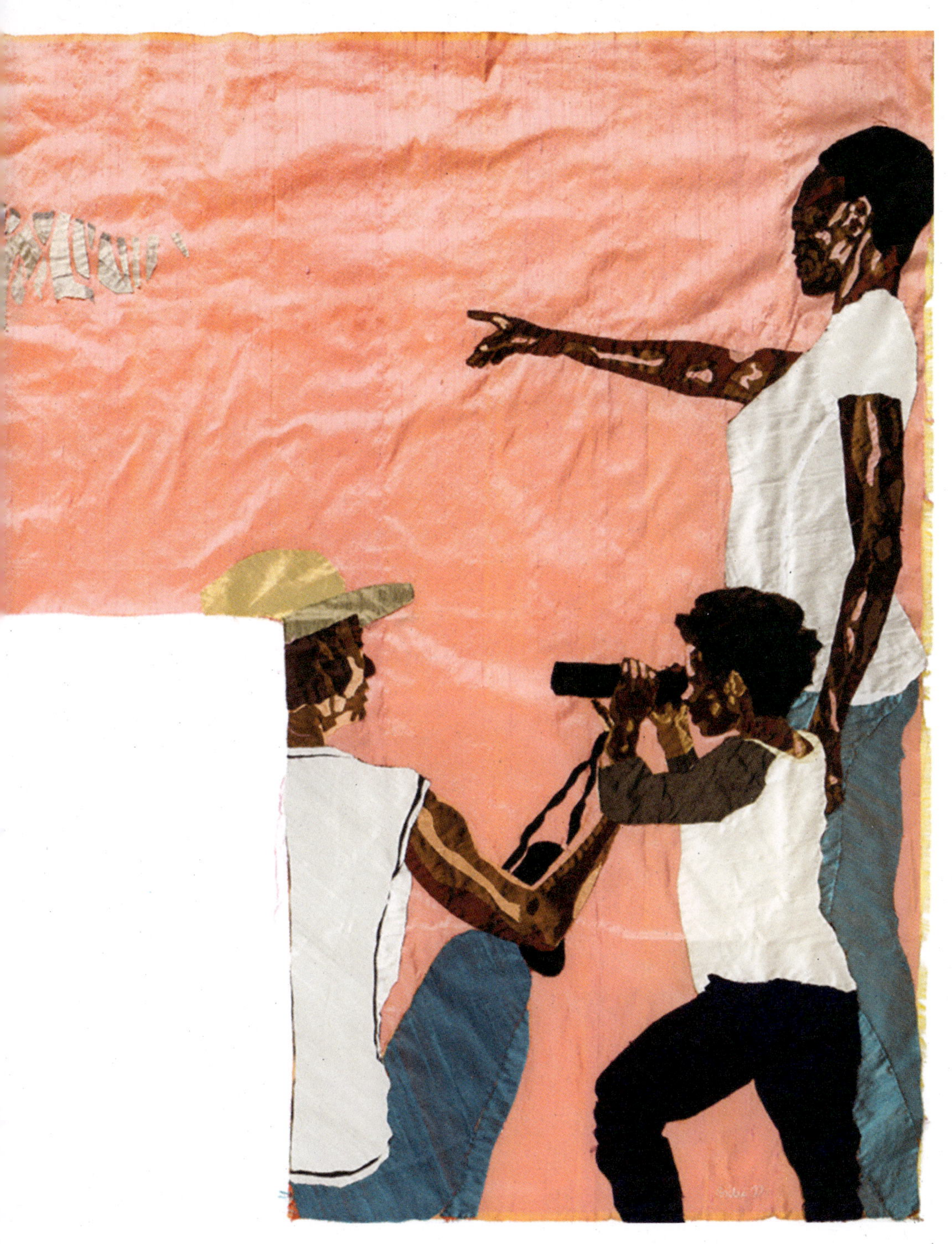

Blessing Ngobeni

Blessing Ngobeni loves the sound of the scissors cutting, and the swish-swish of a brush sweeping across a the canvas. These are the sounds of his creativity coming to life. Although he only started drawing as a teenager, he immediately knew that it was something that would play an important part in his life.

He soon realised that people were drawn to his work and wanted to buy it. This made him feel really good because before that it didn't always feel like life was on his side. When he thinks back on his childhood, he calls it 'complicated'.

After having a few exhibitions, Blessing was able to live and work as a full-time artist. He wants to make art works that show things from his everyday life perspective and connect with people who might have had similar experiences. Blessing also makes works that ask questions about politics, power and money. In his work he uses images to show how our politicians are behaving because he wants to hold them accountable. Blessing uses many different mediums to bring his message across:

sometimes he draws, and paints and makes collages from newspaper articles, and other times he does video and installation work. Installation art works bring together different art mediums into one space.

Art has been such an important thing in Blessing's life that now he wants to help others to have the same opportunity. He has started an art prize to give young artists money to have a place to work and then create their own work.

Blessing has come to believe that art can help those who struggle to speak about their experiences, or what they are feeling, by giving them a new language. In this way you can use art to tell your story.

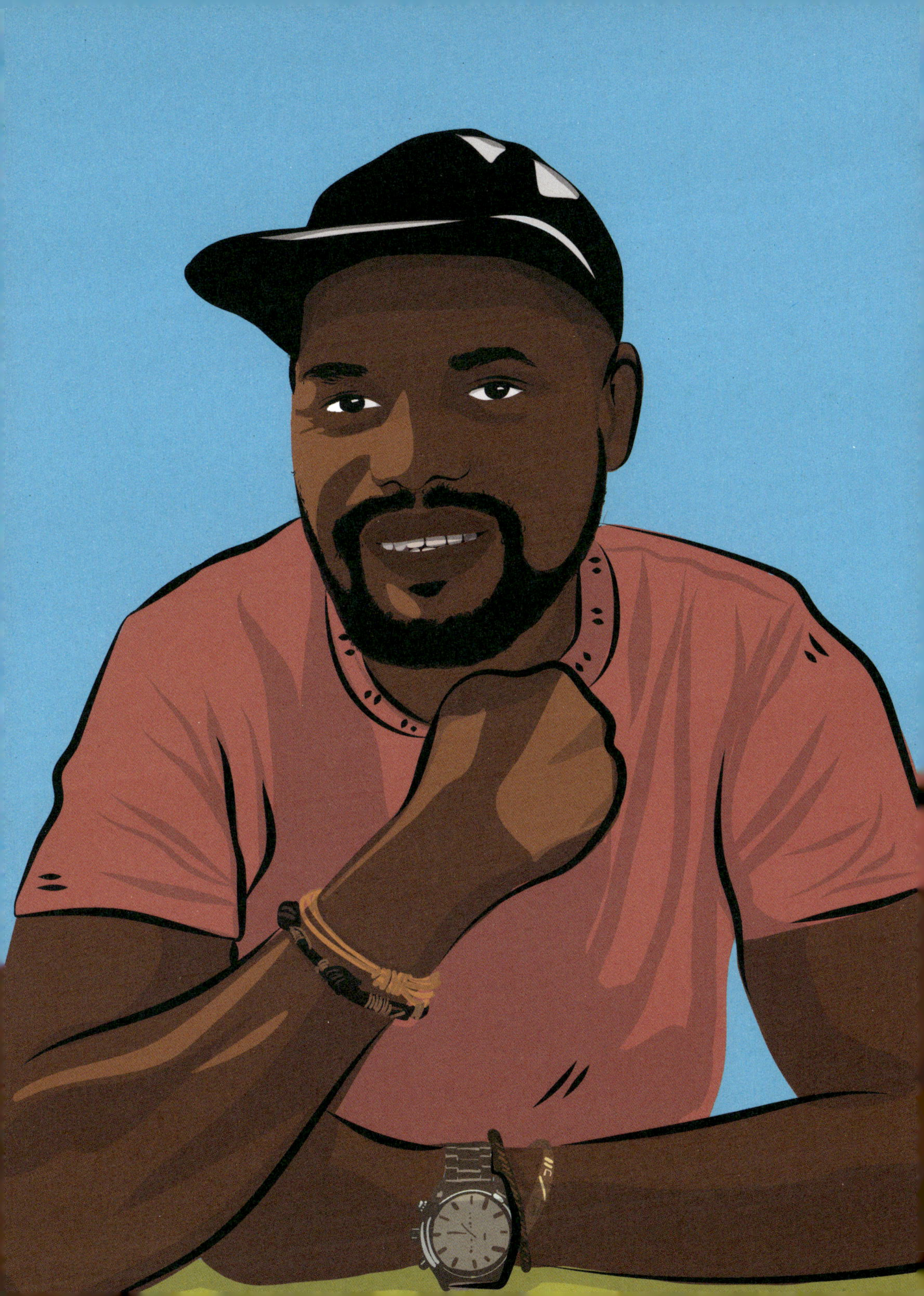

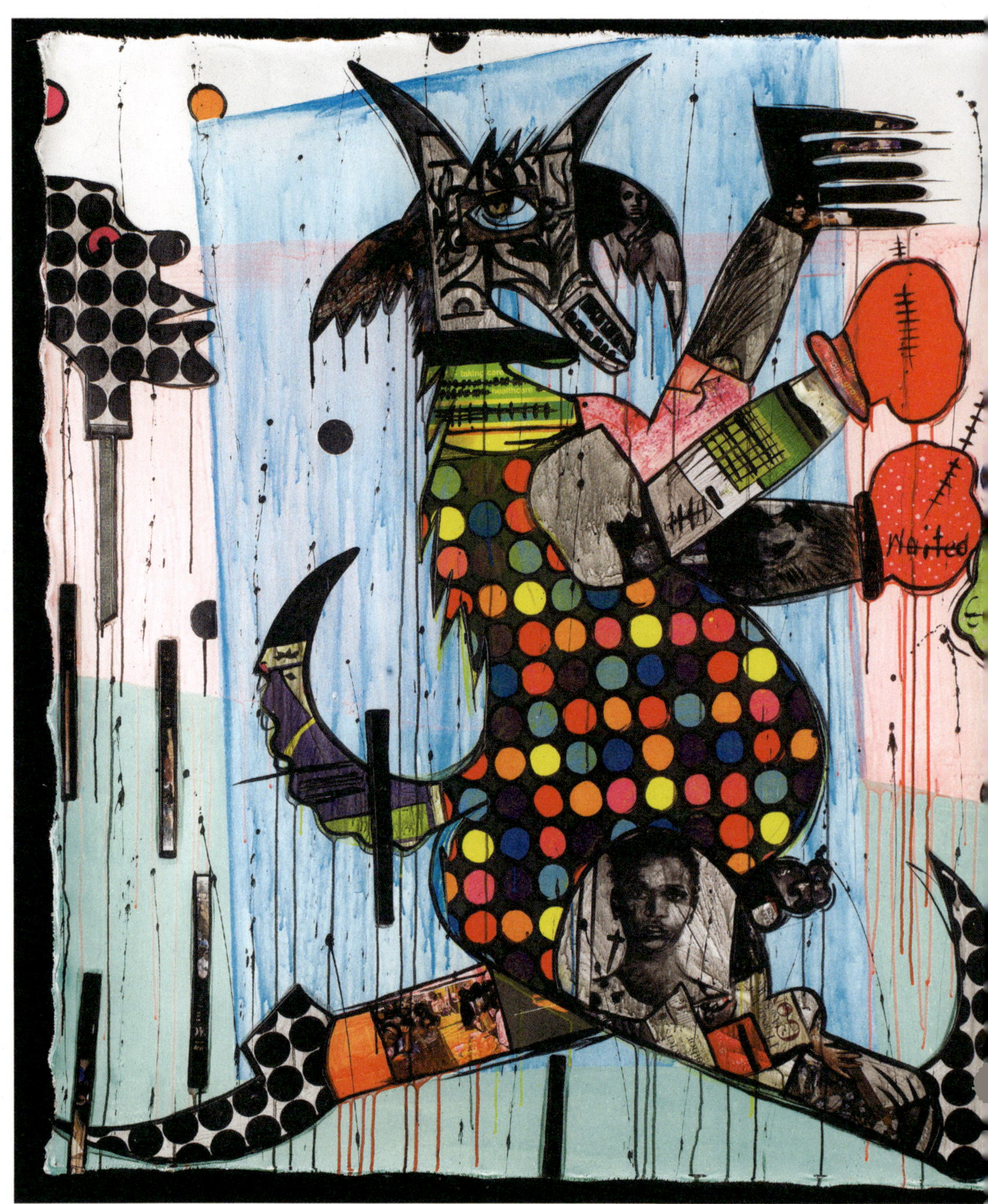

● 'Waited Long Enough', 2018. Acrylic and collage on canvas.
Courtesy of the artist and Everard Read Gallery.

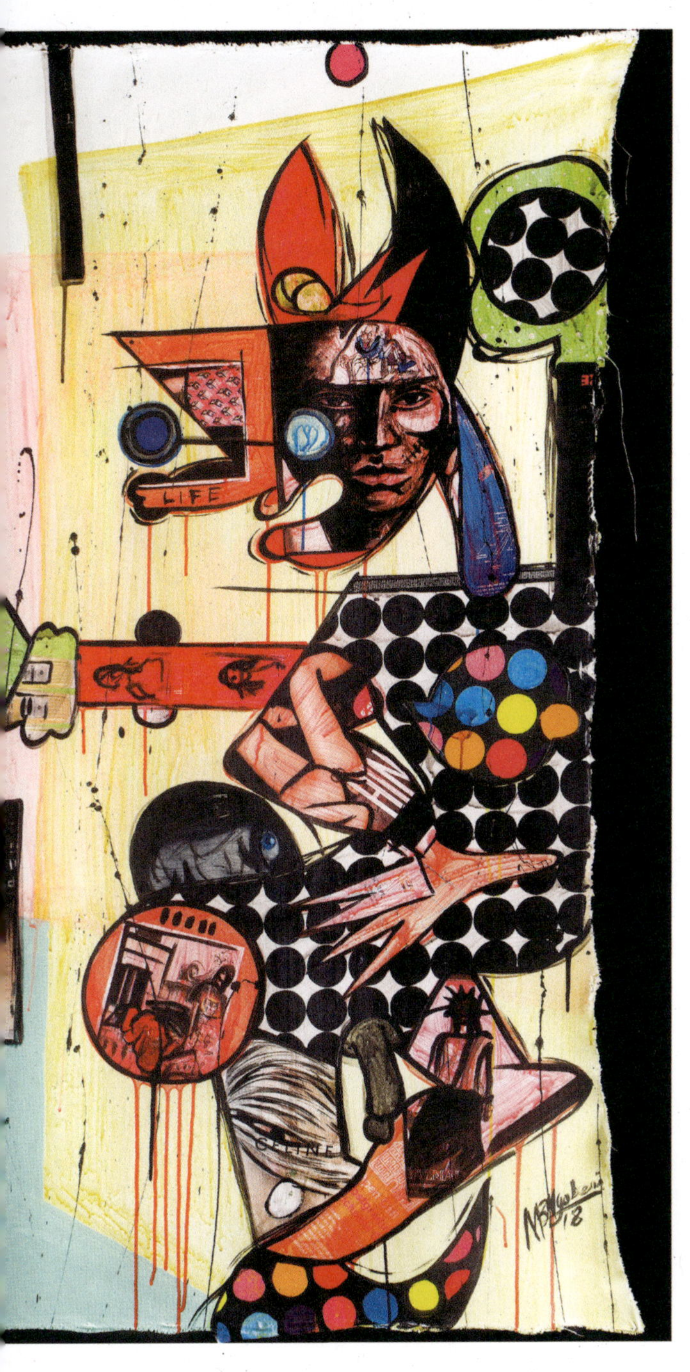

BREEZE YOKO

Breeze Yoko doesn't think art can save the world or change history, but he thinks art gives you a relief from the everyday difficulties of life. He makes his art in public where everyone can see it, because he wants it to give people a break from all the negative things read on street poles and all the adverts by the side of the roads.

Because he likes to work at his own pace and explore the world, Breeze found school rigid and strict and couldn't wait for it to be over. Afterwards, he didn't want a conventional job either. What suited him better was working in the TV industry as an actor and a presenter.

As a teenager he became interested in graffiti through hip-hop and it felt like a culture he knew. Most of his graffiti was done in secret. Sometimes he got caught and sometimes he got frightened, but he never stopped.

One day he overheard a group of young black kids debating whether this one graffiti piece was done by a white artist because it was too good for it to have been done by a black artist. He thought, 'I should be seen doing this kind of art, so that I can be an example to these kids.'

Breeze has developed his own style that is very recognisable. One of his favourite artworks that a company paid him to do is in Khayelitsha. It is on an education building and is huge. A girl is standing in front of Table Mountain shielding her eyes from the sun and looking into the distance. She towers over the surrounding streets, strong and independent.

Breeze has done graffiti all over the world and he often thinks about the lives of children in his pieces. He is also interested in religion, spirituality and politics. Because he creates public art, Breeze wants to make something that the people in the area will like and that will represent their lives.

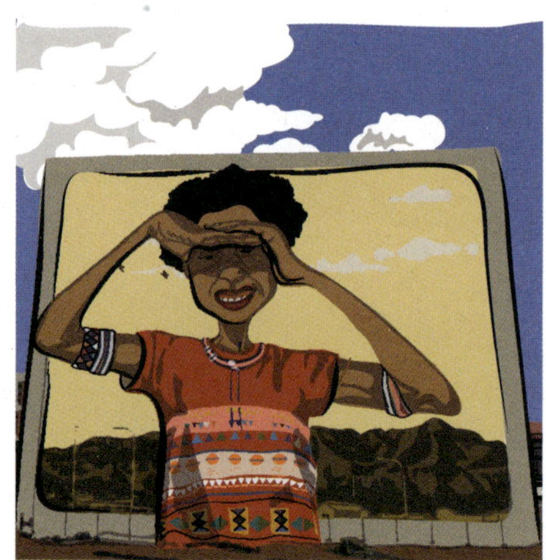

• *Illustration of 'Boniswa', 2016. Graffiti.*

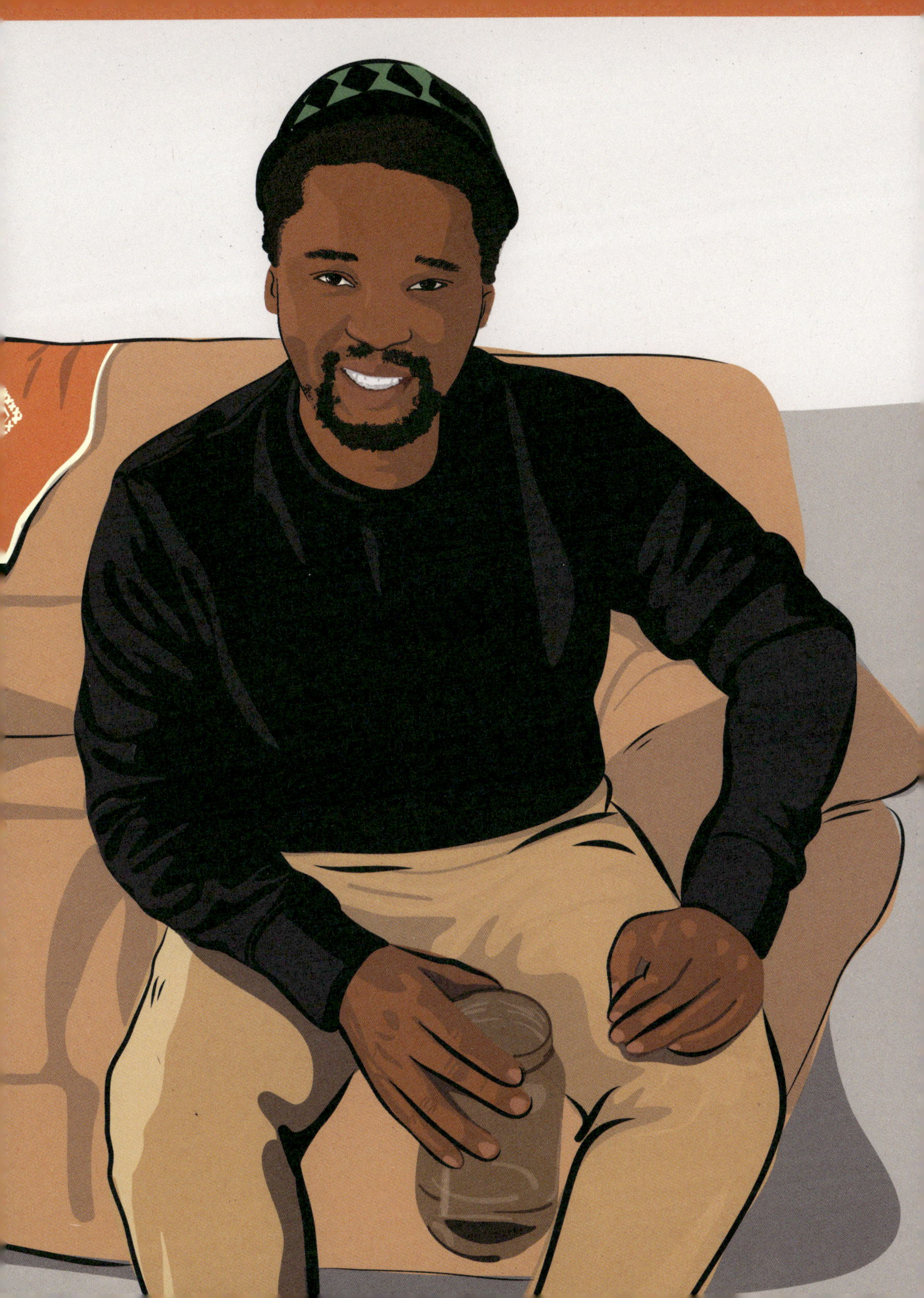

BRIDGET BAKER

East London is a quiet town in the Eastern Cape by the sea. Here Bridget Baker spent the first years of her life, playing and exploring around her house with her siblings. Bridget always liked making things. One day, when Bridget was five, a phone call came for her mother while she was sleeping. Phones don't often ring at three o'clock in the morning, and when they do it is often bad news. This call came through to let her mother know that Bridget's father had suddenly died of a heart attack. Even though Bridget was still small, this event changed her childhood and left her with things that she felt she had to work through.

Remembering and forgetting became very interesting to Bridget when she started making art. When she was in university at Stellenbosch, she used to look at photographs of herself with her father. One photograph was particularly special to her. It was the two of them in a pool and her father was teaching her how to swim. Bridget used this photograph to make a small art piece about memories and forgetting. She remembered that her mother used to rub Vicks VapoRub on her chest when she got a cold. Vicks is a kind of medication that comes in small round tins and is greasy, like lip balm. She took four empty Vicks tins, printed the photograph of her and her father in the pool out four times, and pasted it carefully inside each of these tins. Then she took the Vicks and put a little bit over the first photo, more over the second, even more over the third, and covered the fourth one completely. When you look at these four circles next to each other, the image gradually become more blurry, just like memories grow further and further out of your reach as time goes by.

Although as an adult she has lived all over the world, Bridget has returned many times to the house where she grew up, even after her mother sold it. She has made art about different parts of her childhood, but she has also used art to work through other questions that come to her. Often her work starts with a feeling or an idea that she is not able to figure out just by thinking it through and art becomes a visual way of coming to a better understanding.

She is now a mother herself and will keep using art to think through the big, wonderful change that a child brings to one's life.

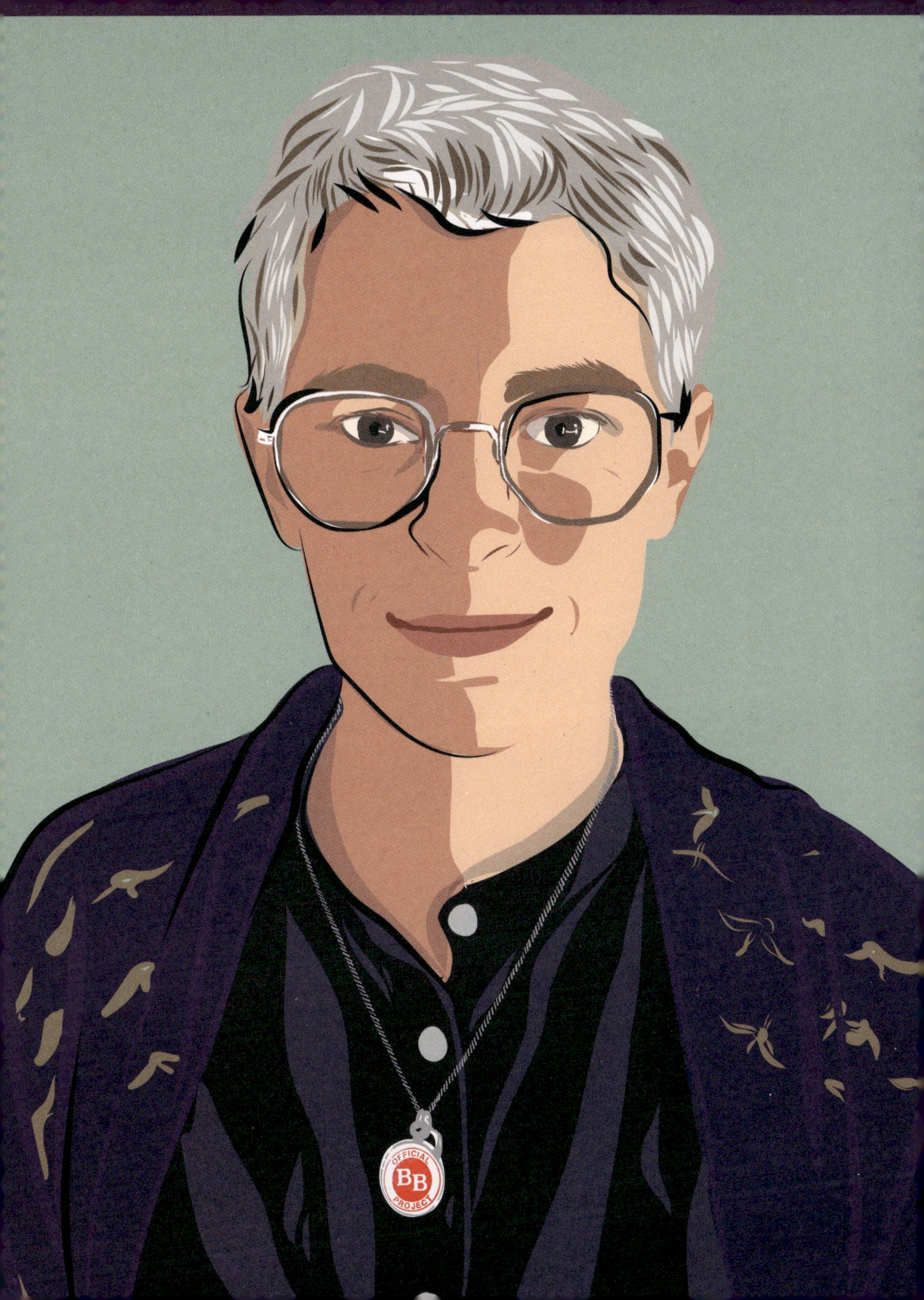
OFFICIAL
BB
PROJECT

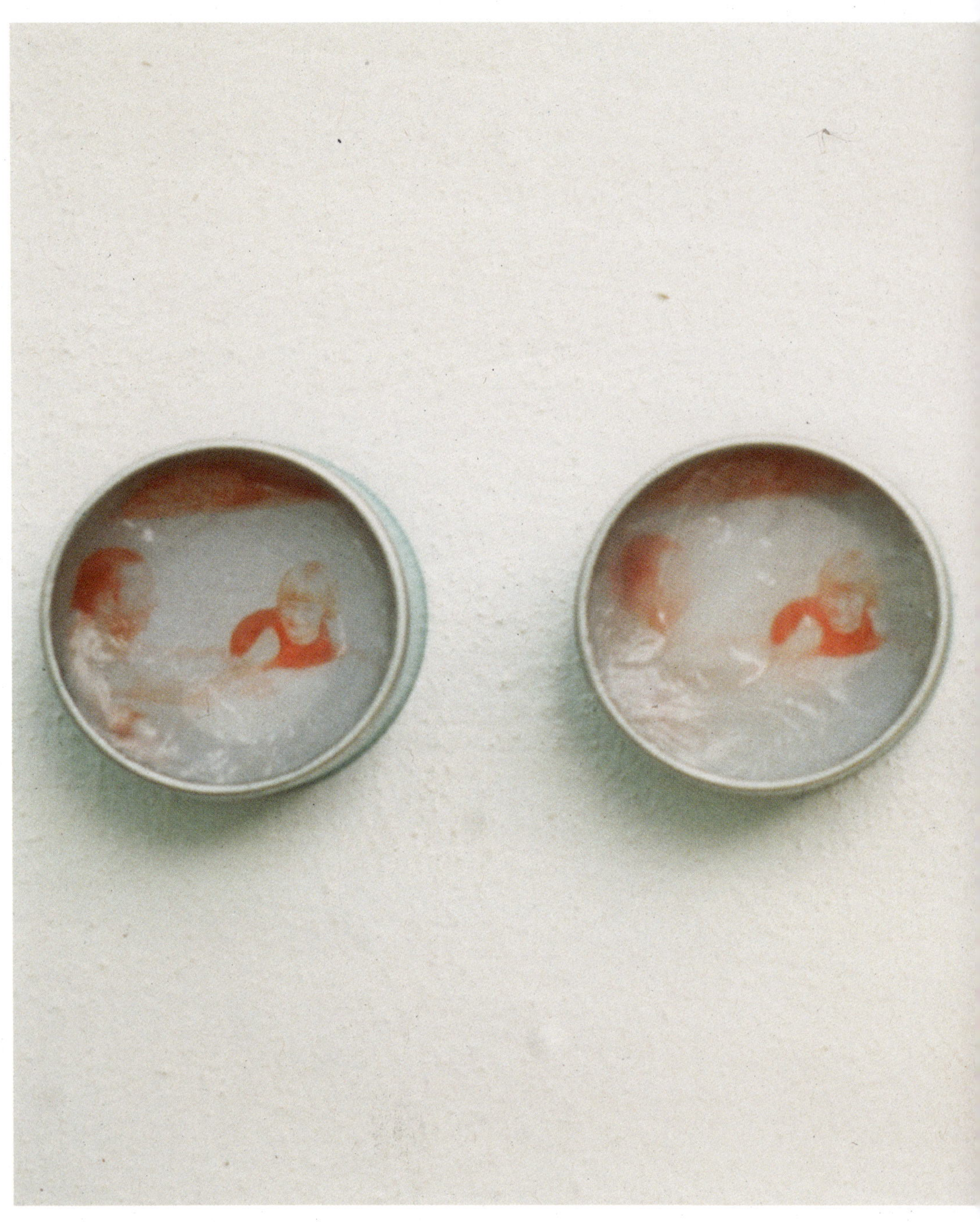

● *'So it goes', 1995. Mixed media. Courtesy of the artist.*

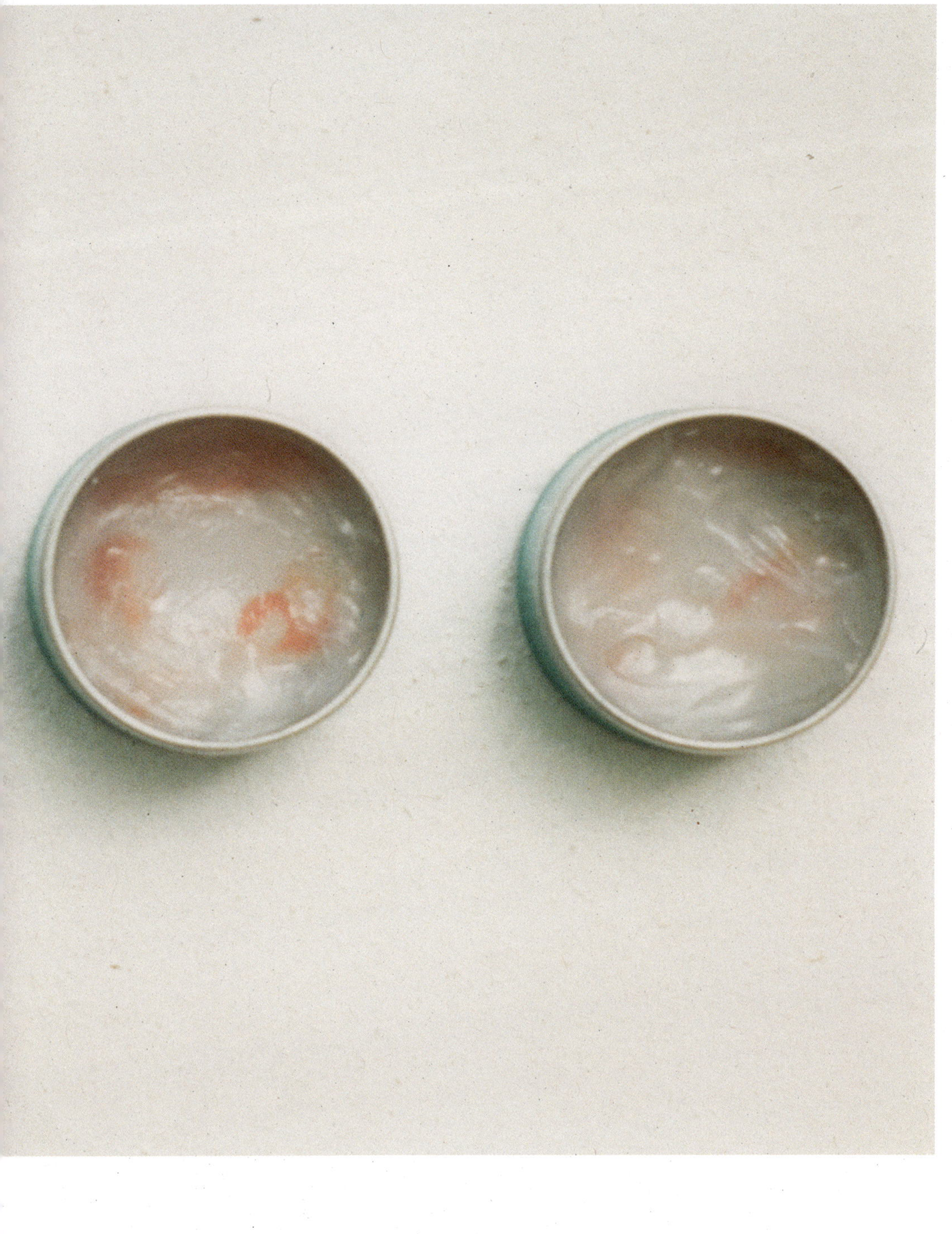

Bronwyn Katz

Growing up, Bronwyn Katz was always drawing cartoons from TV like Spongebob Squarepants, or making birthday and Christmas cards. She was good at drawing, but also very good at maths. After high school, when she had to decide what to study, it was either actuarial sciences or art. She chose art, because it was more enjoyable.

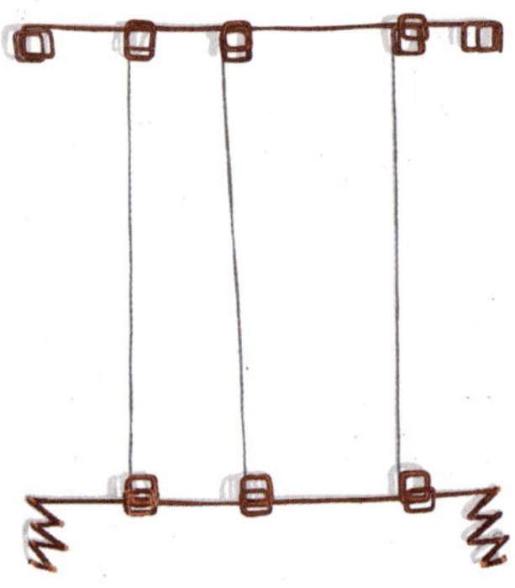

When she got to art school in Cape Town, she found it very hard. Art was not just about painting and drawing well, it was about reading, history, ideas and asking questions. She also felt like she did not come from the right place. Bronwyn tried to drop out twice. But her mother said, 'No way, you convinced us that you wanted to study art, we paid for two years of art school and you need to stick this out!' She is now very grateful that her mother insisted, because in her final year there was a lot of interest in her work and soon she travelled abroad on residencies and for international exhibitions.

The struggles of her first two years at university made her search for her own story and of her heritage in Kimberley. She made works about her home and her grandmother's home and her great-grandmother's home, which were all the same house that the generations had passed on to each other. Bronwyn also made a whole series of works by taking old beds and mattresses apart to speak about the ways that people are connected to the places that they live and come from.

At one point she got frustrated that the art world was too secluded from everyday life. But after going to Mitchells Plain to teach high school students, she realised that once you speak to the children about artworks, they understand them quite easily.

For Bronwyn an important part of becoming a successful artist has been surrounding herself with an ambitious support group of friends. Her journey is the result of lots of people who helped and inspired her along the way. Her work now incorporates video art, sculpture, installation and performance art. And the last ingredient? She calls it a 'leap of faith'.

● *Illustration of 'rooihoek', 2018. Salvaged bed wire, wool.*

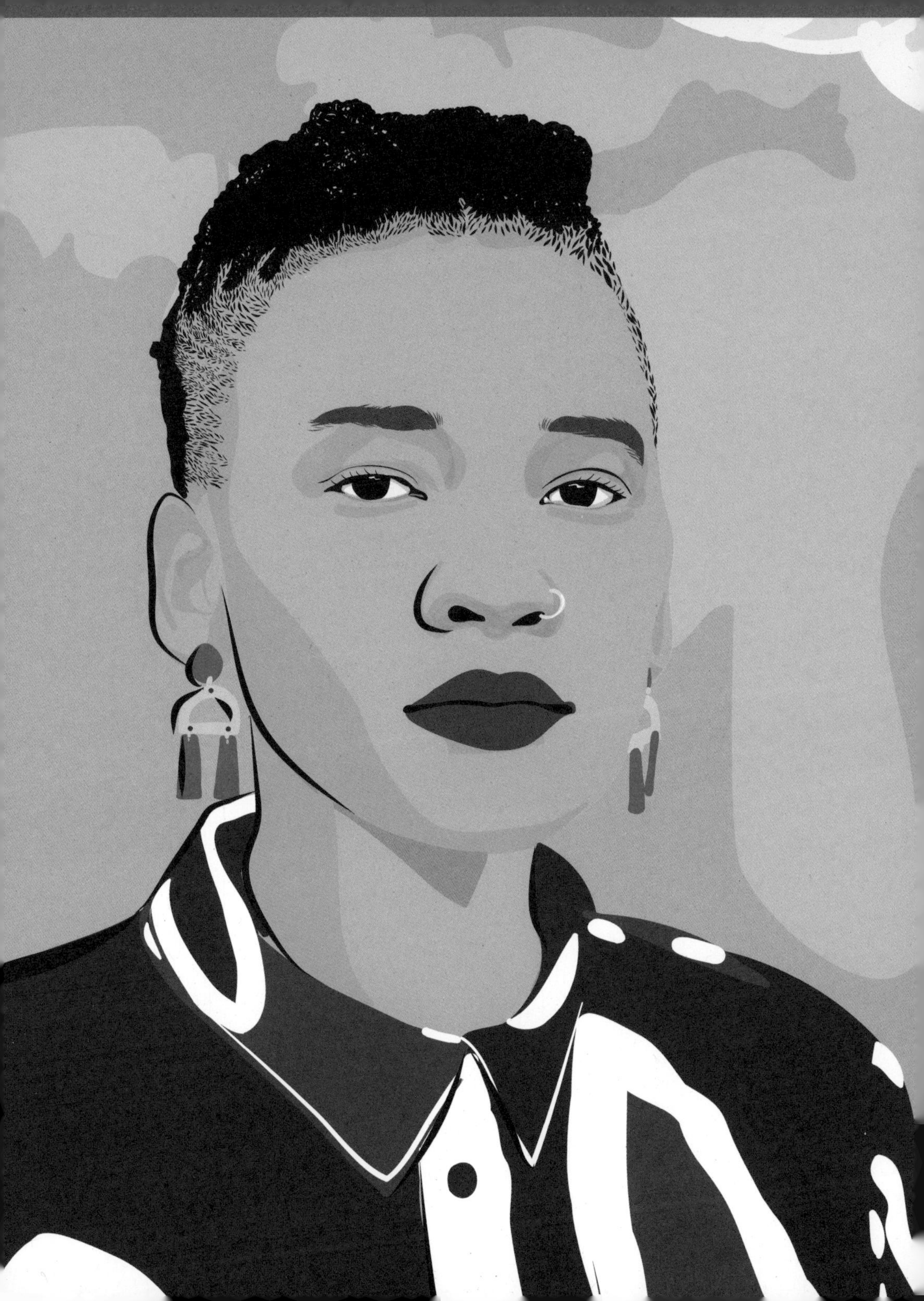

Buhlebezwe Siwani

Sometimes something happens in your life that makes you see the world in a new way. Something like this happened to Buhlebezwe Siwani when she was still in university. She realised that she had 'the calling' to become a sangoma. A sangoma is a spiritual person and traditional healer.

Before this moment, Buhlebezwe had been studying art. Growing up she wanted to be a pilot. She noticed that the pilots' voices that spoke over the intercom were mostly male. She thought she could do that job, but art won her ambitions. When it came time to study she received a scholarship for law and engineering, but she wanted to study art instead.

Buhlebezwe grew up spending half her time with her mother in Soweto and half with her father in the Eastern Cape. Her great-grandmother was jailed at Constitutional Hill in Johannesburg for marching for women's rights. So Buhlebezwe grew up very aware of the political situation in South Africa. She can even remember her grandmother playing pretend voting with her where she had to draw her own ballots. That might be where she developed the strong impression that artists have an important job to do. Art should help people heal from the difficult situations that life has brought them.

Buhlebezwe mostly does performance art, which is a form of art where you use your own or other people's bodies in a space and an audience watches it. She has also made many artworks with a kind of soap from the Eastern Cape that her family used for washing everything from clothes, to hair, to dishes. She carved a figure of herself out of this soap, and molded the soap into the shape of the dish that they used to wash themselves. This art work was shown in Paris as part of a celebration of South African contemporary artists.

After receiving her calling, Buhlebezwe started seeing her art as part of her spirituality. She thinks that people respond to her work because it is very honest.

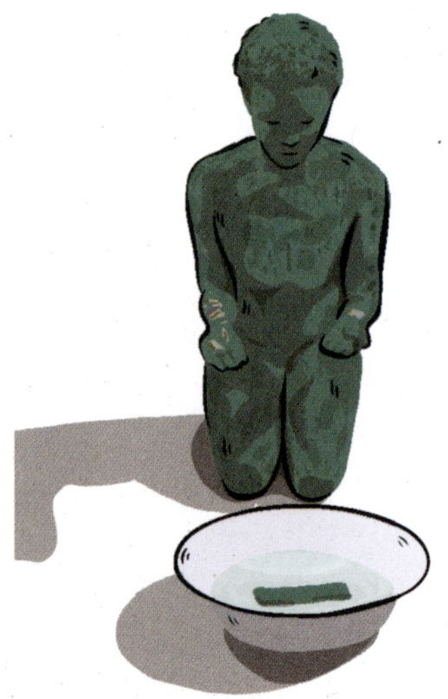

• Illustration of 'Batsho bancama', 2017. Green soap, resin, enamel, steel and rose petals.

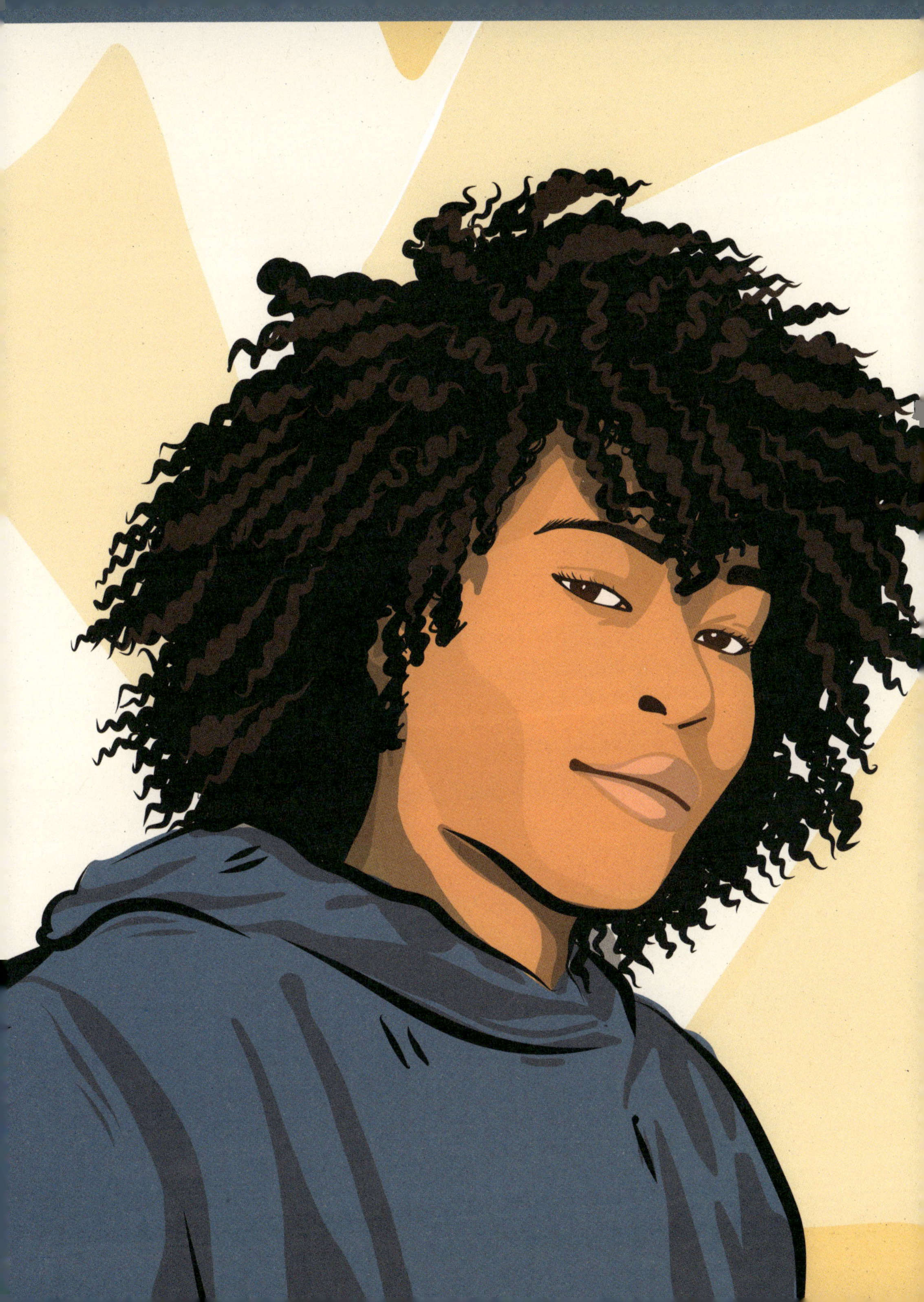

CAMERON PLATTER

Growing up in KwaZulu-Natal, Cameron Platter was a single child and his parents were very busy writers. He had a lot of time to spend by himself drawing and a lot of time in the company of adults. His parents were not particularly strict, but he sometimes felt that he had to grow up fast. When he discovered skateboarding it made him feel more like himself. There was something about skateboarding that had to do with being fearless, independent and cool that he liked. He thinks a lot of his art can still be compared to skateboarding. But it is hard to say exactly why. And that is one of the things Cameron thinks art is there for: to say things in a different language when you can't quite describe it in words.

Cameron was still in primary school when he first felt the magical feeling of making art. He started doing a lot of art and, when he was in high school, he was mentored by one of South Africa's most famous artists, Cecil Skotnes. It was great to see how a professional artist worked and he knew that he wanted to be an artist too. But it was not always easy, because he didn't want to make art that looked like art should. There was something in him that wanted to break the rules and have fun, even when he was asking serious questions about our lives in his art.

He realised that as one grows up there are many rules and manners that parents or elders teach you so that you can behave in a way that they see as proper. That means that some human behaviours, like burping, laughing loudly in assembly and pointing at things, embarrass people, even if they are natural human reactions. Cameron is interested in things that are part of being human, but that people don't want to show or think about. He also likes to make artworks that are bright and colourful that do not always look like serious art. Sometimes he works in sculpture, sometimes in painting, drawing or printmaking and he has shown his art in many countries around the world.

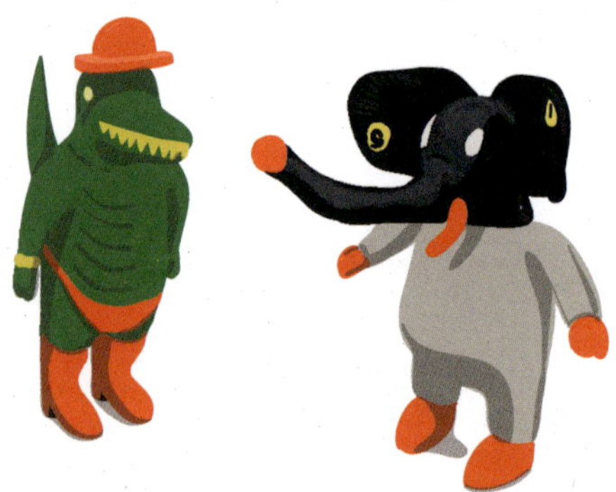

Illustration of 'Three missed calls', 2006. Installation of wooden sculptures.

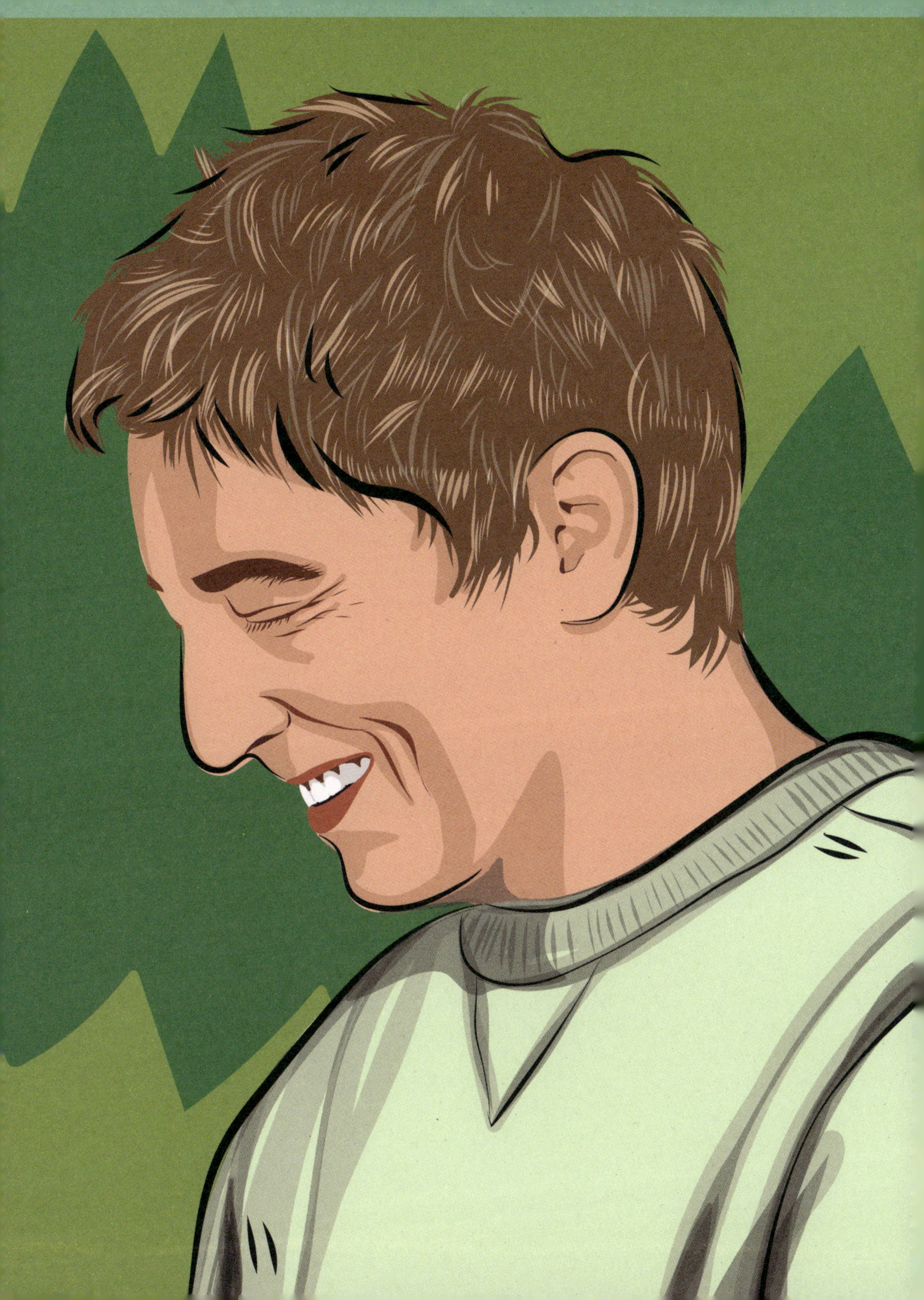

He is now a father of two and lives in KwaZulu-Natal. As he watches his two children, he can see a lot of himself and the way he makes art in his children when they run around like crazy all over their house, giggling, shouting, fighting and just generally behaving like children!

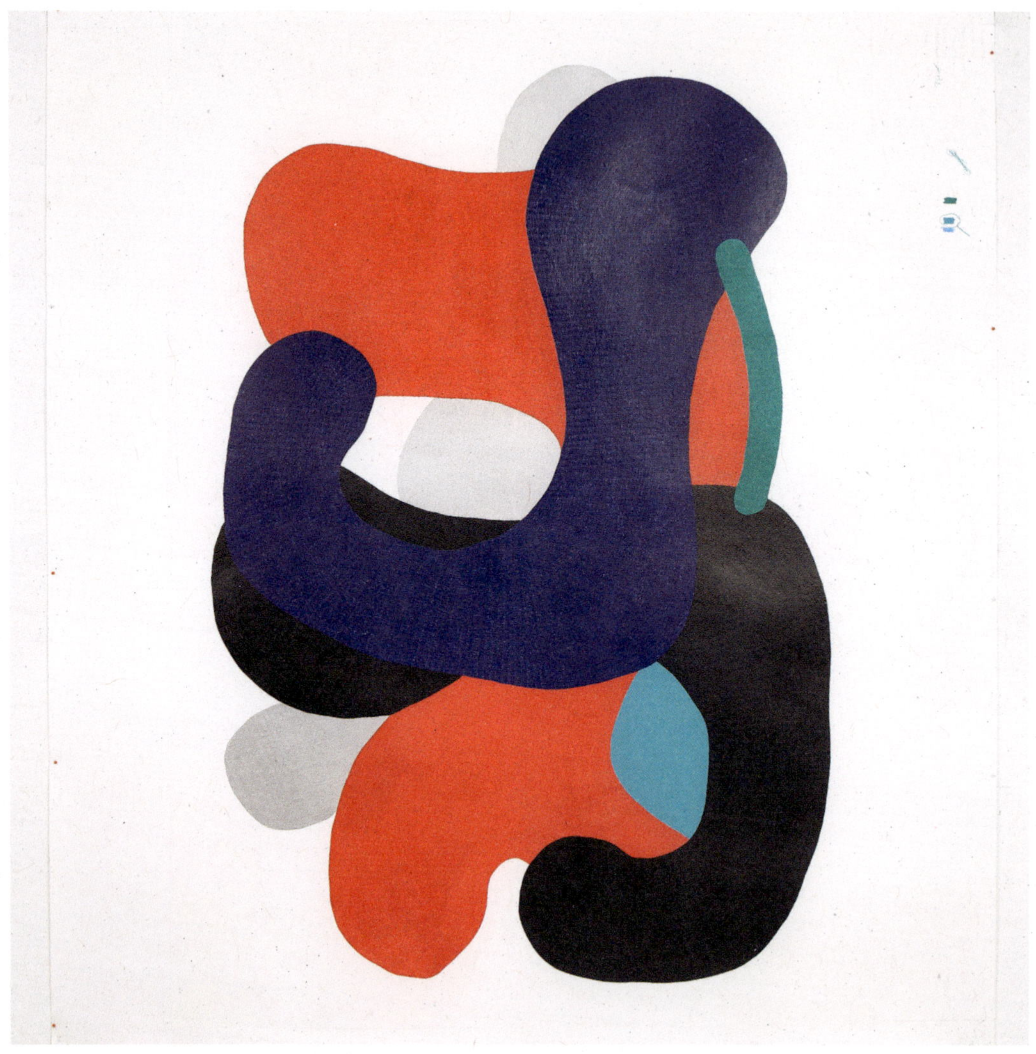

● *Top: Dance Routine, 2019. Pencil on paper. Courtesy of the artist.* ● *Right: 'Thousand Island', 2019. Pencil on paper. Courtesy of the artist.*

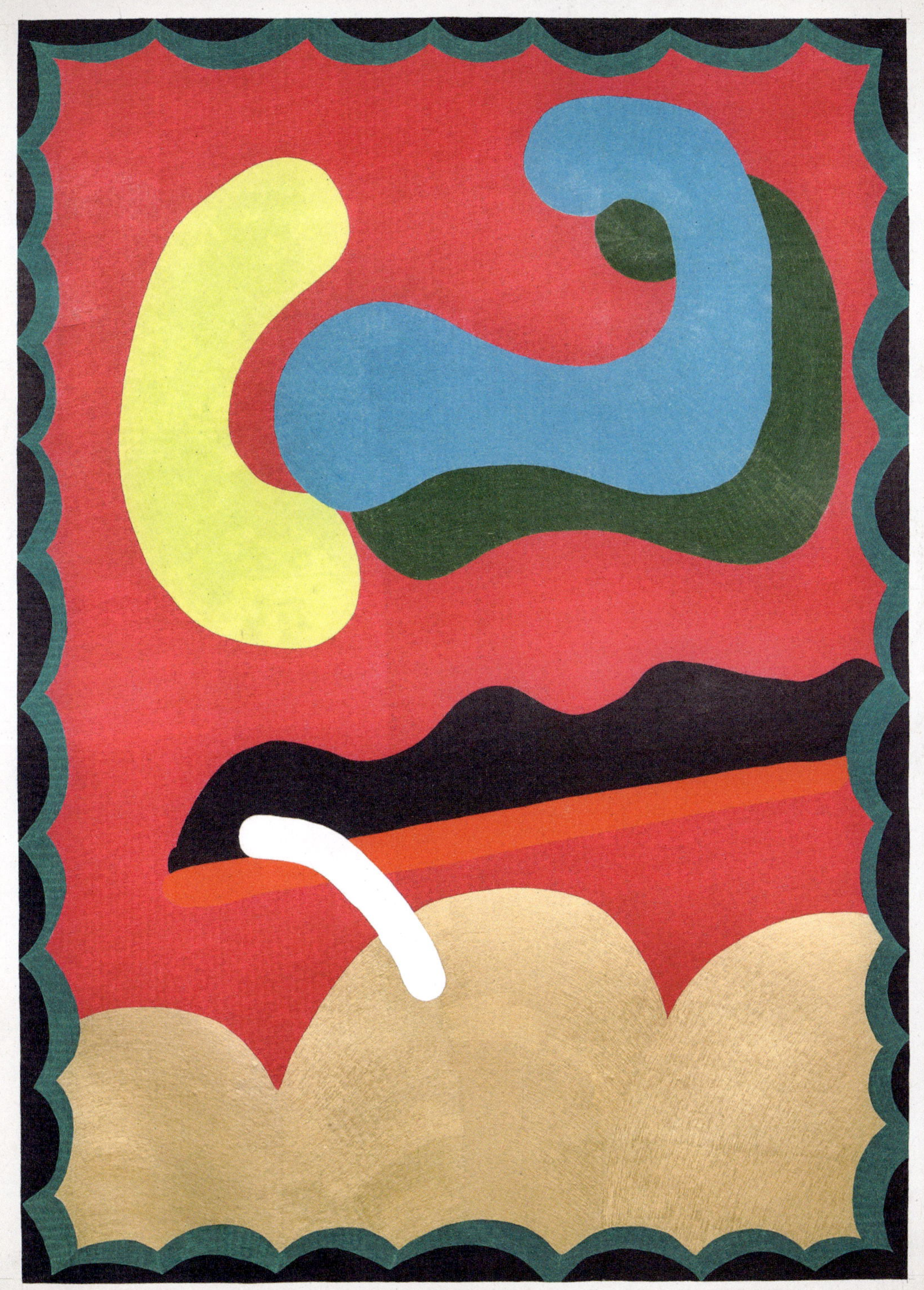

DAVID KOLOANE

The charcoal and pastel drawings by David Koloane are full of information about life in South Africa. David looks at the world around him and creates drawings or paintings that ask questions about how people live and about whether all people are safe, respected and protected. David is one of those people who are many things in one day: a lecturer, an art critic who writes about art works, an art curator and a full-time practicing artist.

A long time ago, David grew up in the township of Alexandra in Johannesburg and he remembers the streets being alive with musical performances, choirs and church bands. David loved reading as much as soccer and socialising and he had all kinds of friends. In his own home he was being brought up by a group of women and next door was a family who didn't have any children and he became their child too.

David loved drawing. At the time, there were so many apartheid rules that governed the lives of black people, David just assumed it was not allowed for black people to be artists. One day a friend took him to an art gallery and he felt he could stay there the whole day.

When he started going to art classes in the city he knew from the moment he walked in that he had found his place. He started going to the studio every Saturday, and even though Saturdays were the busiest days in the township with sports and parties, he kept going.

His friends said, 'You're going to an art lesson on a Saturday? You must be out of your mind!'

Later, after he had decided to join the art classes full time, a buyer of his work created a his first exhibition to showcase what he had been doing. He was very surprised and shy at first, but it was a big success. He went to study in London and thereafter taught art for a long time at the Federated Union of Black Artists Arts Centre.

It has always been important for David to create more opportunities for black artists, especially those from the townships. He was part of the group that founded the Bag Factory Artist Studio as a place where artists could have studios and get mentorships. Until he was in his seventies, you could still see David walking all the way from across the other side of Johannesburg to his studio at the Bag Factory to make art and be an inspiration to generations of young artists.

● This interview was carried out before David's passing on 30 June 2019.

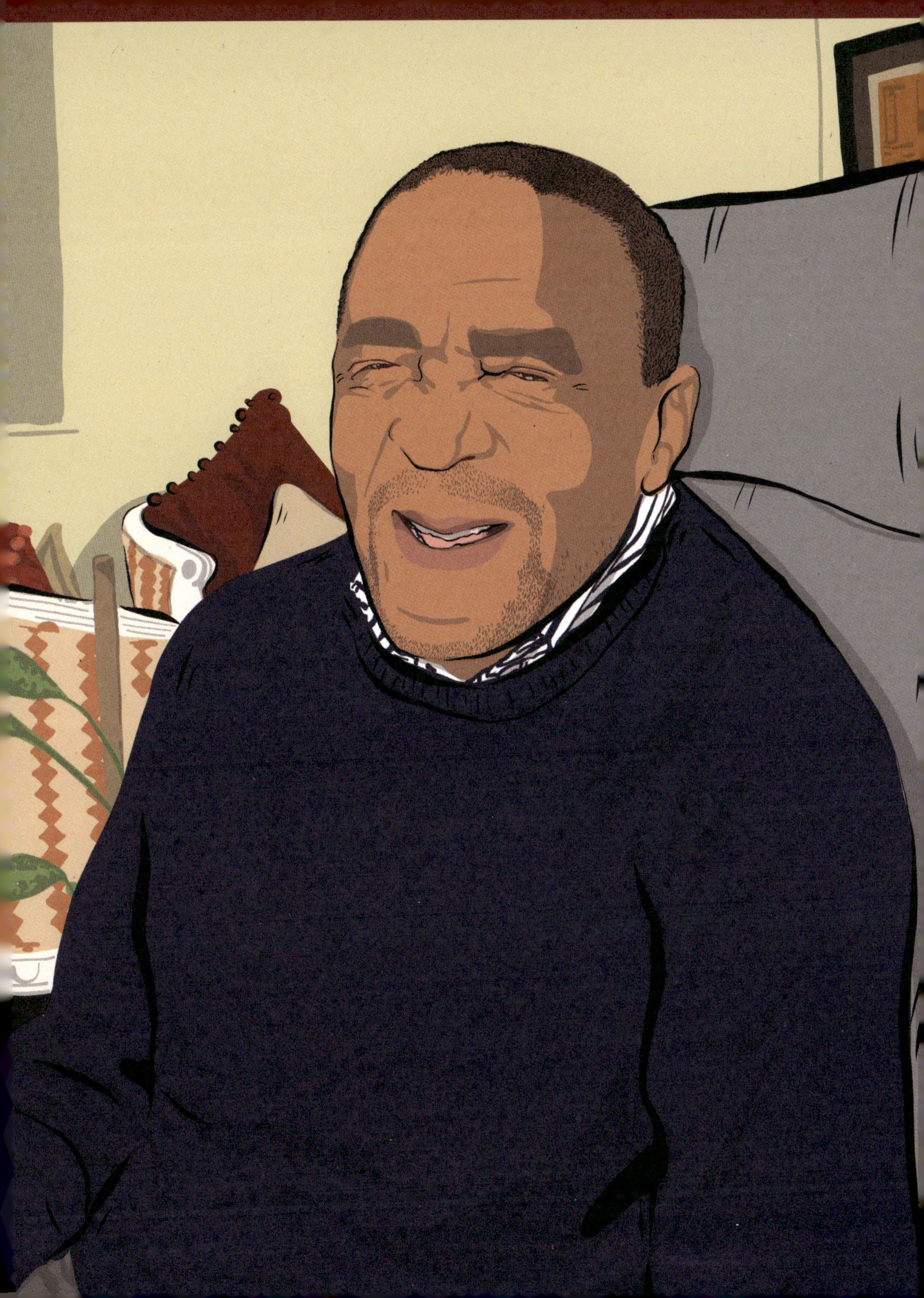

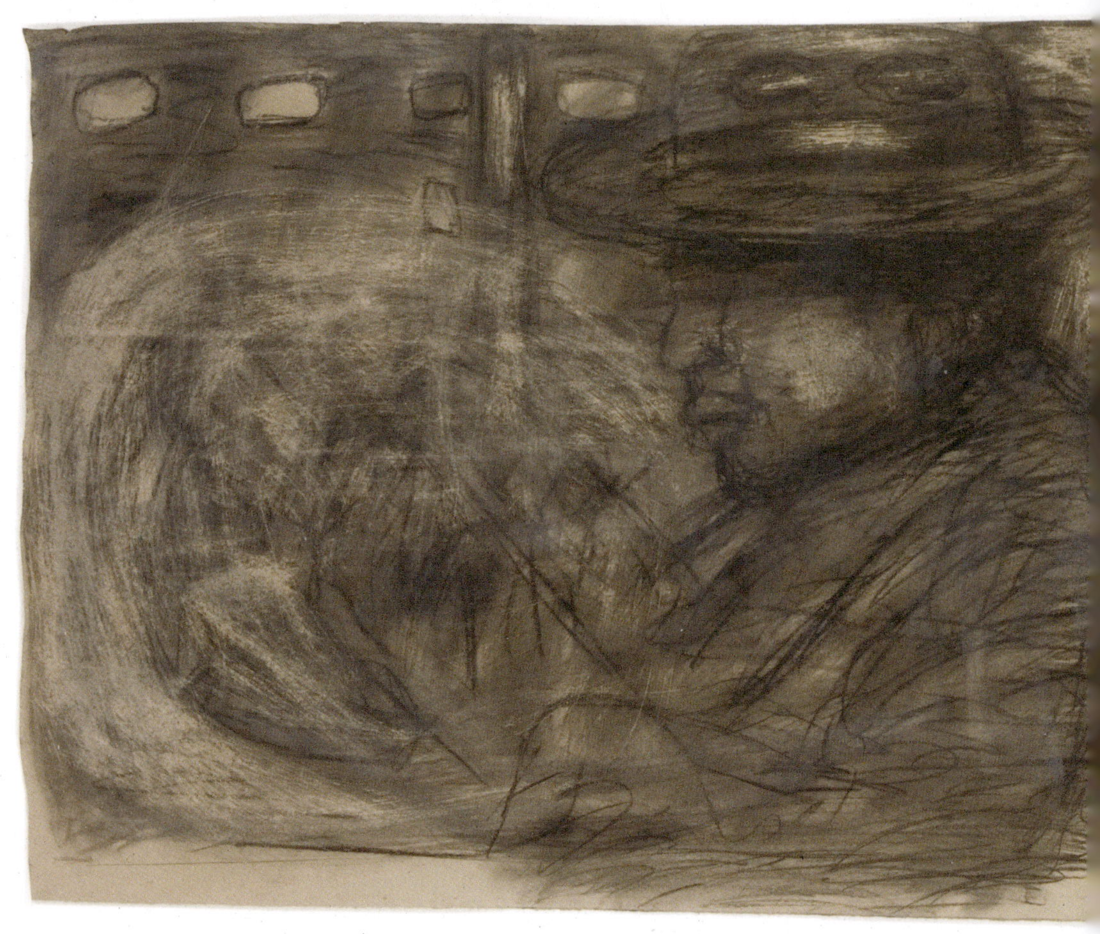

• 'Night Shift', 2010. Pastel and charcoal on paper. Courtesy of the artist and Goodman Gallery.

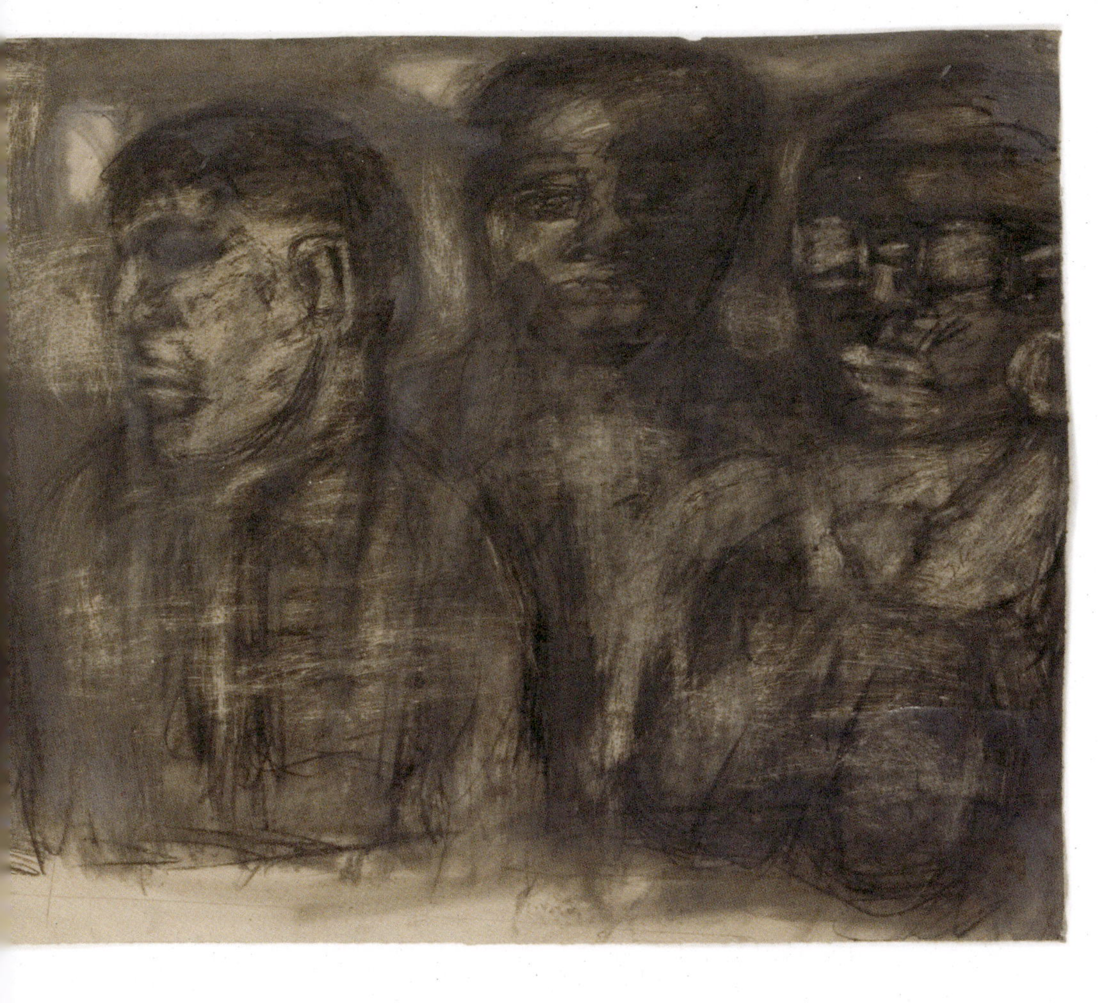

Frances Goodman

As a little girl of only three years old, Frances Goodman already knew that she wanted to be an artist, and nothing else. She was surrounded by art in her home and her parents had many artist friends. She wanted to make objects. She would come back from walks with sticks and leaves and then make little animals with things that you wouldn't normally think of as art materials.

Frances wanted to make work for people like her parents who are not from the art world, but learn to love it over time. As she grew older she realised that art does a very special job in the world we live in. It might not be defending people in court like lawyers do, but it gives more meaning to people's lives.

When she makes her art, Frances thinks a lot about how women are shown in adverts and movies. Are they shown the same way as men? Or are they always less important and less strong? Frances feels that on social media everyone looks perfect and happy, but maybe they are not, they just feel like they have to look that way to be accepted, or to be successful.

She once made a very, very big work about weddings that has been shown all over the world. The piece shows how nervous women are about their wedding day. Throughout the years many women have written to her to say that since they saw this artwork they feel so much better about how difficult it is to be perfect on their wedding day. Frances's work tells them that it is okay and normal to feel as if you have to be the perfect bride, but that it is almost impossible to be that way.

She has also made work where the whole object is made up of hundreds of different coloured false nails. For Frances, these works are about how we make the surface of our lives so shiny with things, but that often underneath that surface people are scared and alone. Art can bring those feelings out into the open and then people can understand that vulnerability is also part of being human.

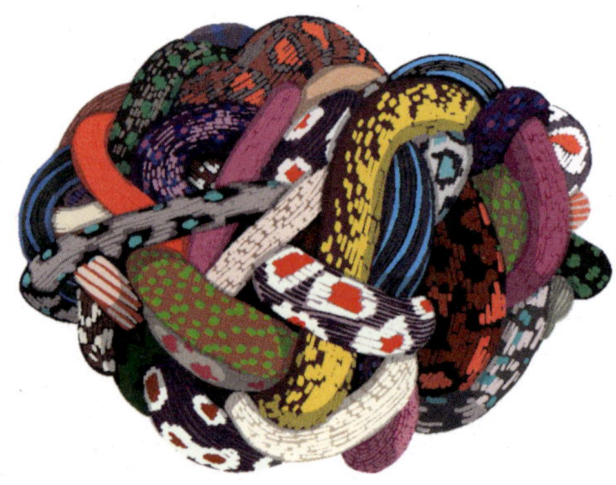

● *Illustration of 'Comfortable Entanglement', 2019. Acrylic nails, wood, foam, resin, silicon.
Right: Illustration from photograph by Jurie Potgieter.*

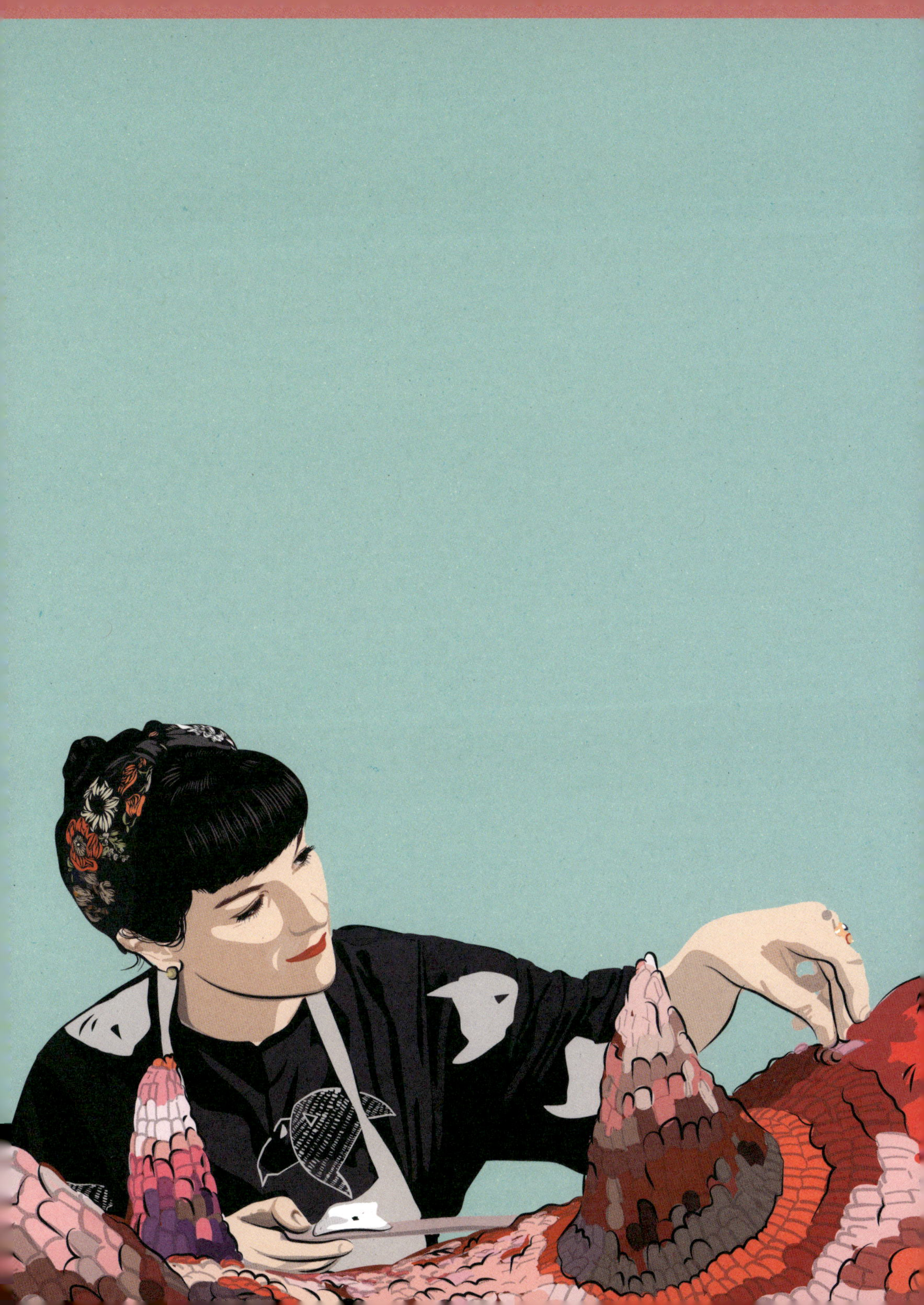

GaBrieLle gOliAtH

Art is not necessarily the first thing that comes to mind when you think of trying to feel better about something really hard that happened to you. It is also not always what you think of when you want to bring change about in the world. There are other ways of doing that. But for Gabrielle Goliath, that is exactly what she wants her work to do. Gabrielle believes art can be a gentler and quieter way of bringing attention to vulnerability. She also believes in the power of art to help individuals heal from past experiences.

Gabrielle never thought that she would be the one in the family who would end up an artist. Her father, an engineering estimator in Kimberley, also played the drums and painted. Her brothers all loved music. She remembers her mother always reading. Sometimes her mother would try and hide herself away to read a bit in between being a mom, but Gabriella always found her and asked her to teach her words. If her father gave her the talents of working with images and music, her mother gave her the gifts of reading, researching and writing. All these elements combine in Gabrielle's work.

Sometimes her art is elaborate with video, sound, installation and performers. In 'Elegy' Gabrielle spent months speaking to people who have suffered trauma and created a live performance from some of what they shared. This installation speaks about suffering, healing and how we are all connected as people.

Other times her work is a simple gesture. 'Stumbling Block' has been performed in many places and in it Gabrielle and some other women lie on the floor on flat boxes covered in grey blankets for seven hours. They often lie in such a way that people have to step over them. What are these lying figures reminding us of? It is a very common thing in cities that we all see every day: people sleeping by the side of the road. Often we turn our eyes away and pretend we don't see them. With this artwork Gabrielle shows how these figures, vulnerable by the side of the road, are always unwelcome.

Gabrielle's work shines a light on difficult aspects of life that we don't always want to think about but are part of the world we live in.

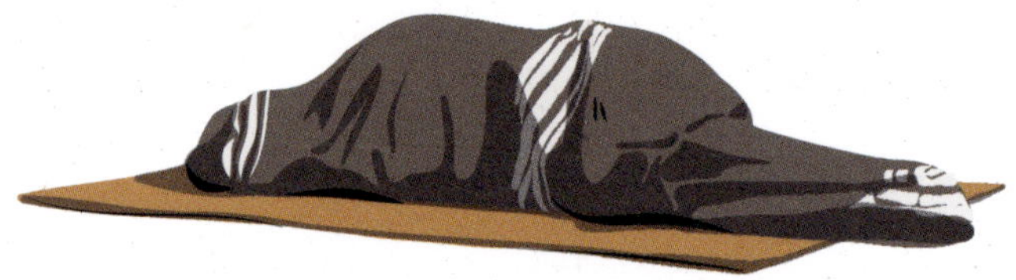

• Illustration of 'Stumbling Block', 2011. Performance.

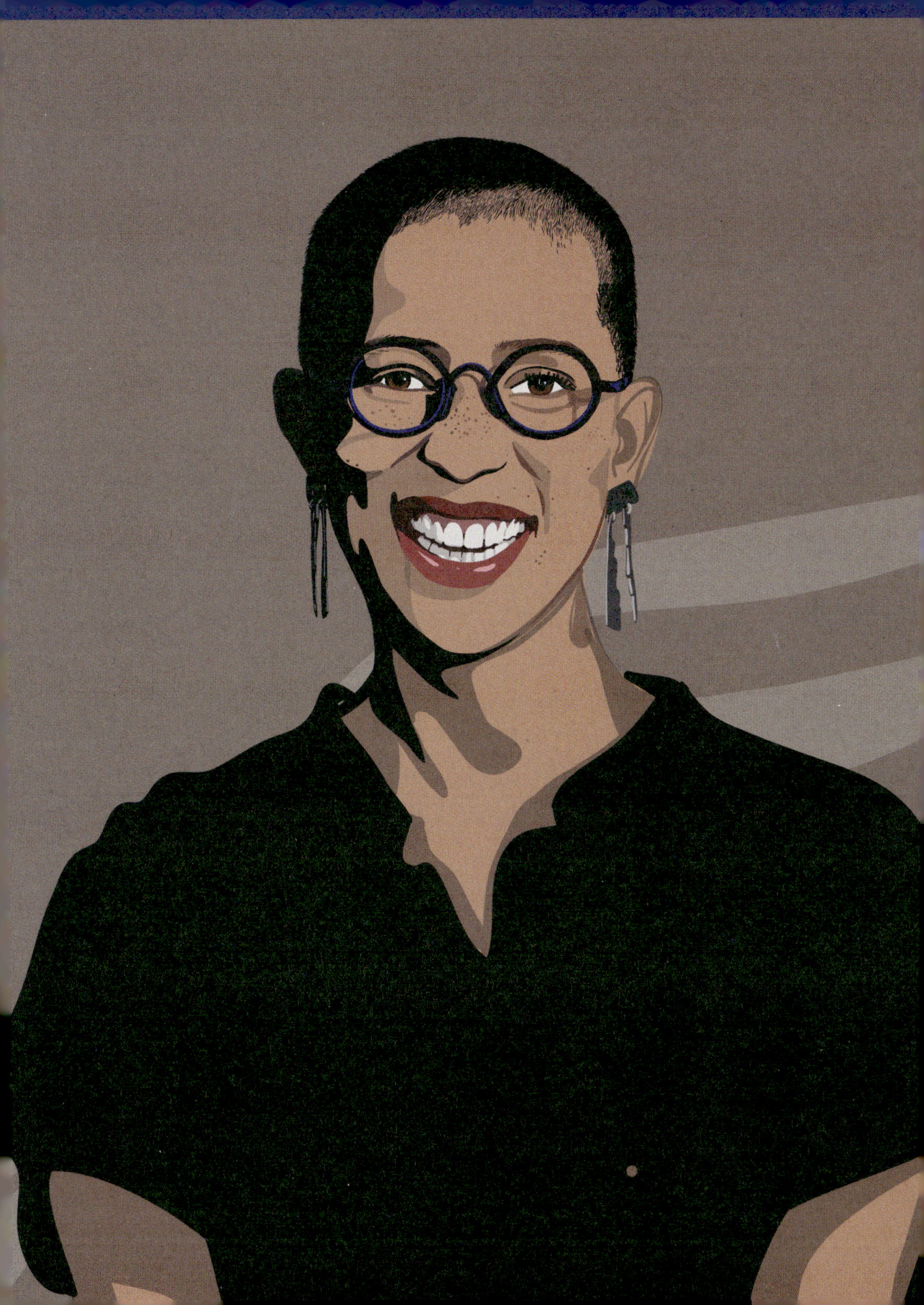

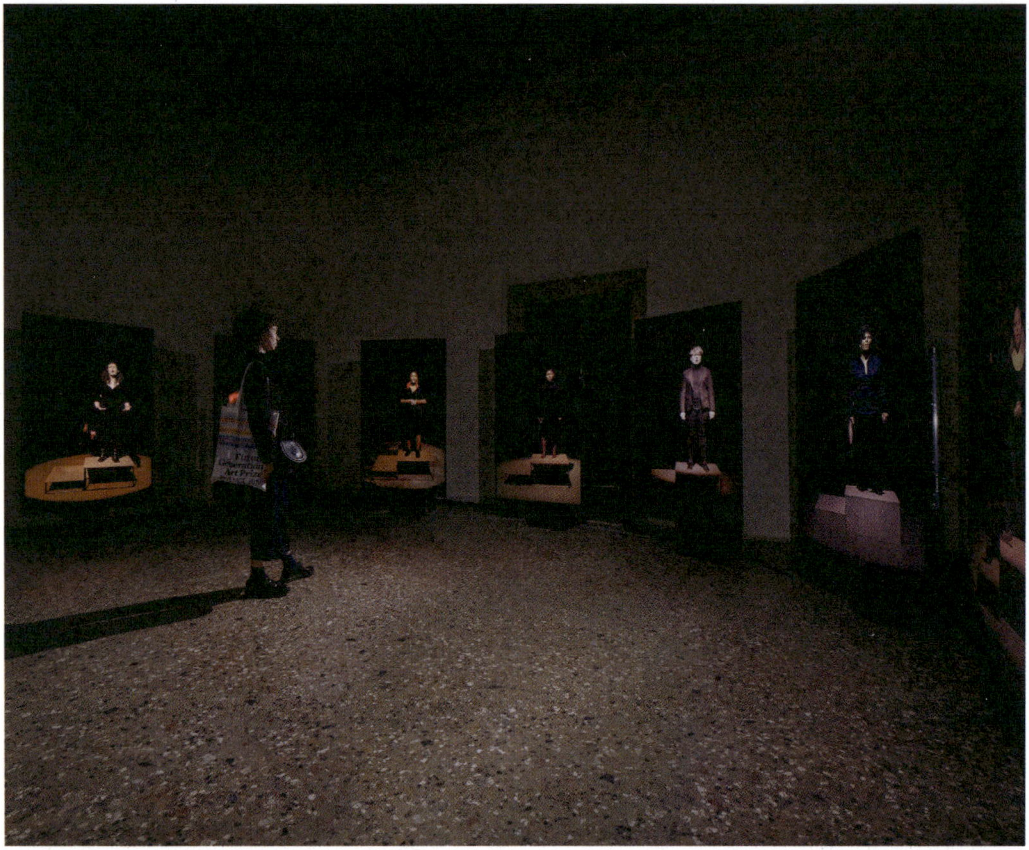

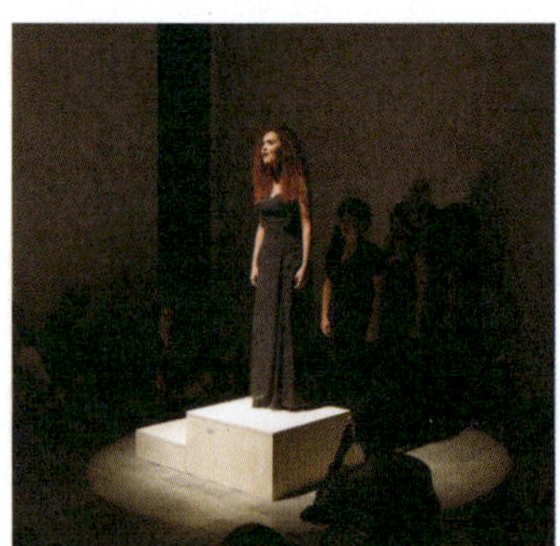
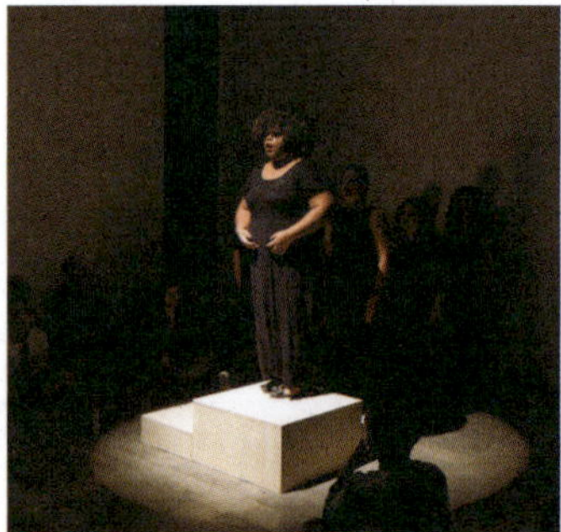
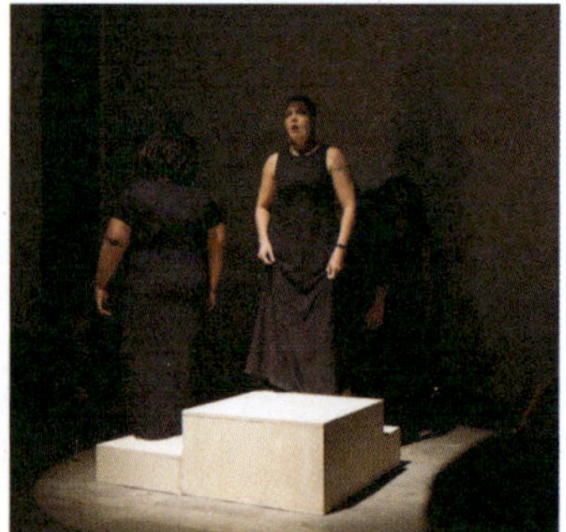

● 'Elegy', 2018. Sizakele Sigasa & Salome Masooa, Verbo Performance Art Festival, Galeria Vermelho & Videobrasil, São Paulo.
Photo: Edouard Fraipont and Stumbling Block (2011–), 2019. Long-term performance.
Duration: variable. Centro Cultural, São Paulo. Photo courtesy of Goodman Gallery.

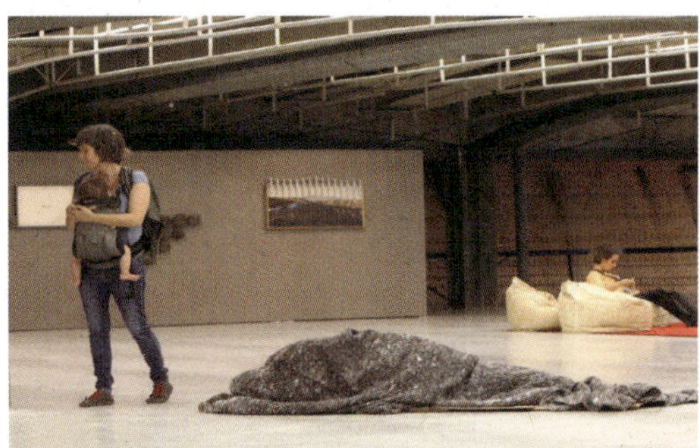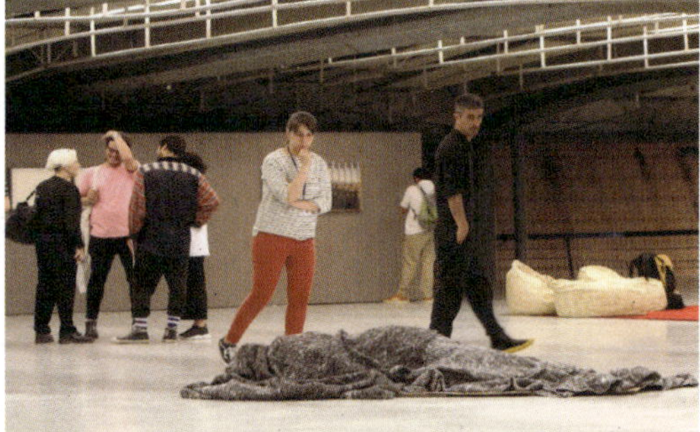

● *'Stumbling Block', 2011. Performance. Courtesy of the artist.*

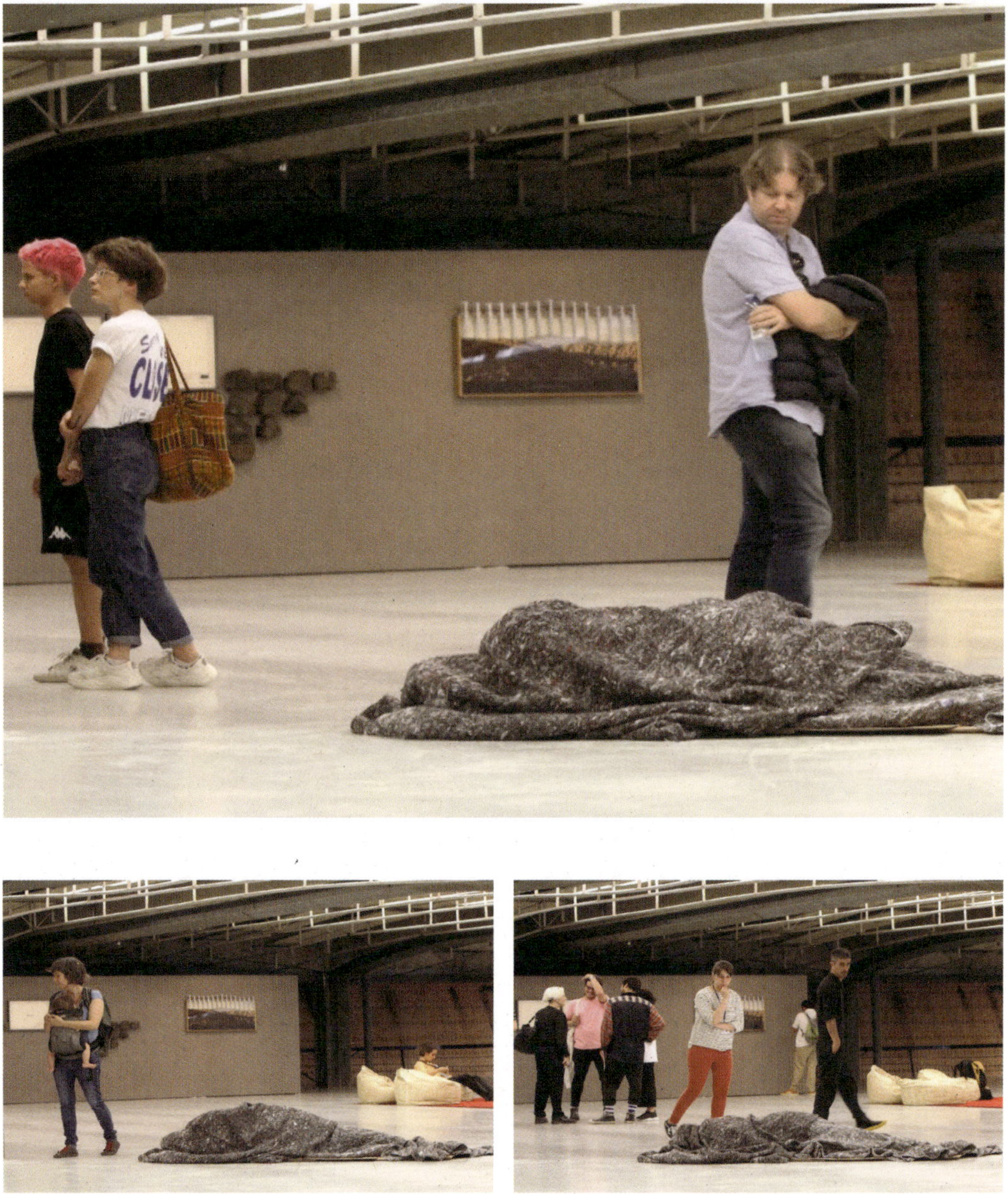

Igshaan Adams

Competition between siblings or friends can be the inspiration for finding something that you're really good at. When he was growing up, Igshaan Adams felt that his brother was good at everything. He was cool and popular and even got into local newspapers for his BMX tricks. So when Igshaan found out that he was good at drawing and schoolwork, he tried extra hard to stand out.

His father used to make pen line drawings and to Igshaan it looked like magic happening in front of his eyes. His aunts were also always making things in especially creative ways, like turning a pillowcase into a lampshade or using plants to decorate church posters. In his own artworks, he still uses materials that are close to hand and not expensive, like paper, or cloth.

Igshaan went to Cape College and learnt how to paint and draw. But he was extremely shy and didn't feel good about himself. Some of these feelings came from difficulties that he faced while growing up. He also needed to earn money, so he started just drifting around. A few years later, he went to a holiday school art workshop. The teachers at the art school saw his work and thought it was so good they gave him a scholarship to study art there.

As soon as he got this opportunity he started only making art. It wasn't long before he won prizes and important galleries started exhibiting his work. Igshaan wanted to use art to understand who he was and to work through the many difficulties he had experienced. He also used it as a way of healing the relationships with his close family. He did art performances with his grandmother, who raised him, his sister, his brother and his father. After the performances many of the viewers feel moved and come to talk to him about their own lives.

Igshaan believes that art helps you to know yourself better and it can bring a person peace. He thinks everyone should draw or paint even if they don't think they are talented. The important thing is the process of art.

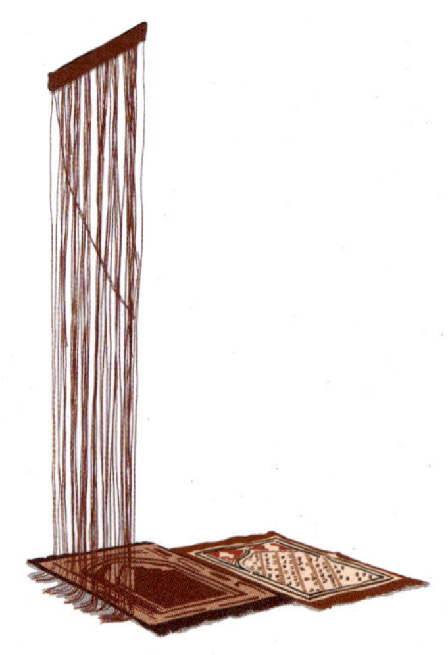

• *Illustration of detail from '69', 2013. Mixed media.*

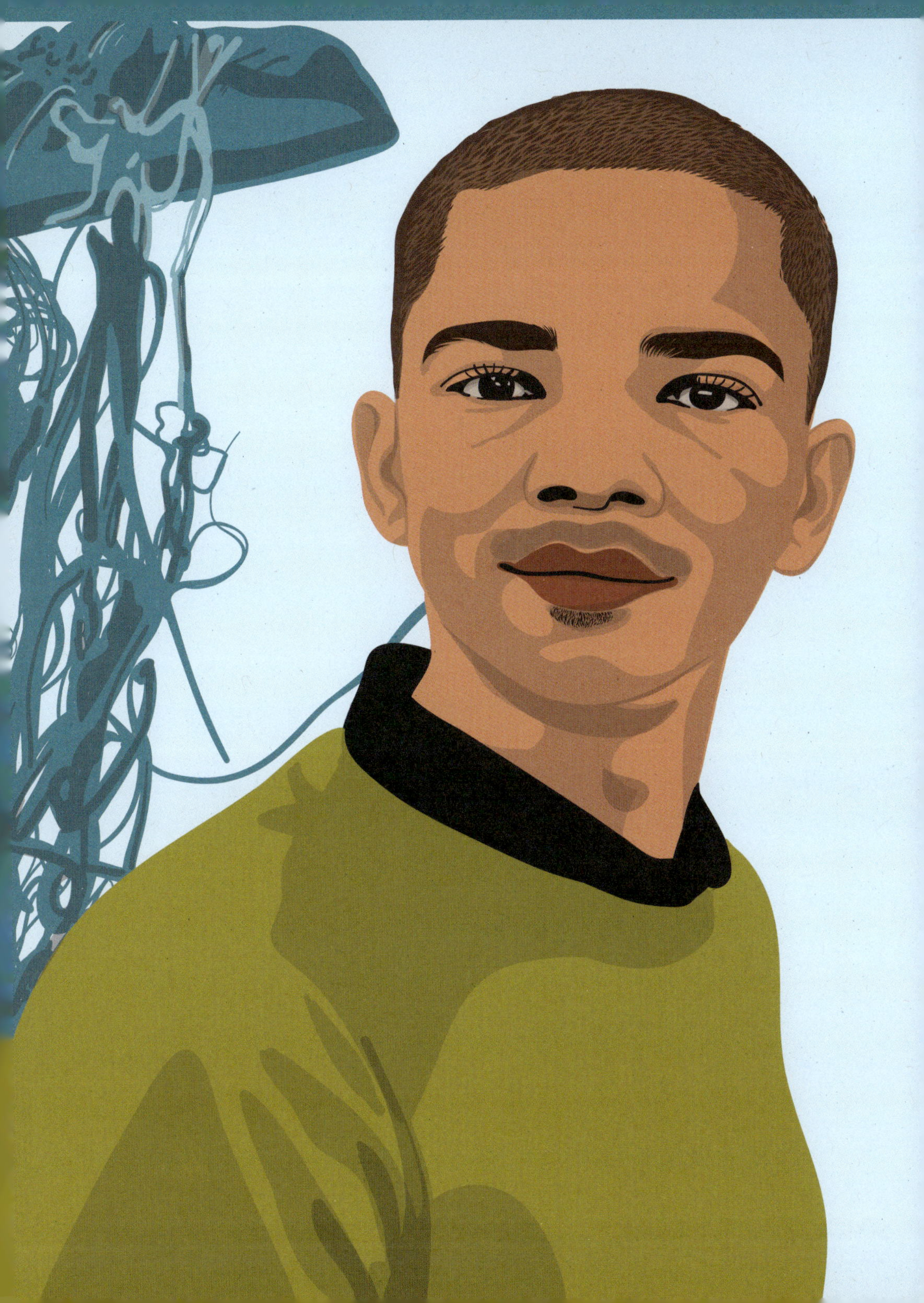

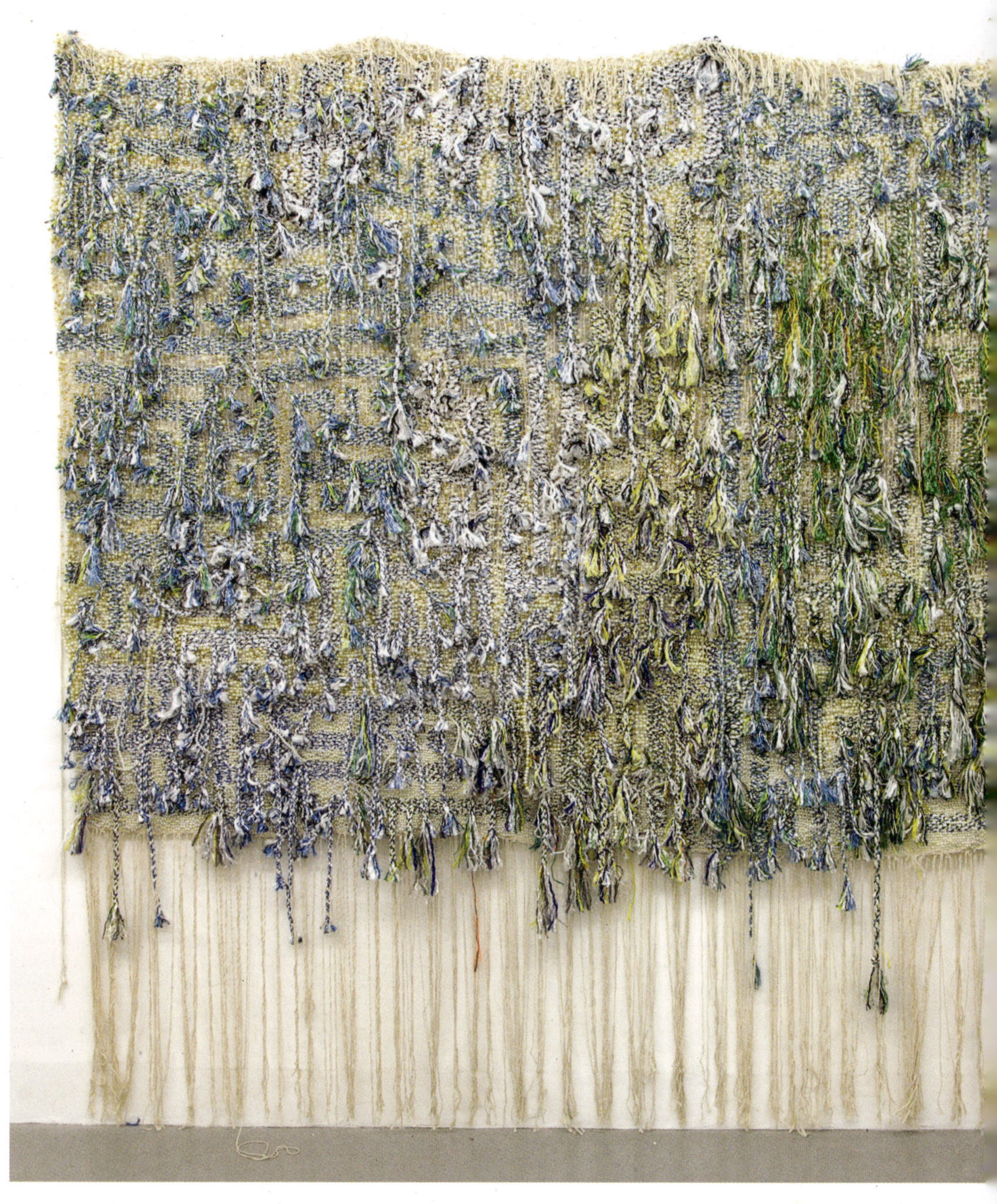

● 'Surah al-Kafirun III (part one & two)', 2016. Woven nylon rope, beads and string, at Frieze NY. Courtesy of the artist and Blank Projects.

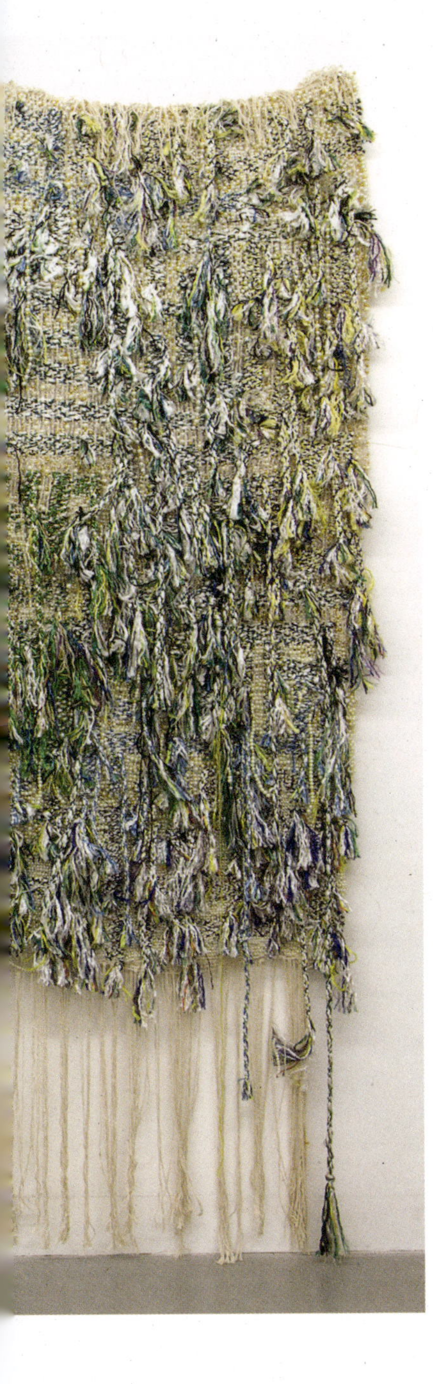

Jo Ractliffe

When Jo Ractliffe was growing up, she knew she wanted to do art. Her mother was a sculptor and she also wanted to do something in the arts so she went to study painting after school. She tried her best, but didn't think she was very good. Then, one night she attended an evening photography class. She can still remember how fascinated she became. At once, almost like the click of a camera, she thought: 'This is it.'

Although things have changed a lot, there was a time when there wasn't that much photography in art galleries or museums. Because Jo didn't make paintings or sculptures, there were many times when Jo felt that she did not know where she belonged. She mainly took photographs of empty landscapes with no people in them. The other photographers were confused and they asked her: 'What are you photographing? This isn't photography.'

Jo likes to photograph landscapes to understand what the landscape is saying about what has happened there. She goes back to a place that she has photographed many times to look at it again and again. So she works very slowly and it sometimes takes years for the actual artwork to be finished. These works were strange to other photographers and she was worried that she might never find people who were interested in what she does.

Then someone said to her: 'What is important in making art is to keep on making the work, not caring whether people like the work or not'. That made her feel that she could do whatever she wanted. And since then she has exhibited her work in international museums all over the world, because, after a while she did find people who thought what she was doing was important.

Jo has also always enjoyed being a lecturer and looking back now she sees herself as both a photographer and a teacher. She has realised that once you are someone's teacher you remain their teacher for life and she has loved being part of her students' art and helping them understand her art through workshops and lectures.

• Right background: Illustration of 'Vlakplaas: 2 June 1999 (drive-by shooting)', 1999. Pigment print on cotton paper.

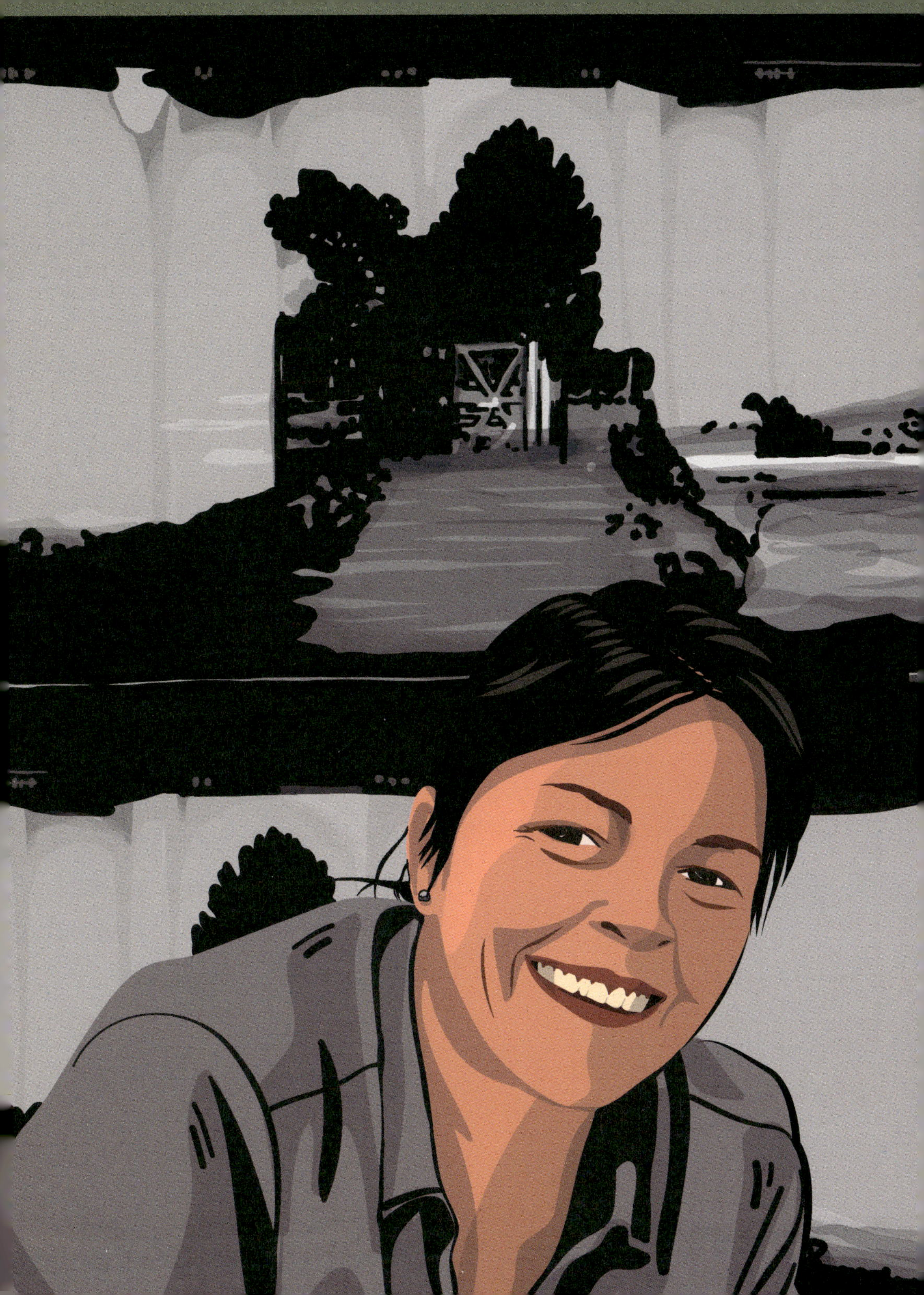

JULIA CHARLTON

Julia Charlton's story is also the story of one of the biggest art museums in South Africa, The Wits Art Museum. also called WAM.

Art came to Julia by default. She had sisters who were good at music and ballet. So she thought if she tried art it might be something that she could be good at. She spent a lot of time in high school and university studying art up to a very high level. Looking back on those years she wonders what her younger self thought she might do with all those art degrees in the end but somehow it wasn't a big problem back then. After that she just started working in various galleries and art shops to make a living.

Julia ended up at the Gertrude Posel Gallery at the University of the Witswatersrand. Five years later, the university decided to close it. The team was given a basement to work from and to store everything in, while they waited for a new space. But they never knew if they would ever get a new space. One day Julia came to the gallery and realised that the whole basement had flooded and her spirits reached a really low point.

Julia and her team went around asking big businesses and people in the art community for the money they needed to complete a new art museum building. It took a lot of patience and determination and ten years to raise the funds.

The Wits Art Museum has become a place where questions can be asked about the big collection of African artefacts, such as masks and figures, that Wits owns. Many of these objects were gathered by anthropologists in the 1920s and 1930s. Wits can display these objects and spark new debates about what these objects mean. Some people wonder whether these objects belong in a museum in the first place, because they were taken away from the people who originally owned them.

Julia has seen all kinds of people come to the museum and they run many programmes for children to learn about art, or to make art themselves, especially during school holidays. Today WAM is a free space and the whole art community has come together in different ways to help to create a success out of it.

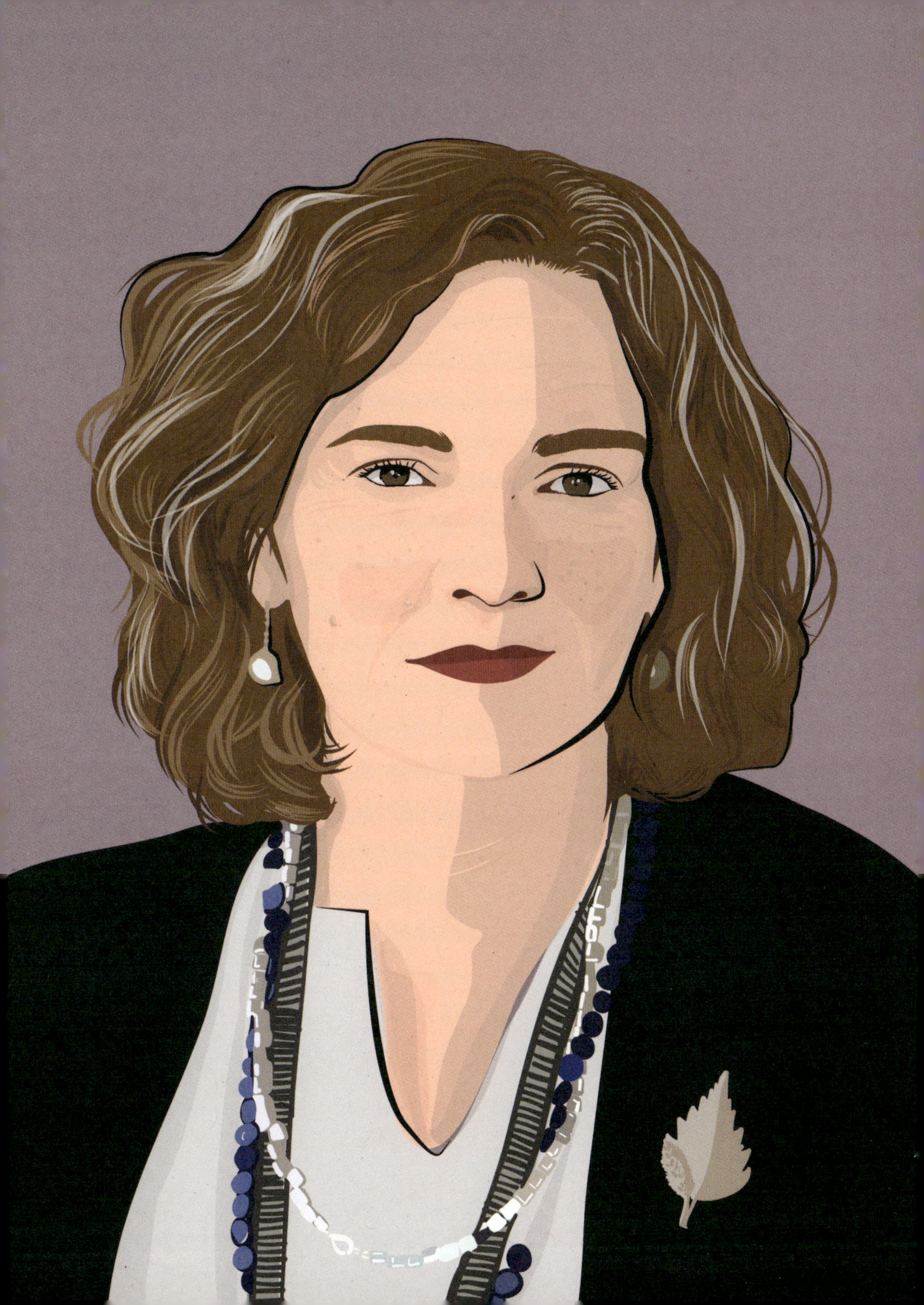

JUSTIN DINGWALL

Justin Dingwall felt different from other kids growing up. He was skinny and shy and the shyer he got, the more he was bullied. His parents sent all three sons to a technical high school to learn a trade. Justin was very good at fitting and turning, which is a way to make things using machines.

Justin's favourite childhood memories were of drawing. His parents were very supportive and caring. Justin thinks his father would have been an amazing artist, but he was never able to follow his dreams. He never had the opportunity to work in the career that he wanted and Justin's parents didn't want that for him. His mother encouraged him to look at something creative and said: 'Let's go look at the photographic department.' He took one look and knew that it was just what he had been looking for.

Photography was a way to combine Justin's keen mechanical skills, and his visual way of understanding the world. He quickly became very good at taking photos for magazines, fashion and adverts and soon got lots of jobs.

In his spare time he started his own photographic projects. One day he had to take a portrait of a gallerist and took the chance to show her his art photographs. She loved them and said he could have an exhibition at her gallery. That was the start of an art career in photography that he still manages side by side with his commercial work.

Justin feels it is important to bring awareness through art. He has done a series of work focusing on albinism. He also created a body of work where he wanted to speak about the xenophobic attacks that were happening in South Africa. He then did a series of work to highlight the suffering of those with vitiligo. Vitiligo is a disease that creates white patches on the skin. These works took years to make and the models he worked with became very famous in the process.

Through his childhood and in his art he has learnt never to let obstacles stand in your way.

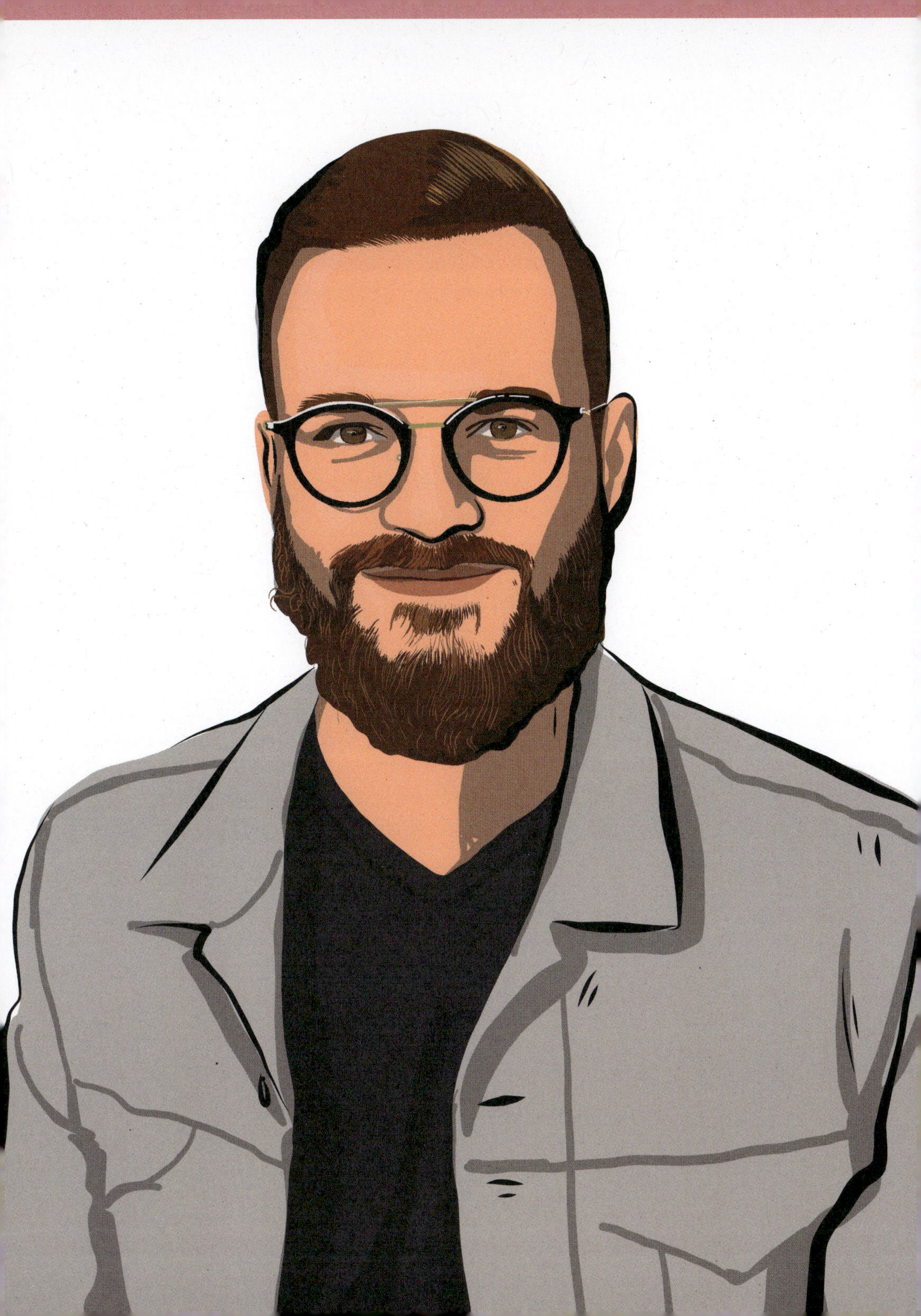

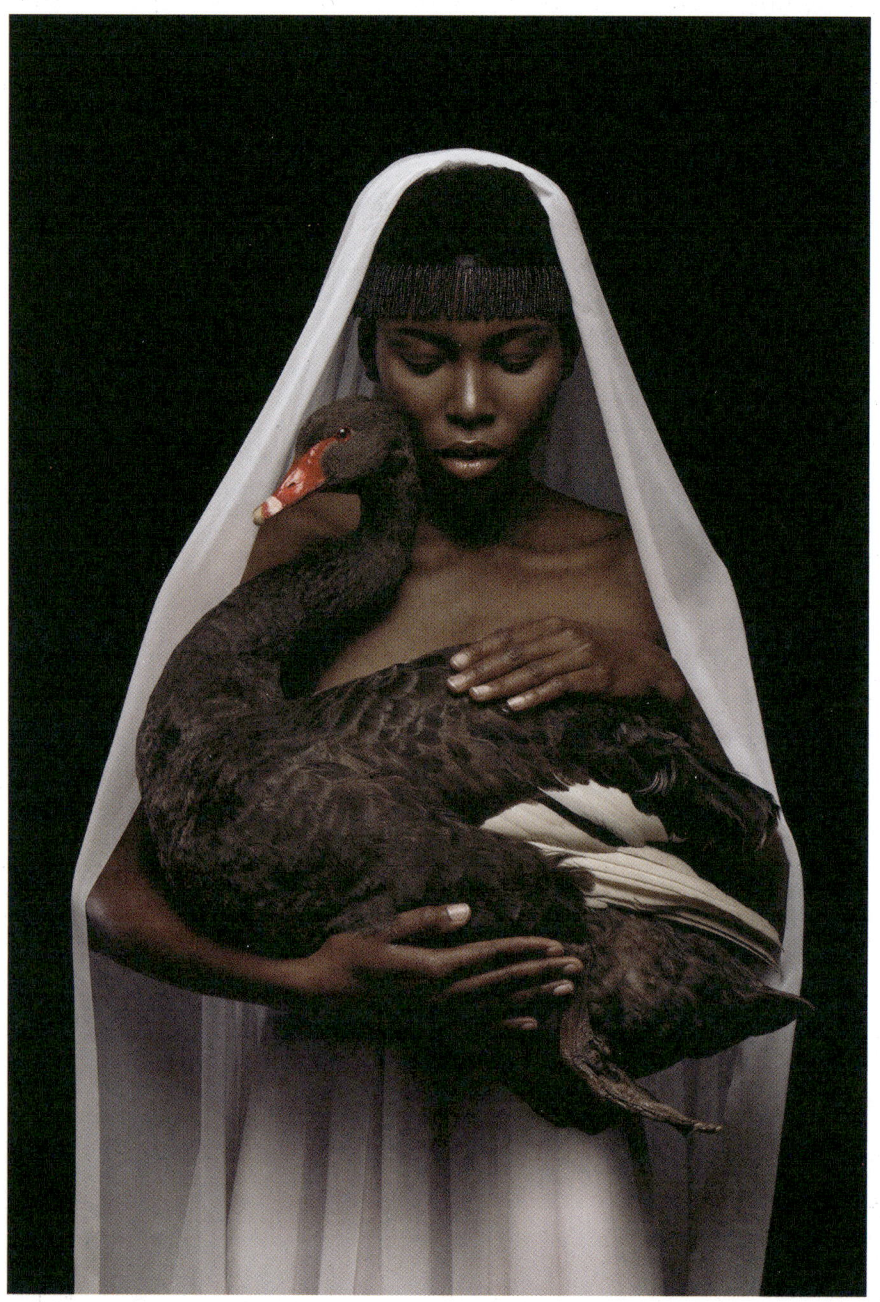

• *'This is a black swan', 2016. Photograph. Courtesy of the artist.*

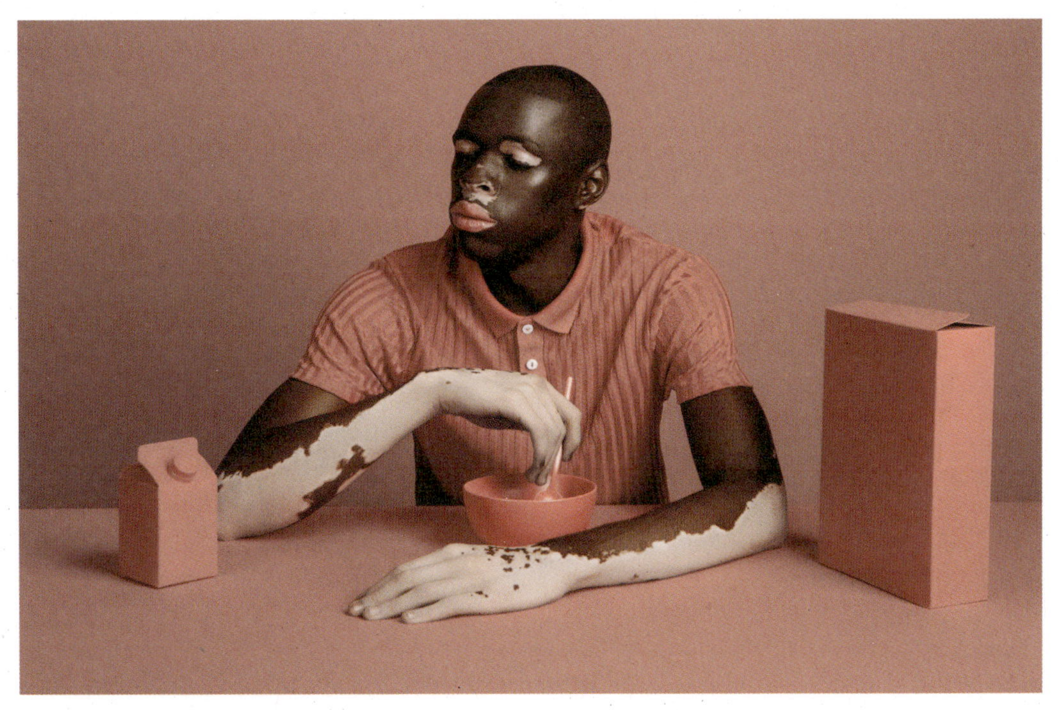

'A seat at the table' Ruby II, 2018. Photograph. Courtesy of the artist.

JYOTI MISTRY

Looking out from the window on the seventh floor of the building she lived in as a child, Jyoti Mistry felt like she could see the whole world. All around her were highways, bus stations and taxi ranks because the building was right in the middle of a spaghetti of roads coming together. Jyoti would spend many hours going through the stacks of her mother's magazines to cut out all sorts of pictures and stick them on paper in new arrangements, making collages. She thinks her mother could have been an amazing artist in another life because of her painting and drawing skills, but being creative came out of necessity because it kept three little children busy. Both being at the window looking down on the movement below and the putting together of cut-out images were influences on the filmmaker that Jyoti would become.

Another big influence was her dad's confectionery counter in one of Durban's cinemas. He sold candy and they could slip in and watch films as they were growing up. When Jyoti decided to study film much later on, her parents thought that was a wonderful idea. They all loved the cinema but they knew no one from South Africa who made films. A Fulbright scholarship took her to study in New York and then she started making films.

Jyoti exhibits in art galleries and museums using projectors and sometimes several TVs to show her work. Much of her time, since coming back to South Africa, has also been spent teaching. She says it's fun to be different people on different days: sometimes a filmmaker, sometimes an artist and sometimes a teacher.

For Jyoti, even her teaching is a form of art making because she spends a lot of time thinking about how to make her classes inspire and excite students. One of her favourite things in the whole world is watching students fall in love while creating films for her courses together. She is only half-joking when she says her courses bring people together who are like-minded!

When she makes her work, her main interest is answering a set of questions that she is curious about. Jyoti doesn't start with something she wants to say, but rather something she wants to ask and wondering if maybe there are others who are asking the same questions.

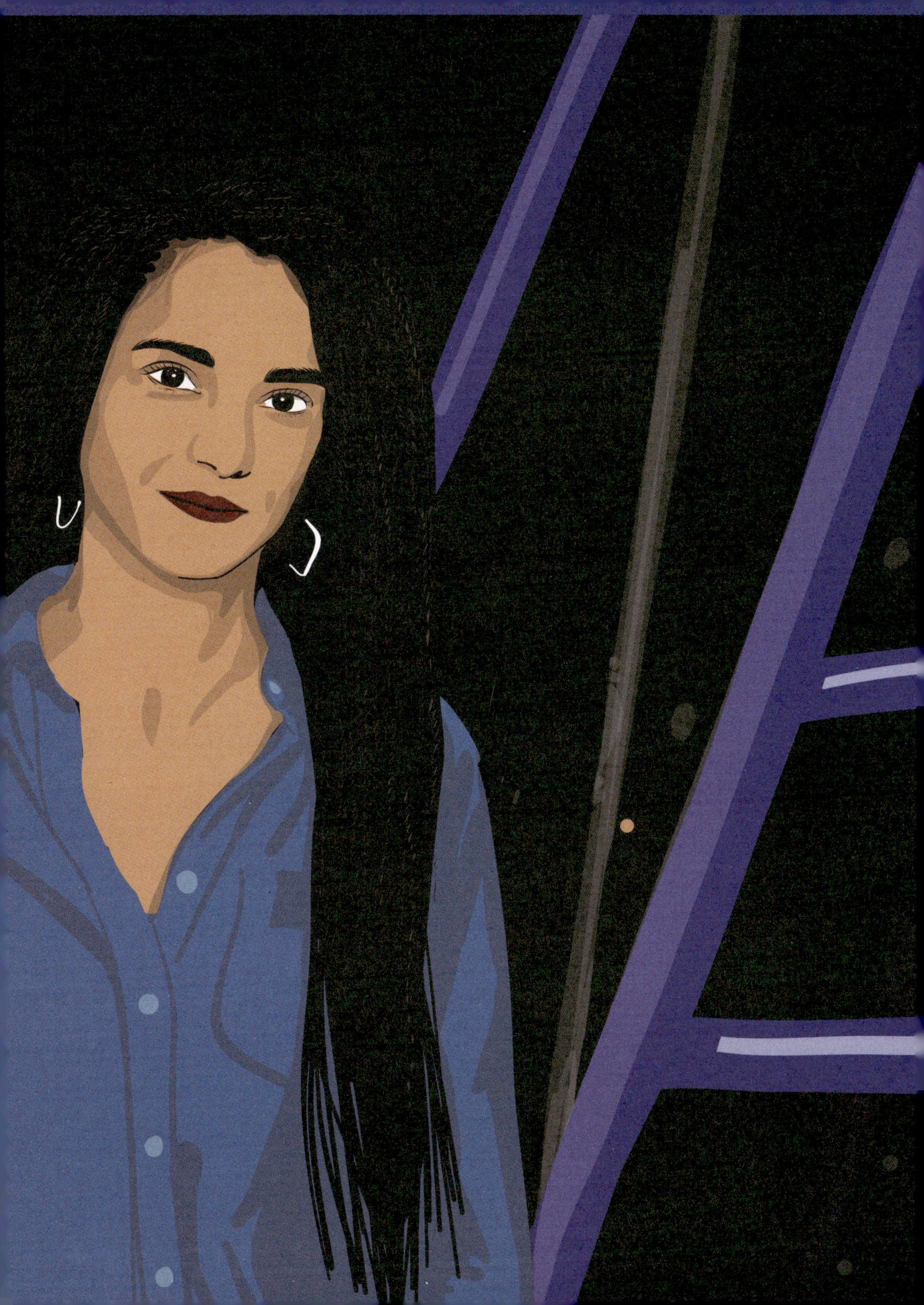

KAREL NEL

One day when Karel Nel was about six, he neatly placed 12 empty bottles in a row. During the following days he would put little bits of rocks in one bottle, another bottle got some leaves, in another bottle he put flowers and so he went. That was the start of the many different collections that Karel has built up and it gives us a clue to his interests in nature, observation and research.

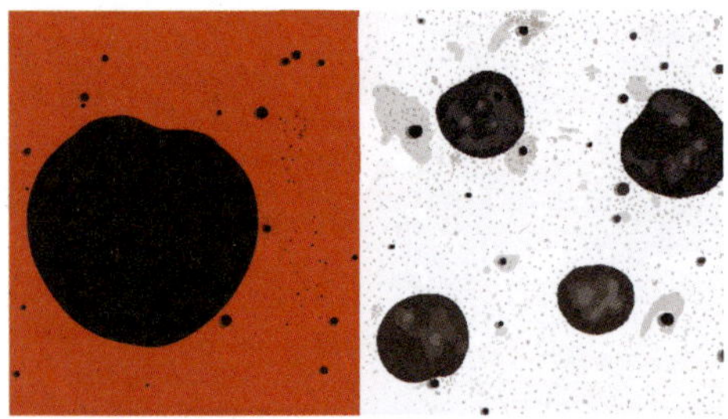

The house where Karel grew up was in a rural part of Johannesburg. It was a hive of interests with Japanese prints and Zulu beadwork on the walls. His own home is built on the same property, and is a place to share with paleo-anthropologists, fellow artists, collectors and all his friends from across the world.

As a very young boy, Karel always had a bunch of colour pencils with him and, long before he could count them, he would know immediately if one was missing! He used these to draw everything around him to get to know the world better. He was also fascinated with the world inside of himself, or his internal world. He used to draw pictures with his eyes closed. Those drawings looked like those funny shapes and colours that appear when you rub your eyes.

Today Karel is the only artist in a group of 120 or so scientists in the COSMOS project. The astronomers are finding out information about one small area of the universe that you can see in our night sky. Since they started, they have found 1.5 million new galaxies there. Karel travels once a year to join the scientists at a work conference. He has made many artworks about what he learns. In some works, he uses ancient coal dust and salt. Others are fresh interpretations of the images that the telescopes send back.

Karel's interest in culture, history and astronomy help him to a better understanding of his position in the world. He also tries to understand simply by looking inside himself. He thinks this is something that children do automatically, through drawings of their homes or families. How do you draw your place in this universe of ours?

• Illustration of 'Sound Syntax', 2008. 540-million-year-old black carboniferous dust and salt and vermillion pigment.

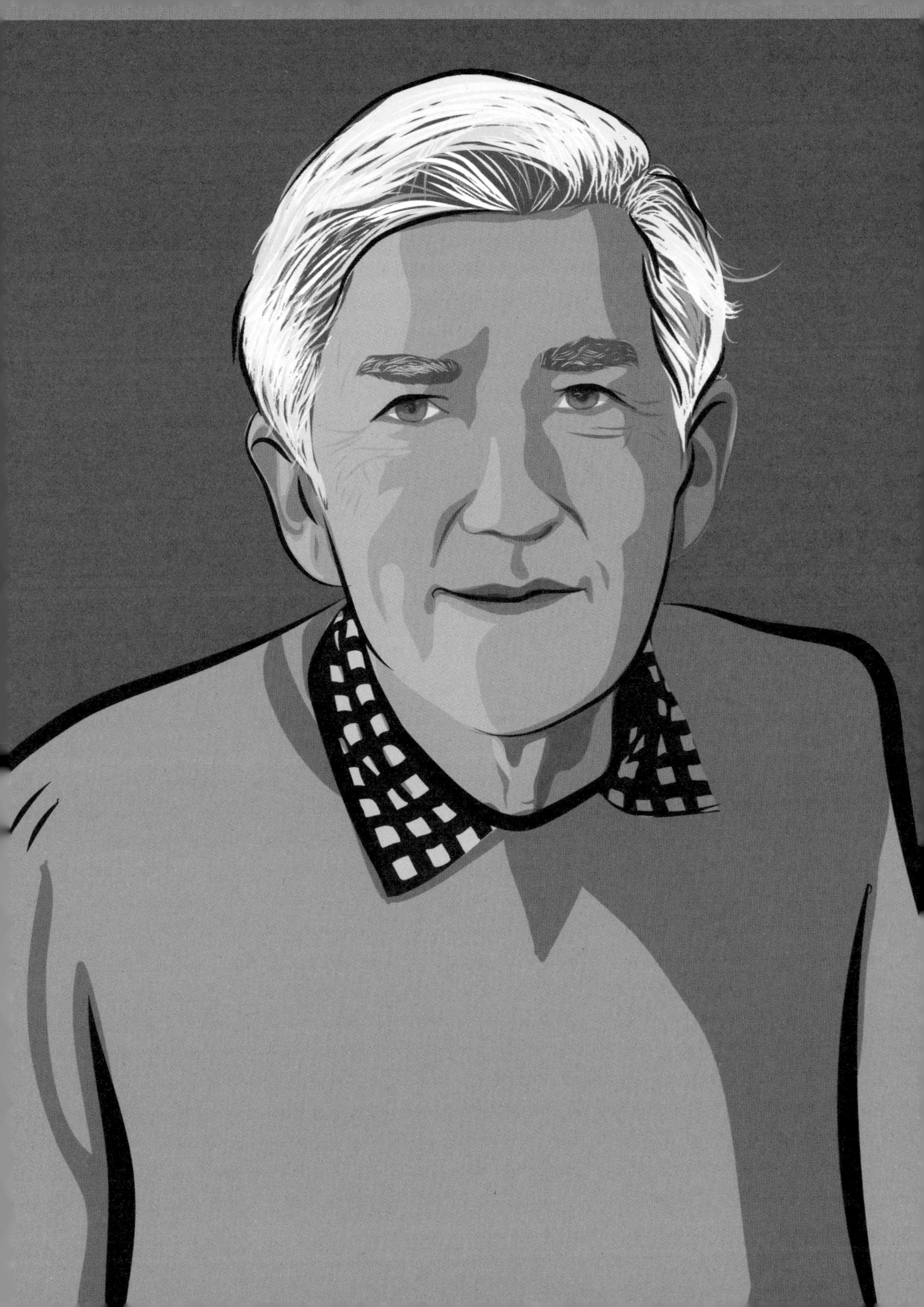

KELEKETLA! LIBRARY

There was once a boy who grew up with lots of stories in his head. In the evenings the adults in the community would gather in circles and take turns telling stories. One person would start: 'Keleketla...'. That means 'once a upon a time' in Northern Sotho, and they would tell a story. Then someone else would say 'Keleketla...' and tell the same story in a different way. Then others would add their versions. The next day might hold a new story, or a new version of an old story. These stories helped him to understand the world and where he comes from. As he got older he wanted to add his own stories, so he started writing.

It was when he moved to the inner city of Johannesburg that he started meeting like-minded storytellers. They would stand in a circle and rap, filling in and adding to each other's flows and so creating new stories of their own. They decided they needed a place where people could read old stories and texts that are important for who they are, as well as to create new stories that help them understand each other and themselves. They created a library and selected important books that visitors could loan and return. They held afternoon art classes for children in the community and travelled around the world sharing their stories. As a library, 'the boy' also created artworks by collaborating with other artists.

This is a story about an art space in Johannesburg called Keleketla! Library. The two men who created this space, Rangoato Hlasane and Malosa Malahlela, have always thought of it as a young black boy. What does it mean for a space to have a story that could be the story of a young black boy? It means that the library was created to answer some of the needs of this specific child. But it has grown to much more than that to incorporate many other children and also adults, as the works that Keleketla! Library makes travel all over the world.

Keleketla! has published books, collaborated with musicians to make art installations and frequently have events at their space to keep creating new and relevant stories.

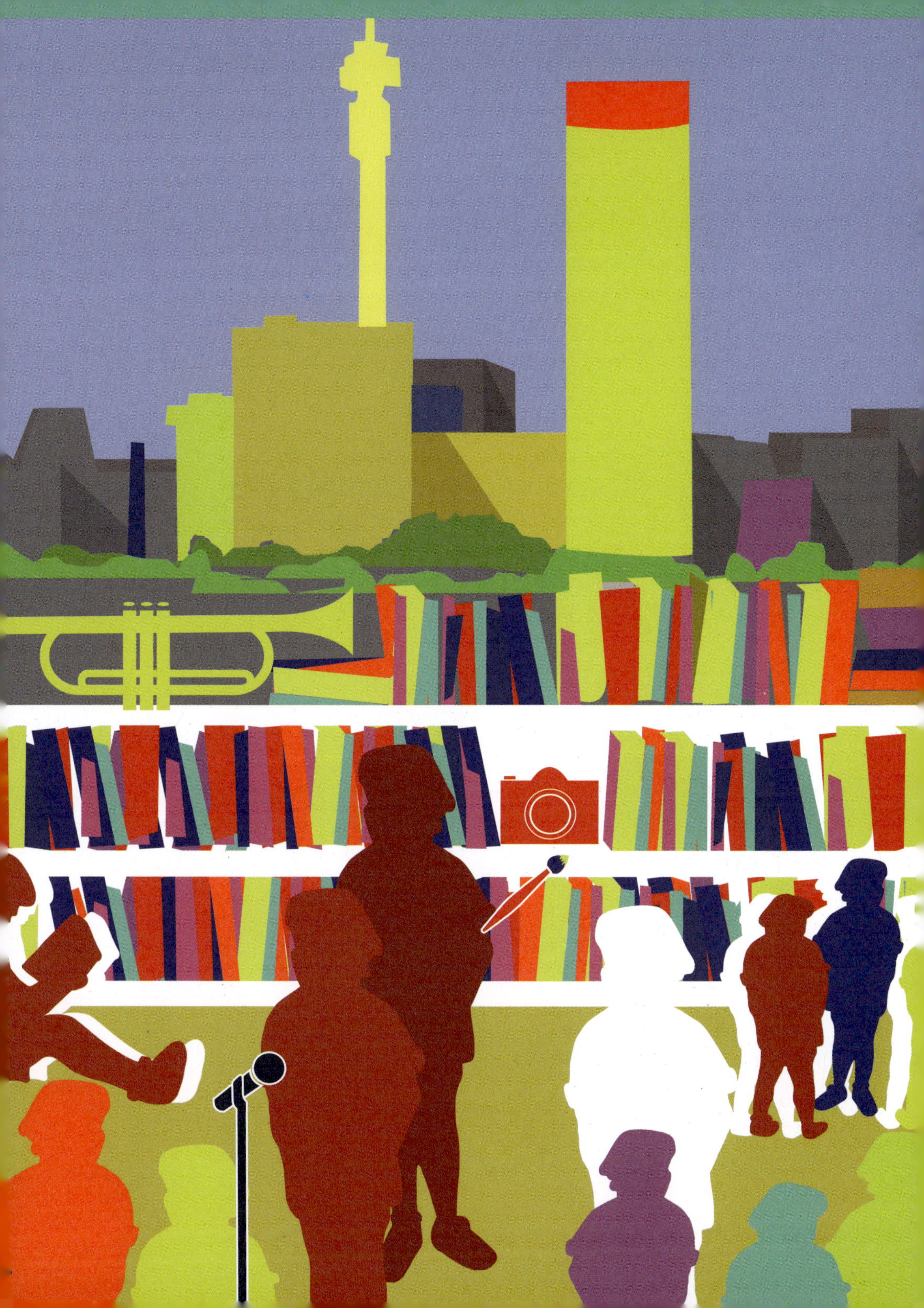

KEMANG WA LEHULERE

A life in theatre is what you would have predicted for Kemang wa Lehulere if you had watched him as a child. From a young age he was completely swept up by the magic of directing, props, lighting, sound and acting. He took acting classes, had a casting agent and even tried to create a theatre group with his classmates, although no one but he and his teacher showed up. He was a politically aware child and in his house the evening news was not just watched, it was also discussed among the family members.

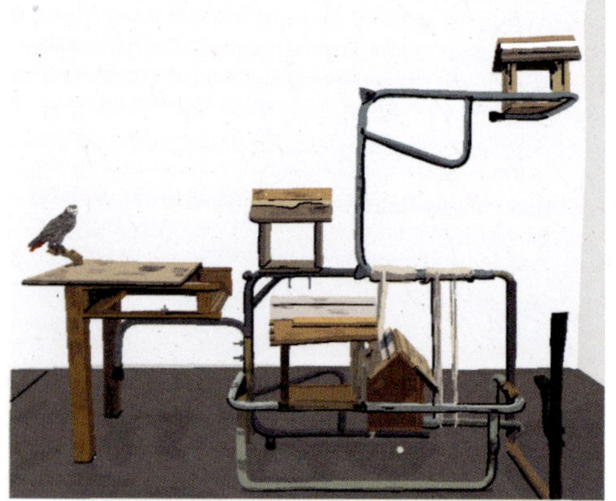

After matric he enrolled at the Community Arts Project in Cape Town to study theatre. Although he enjoyed it, he slowly became more fascinated with visual arts through friends, because it was something he wanted to learn more about.

Just like in theatre, Kemang's work has props that help us to read the story that he is telling through his art. He has made video works, installations and even compiled a whole jazz album for one of his exhibitions.

Sometimes he incorporates drawings and sometimes he performs himself. He has made many works that use old school desks to create different objects. Through these desks, he speaks about education in our history and our present.

The title of his first solo exhibition in an American museum shows that sometimes Kemang is still surprised by everything that has happened to him in the art world. For this exhibition he made one work where he illustrated notes from a song by South African jazz musician Faye Faku out of hair. The song speaks about the life of South African activist Steve Biko. The hair reminds you of the way people in South Africa were classified into different races because of how their hair looked. He called the exhibition, 'In All My Wildest Dreams.'

Kemang feels that art has a political job to do. And while people might say art can't change the world, he thinks it can change individuals, both those who make it and those who engage with it.

• Illustration of 'My Apologies to Time', 2017. Installation, mixed media.

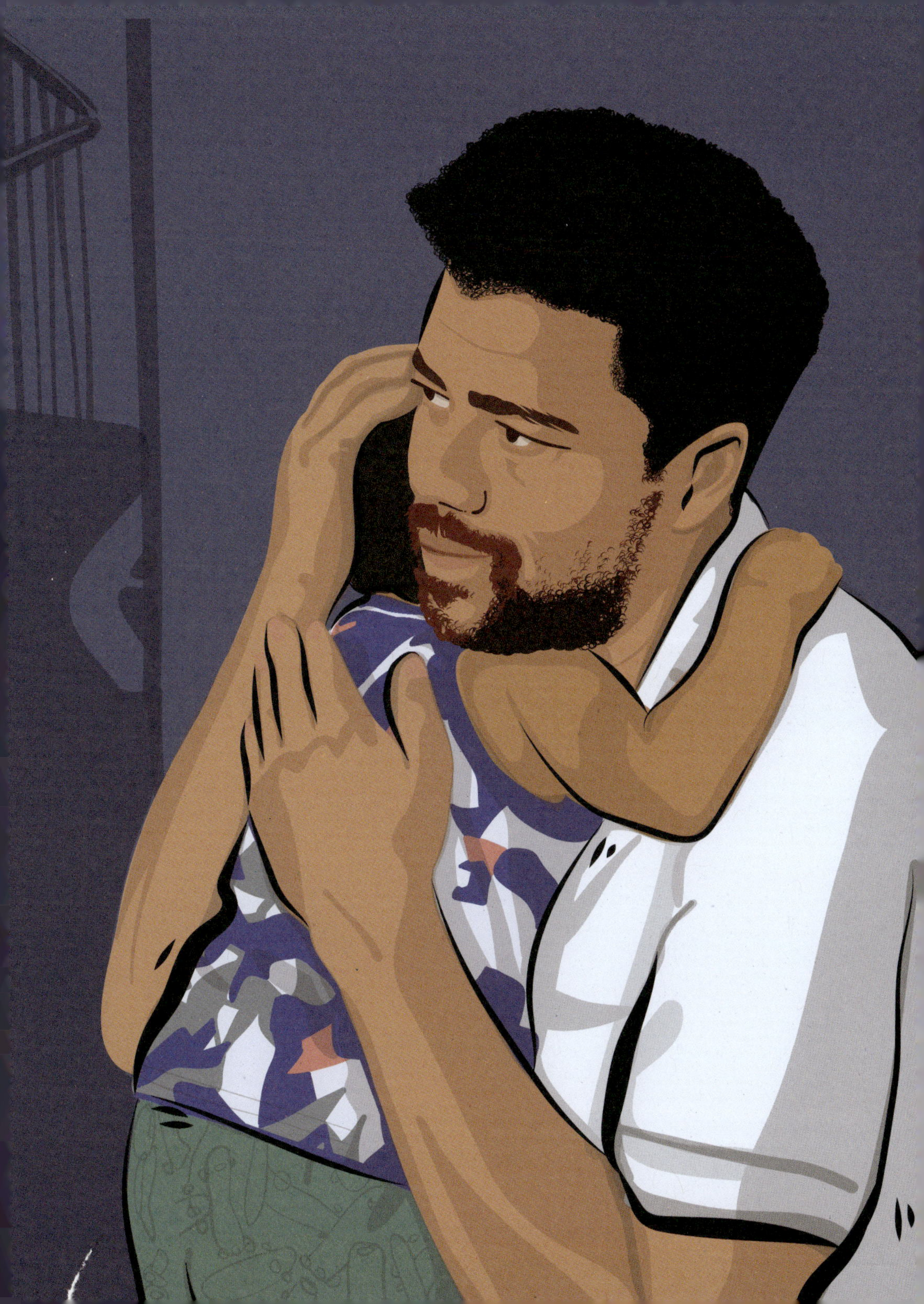

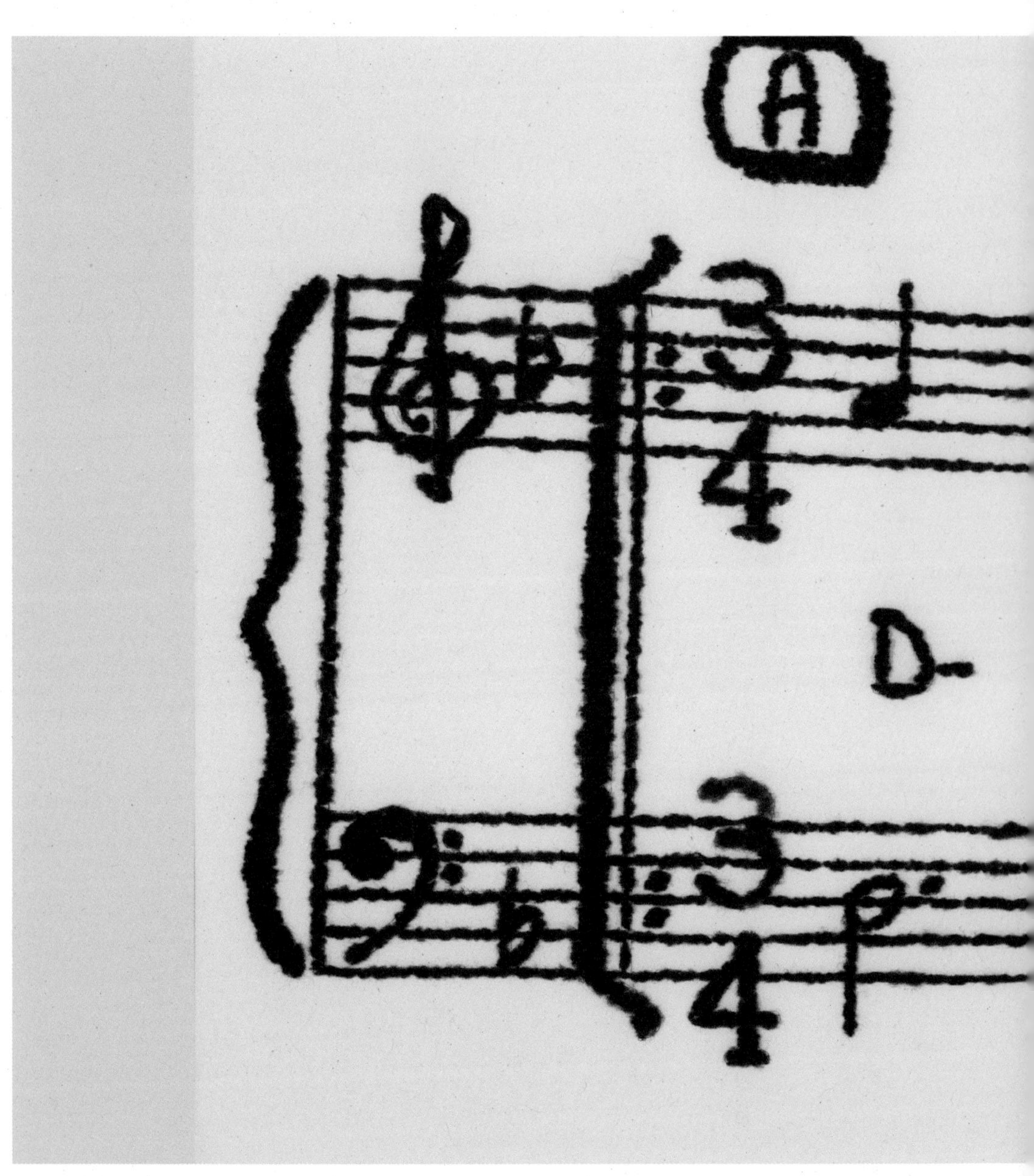

• *'Broken Light (Feya Faku) 1', 2016. Hair, graphite and paint on canvas. Courtesy of the artist and Stevenson, Cape Town and Johannesburg.*

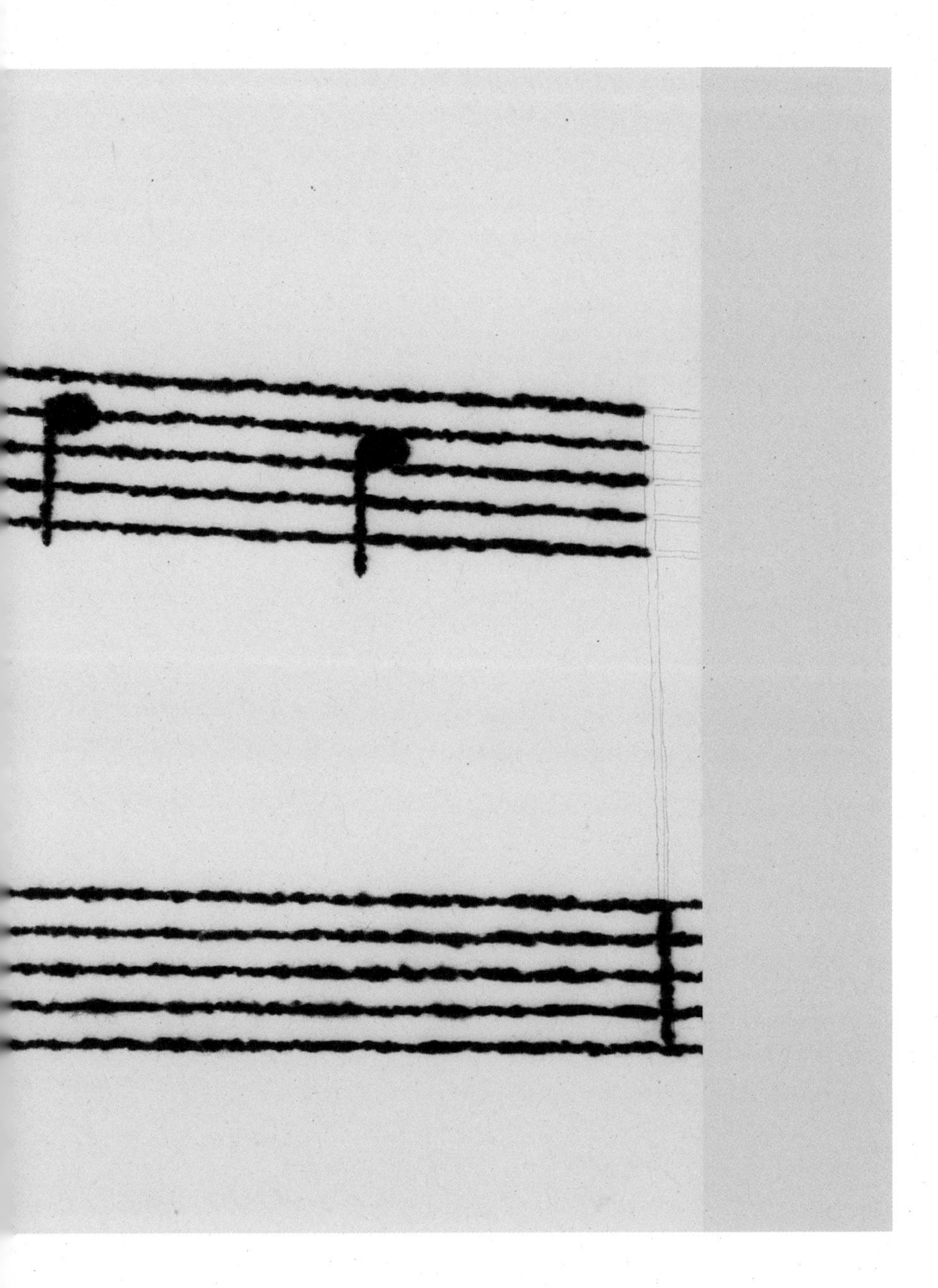

LADY SKOLLIE

Picture a small town in the Western Cape. There is a safe house with a mother who is a teacher and a father who is a lawyer. Two beautiful daughters go to a school with mostly white Afrikaans children. The parents are hard-working and expect the same of their children so that they can create a good life for themselves. The two daughters are talented and win first prizes in the music Eisteddfods. One plays the clarinet and saxophone and the other sings beautifully. They come first in local school beauty pageants where they win sessions at a tanning salon meant for people with lighter skin than theirs. They go to university and get good grades.

Laura is one of these two girls, the one who plays the saxophone and has beautiful, long curly hair. But one day, she realises that she is a different person inside. She doesn't want to pretend that everything is okay with the world as long as you are earning a good salary and not getting into trouble.

She realises that she wants to speak about the unfairness that she sees all around her. And so she does. She shaves off her hair and starts speaking publicly about what she believes in. She changes her name from Laura to Lady Skollie. A 'skollie' is a stereotyping word, often used for, so-called Coloured people to mean that they are sly.

Today Lady Skollie is a DJ, an activist, a public speaker and an artist. When she makes paintings, she imagines that she is creating a giant cave that she is filling with cave drawings, just like at the Sterkfontein Caves. She uses forms, colours and images that come from mysticism, like the shape of the sun. In her paintings she asks many questions about her life, such as where she comes from, her relationships, pleasure and power.

The confidence that was nurtured when Lady Skollie was growing up has made her a fearless woman with a massive amount of energy. She does not care what people expect of her or how she is supposed to behave. What is important to her is to tell the truth and to tell it loudly. She believes if you want to be heard, you must not make any apologies for who you are and what you want to say.

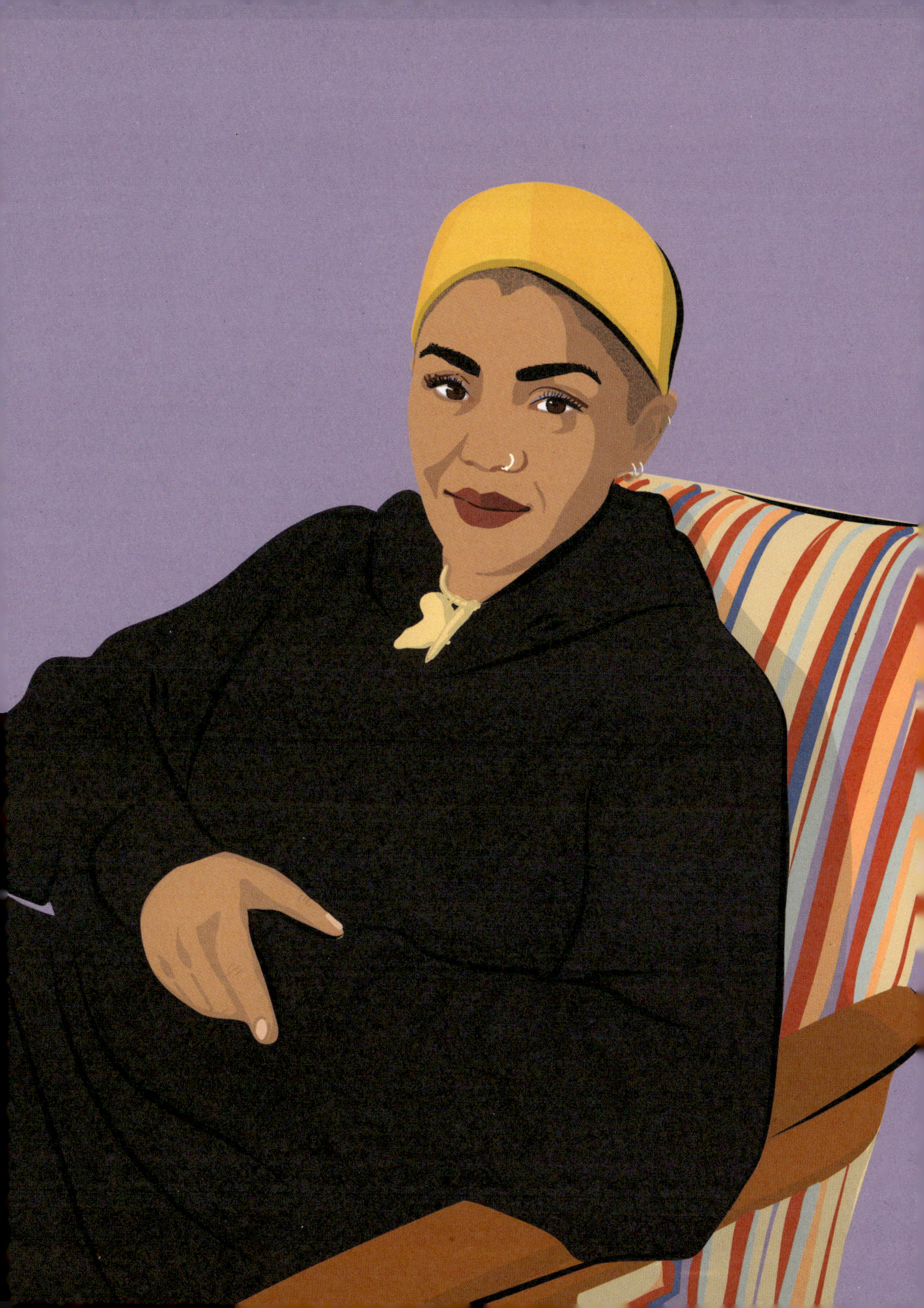

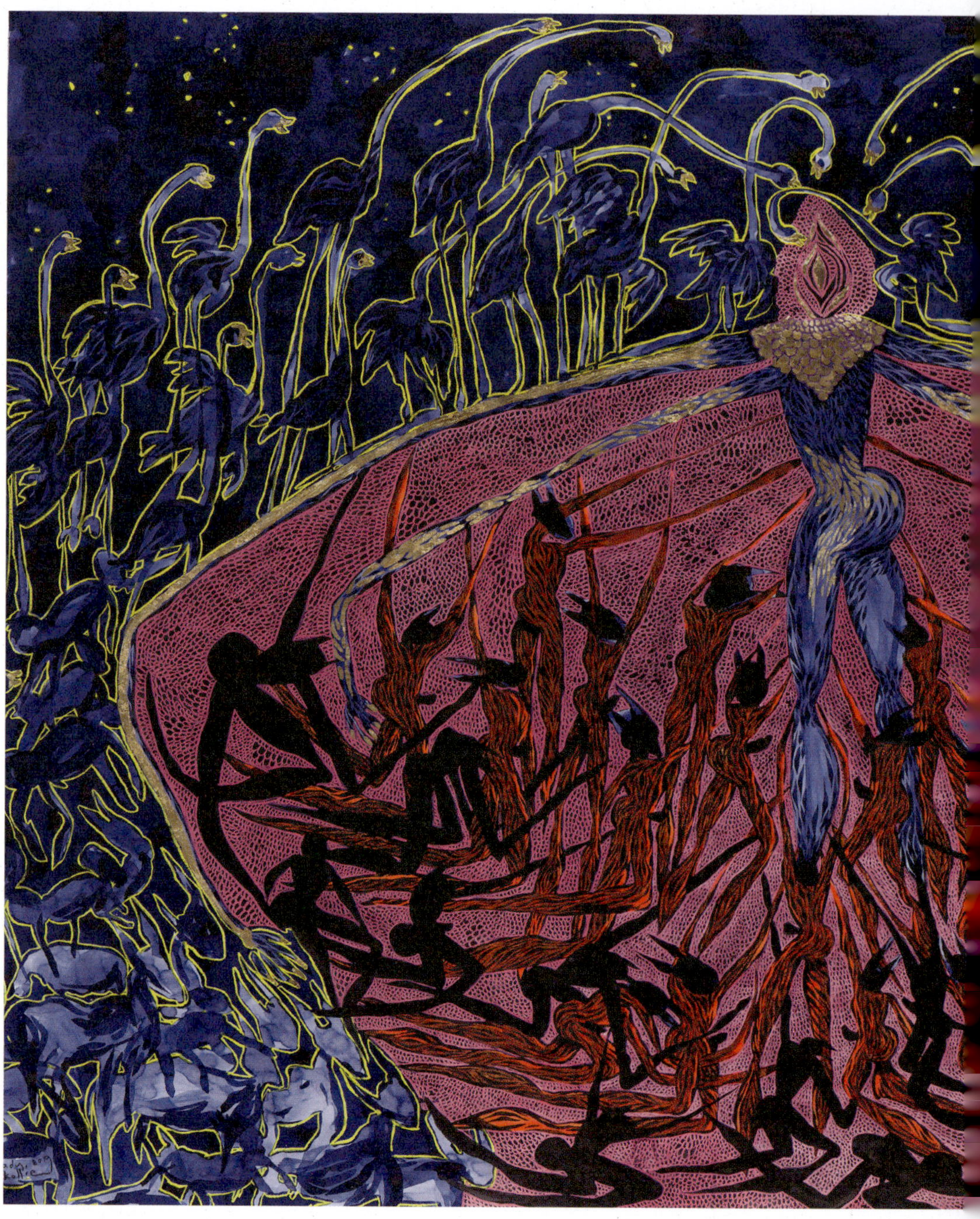

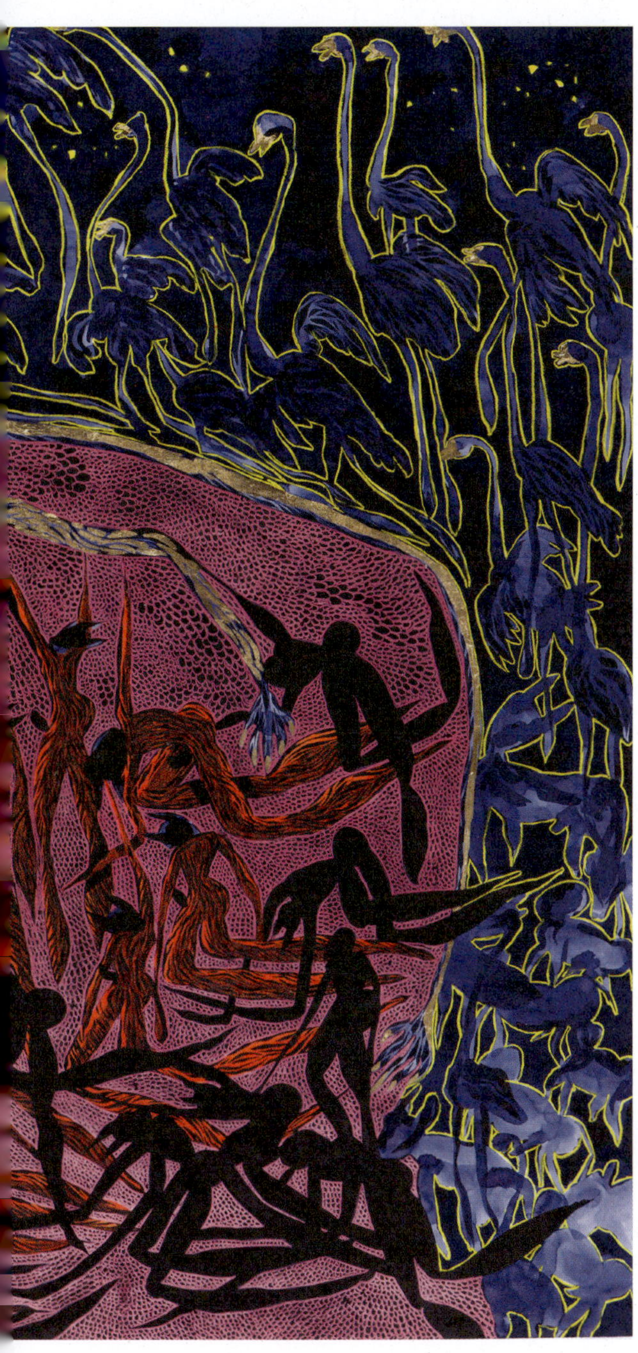

''n Skans teen die donker (protection against the dark): I collect them all together under my arms, lifting us all up together, up and away from the past', 2019. Mixed media on Fabriano. Courtesy of the artist and Everard Read Gallery.

makgati malebatsi

Once there was a girl who grew up in a difficult time and place in history. Makgati Malebatsi grew up in a township south of Johannesburg that is famous for the political violence that went on there. The place is called Sharpeville. As she was growing up adults would point to different houses in the neighbourhood and say 'In that house the father was shot in 1969,' or 'That family lost their child in the riots of 1969.' Things were dangerous and the world around her was bleak. Makgati longed for a different world.

Luckily, when she finished school, with her smarts and sparkling personality she became a marketer for many of South Africa's big companies. She loved her job, but still thought that there must be something more interesting out there.

One day she was visiting friends from Senegal and Algeria. They had a visitor from New York. When she saw him coming into the lounge, she didn't know that this man would change her life forever. He said to her, 'I don't know how to drive and I have a few meetings, can you drive me around tomorrow?' That was the start of a long relationship.

This man was one of the most important African curators, called Okwui Enwezor. She suddenly found herself in the very centre of the African contemporary art world. She felt totally lost in this new world and felt shy because she didn't understand the conversations around dinner tables. Makgati had no idea what a curator even was!

She started reading and teaching herself everything about art. She travelled to all the big international art exhibitions, all over Africa, America, Europe and China. She still had her job in marketing, but she realised her heart was not in it and her boss said to her: 'Why are you here when your head and your heart is somewhere else? You should work in the art world.'

She thought, 'There must be people like me who feel too scared to ask questions and who want to know more, but don't know how to start.' That is when Makgati made it her mission to guide others to become art buyers and art lovers.

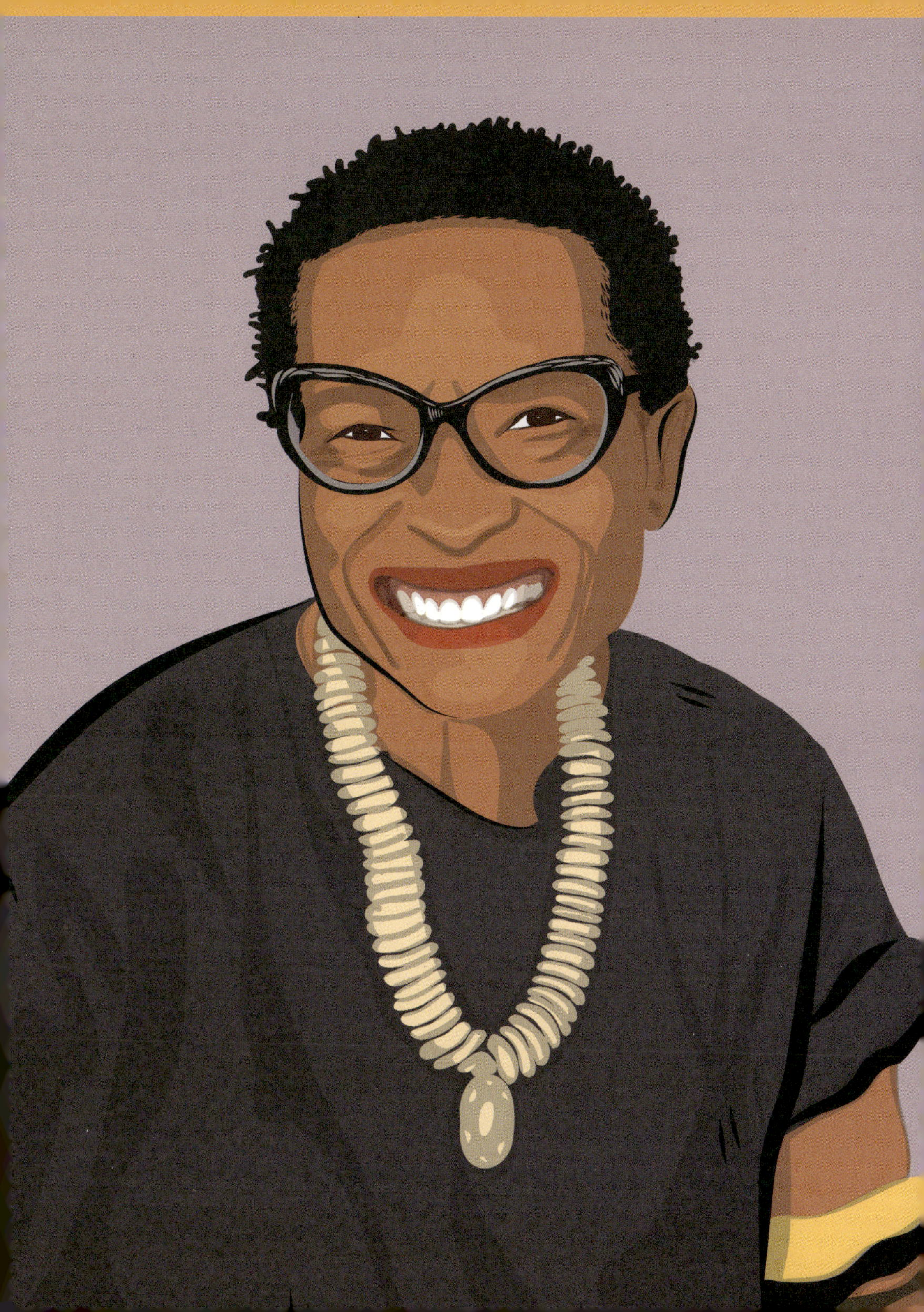

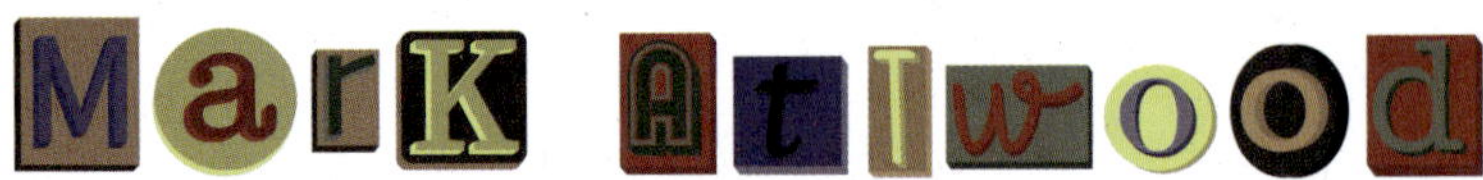

Once there was a boy who grew up spending a lot of time in his father's printing shop. His father printed books, brochures and pamphlets. Mark Attwood knew that he would probably also work in this shop when he grew up. But something bothered him about this job. He kept seeing thousands of pamphlets or programmes printed. They were only used for one show or event and then it all landed up in the dustbin. He didn't like that kind of waste.

One day he got his hands on a book that became very special to him. It was a book about lithography. Lithography is a way of printing that was invented around 200 years ago and was once the most popular way to get lots of copies of something printed quickly.

Mark knew immediately that this was what he wanted to do. He knew that artworks are very different from the pieces that he saw being printed and thrown away when he was little. Artworks are things that people treasure.

As soon as he could afford it, he got a bank loan to buy his first printing press. It was huge and had to come on a ship from America. By then he had already decided to live on a farm in White River, Mpumalanga. There he has his own house with his family and some cottages for artists to stay while they work in his studio to make lithographs. Lithographs work best for artists who paint or draw. He called his business, The Artists' Press.

Mark offers a specific service to the art community. At White River, artists are able to get away from all the distractions of city life, to have a calm and focused space to just make things with their hands that others will love and buy. In the more than twenty years that Mark has run The Artists' Press, he has worked with almost all of South Africa's famous artists to create hand-printed editions. And because he prints by hand, and not just by pushing a button on a computer, every single print is still unique.

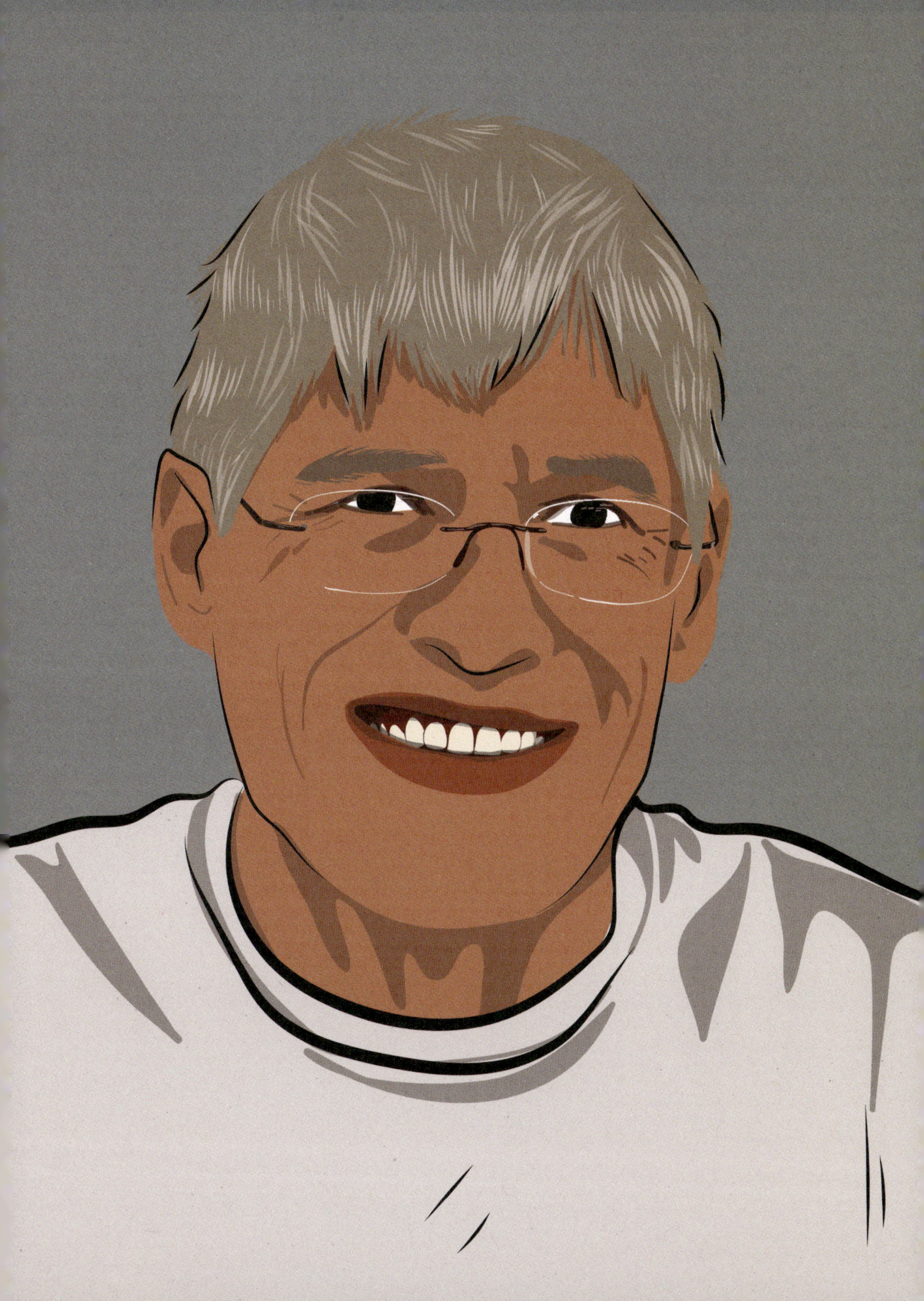

MIKHAEL SUBOTZKY

What does it mean for your life if your father is a teacher at a good school, your mother is a doctor and you grow up in a nice house, in a nice neighbourhood? It probably means that you feel safe and that you might have many options for your future. You might also have many opportunities to become successful and develop the talents that you have. This is how Mikhael Subotzky grew up in a quiet suburb in Cape Town and, in his artwork, he asks these questions about his own white privilege.

Mikhael was always very good at the sciences. When he was still in high school he did a biology project that won him prizes at science fairs and took him overseas. Just as he was about to enroll in medical school, he impulsively decided to take a year off to travel around the world. That was when he started taking photos and, when he came back, he went to art school in Cape Town.

From early on he wanted to go into poorer areas where people with his background would not normally go. He used his photos to show the lives that were lived in those areas. But after a while, he started to wonder whether it was okay for him to photograph people with so little power.

One of his most famous exhibitions was inside the prison cell of former president of South Africa, Nelson Mandela. He wanted people from the public to feel what it was like to be in a prison, what it sounded like, what it smelt like. He also took many photographs of the prisoners.

More and more, he started thinking that he should spend time looking at his own life in his art. Mikhael realised that it is important as an artist to be brave and open-minded. He believes you should always ask the difficult questions about your own life and the world you live in, even if those questions are very personal and uncomfortable.

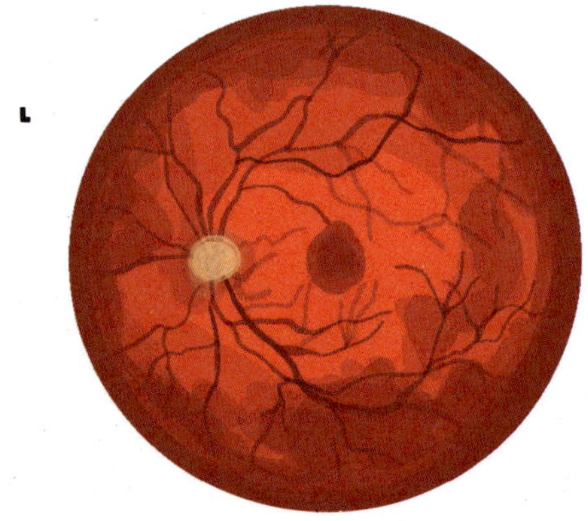

• *Illustration of 'Self-portrait (with the help of optometrist) L', 2012. Inkjet print mounted to Diasec.*

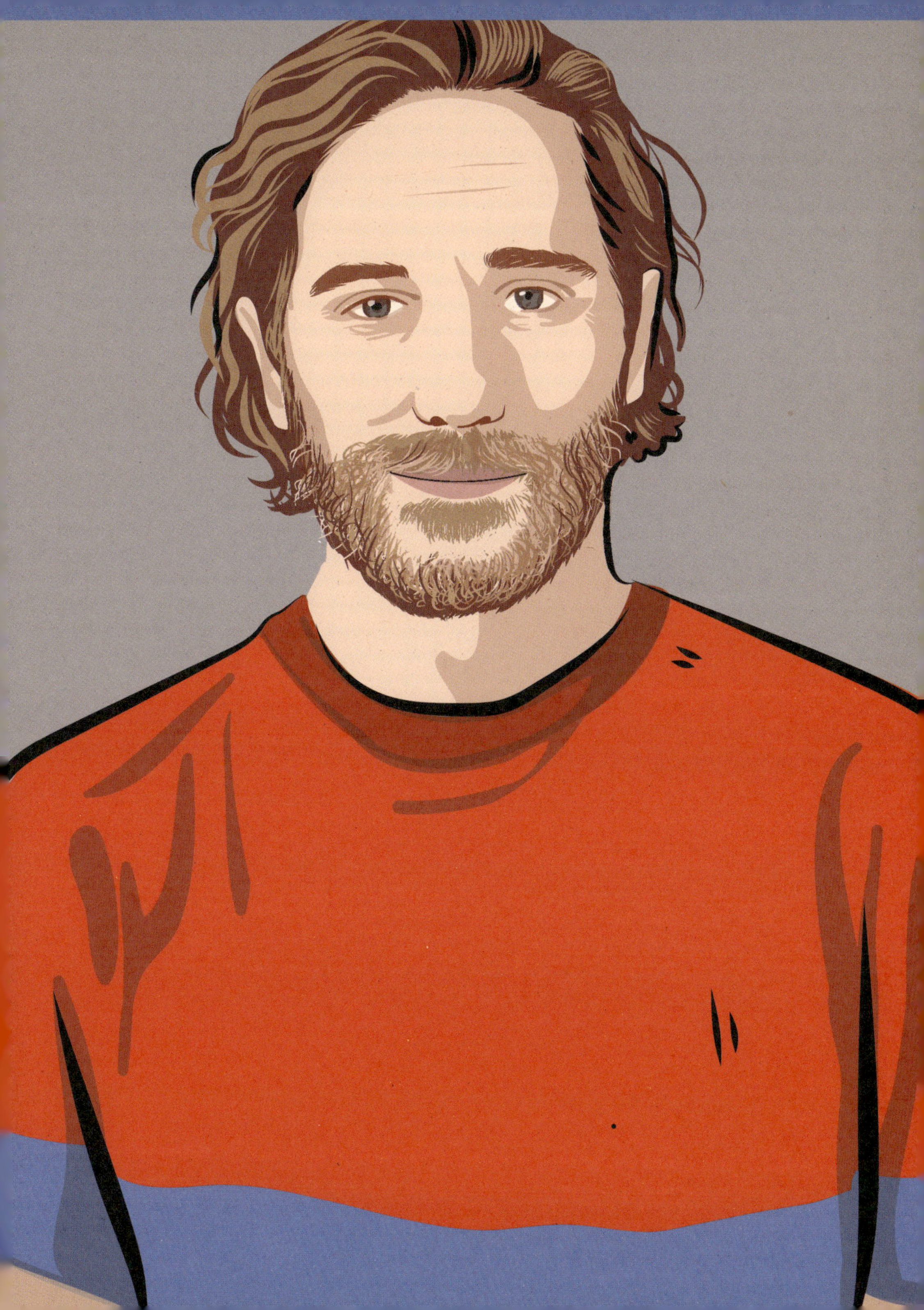

MMAKGABO MAPULA HELEN SEBIDI

When Mmakgabo Mapula Helen Sebidi starts an art work, she splashes colours all over the surface. She loves that part of the process, it is loose and feels free, but it is not what she wants to show the world. She then starts building the picture up with paint. She believes her hand is controlled by her spirit ancestors. It takes a very long to make a work because she enjoys the process of making and creating it so much that it is hard for her to stop.

If there is one person in Helen's life who taught her everything that has been important, it was her grandmother. Her grandmother never lived in a big city. She lived near Hammanskraal, growing her own food and rearing farm animals. Working and being creative was very important to Helen's grandmother.

Her grandmother used to say to her: 'This home we live in now is not your house, I want you to build your own house within you'. Being close to the world of ancestors and spirits was a central part of her grandmother's life.

Helen's grandmother taught her that it was very difficult when men and women had to go to the cities and leave their houses and children behind to make money. When people left, families were broken and traditions were lost.

Unfortunately, when she was 16 years old, Helen had to leave her home to make money too. Helen felt that the work prevented her from ever learning any valuable skills. She went from

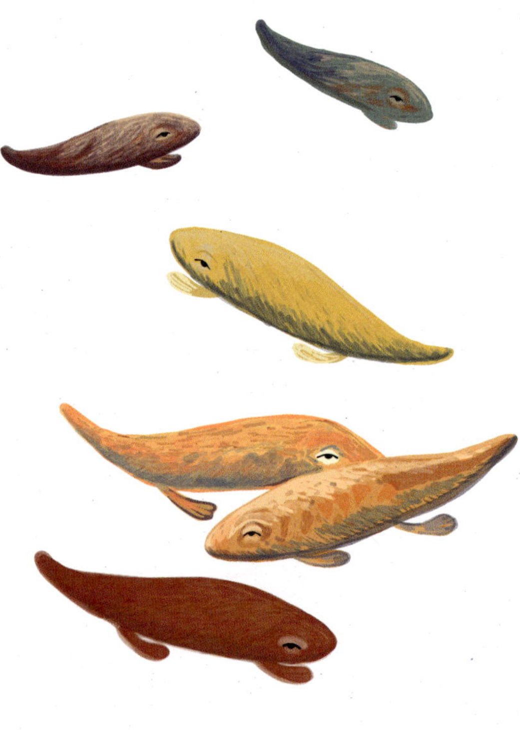

● *Illustration from 'A Girl Meets Her Spirit Parents', 2014–2015. Oil on canvas.*

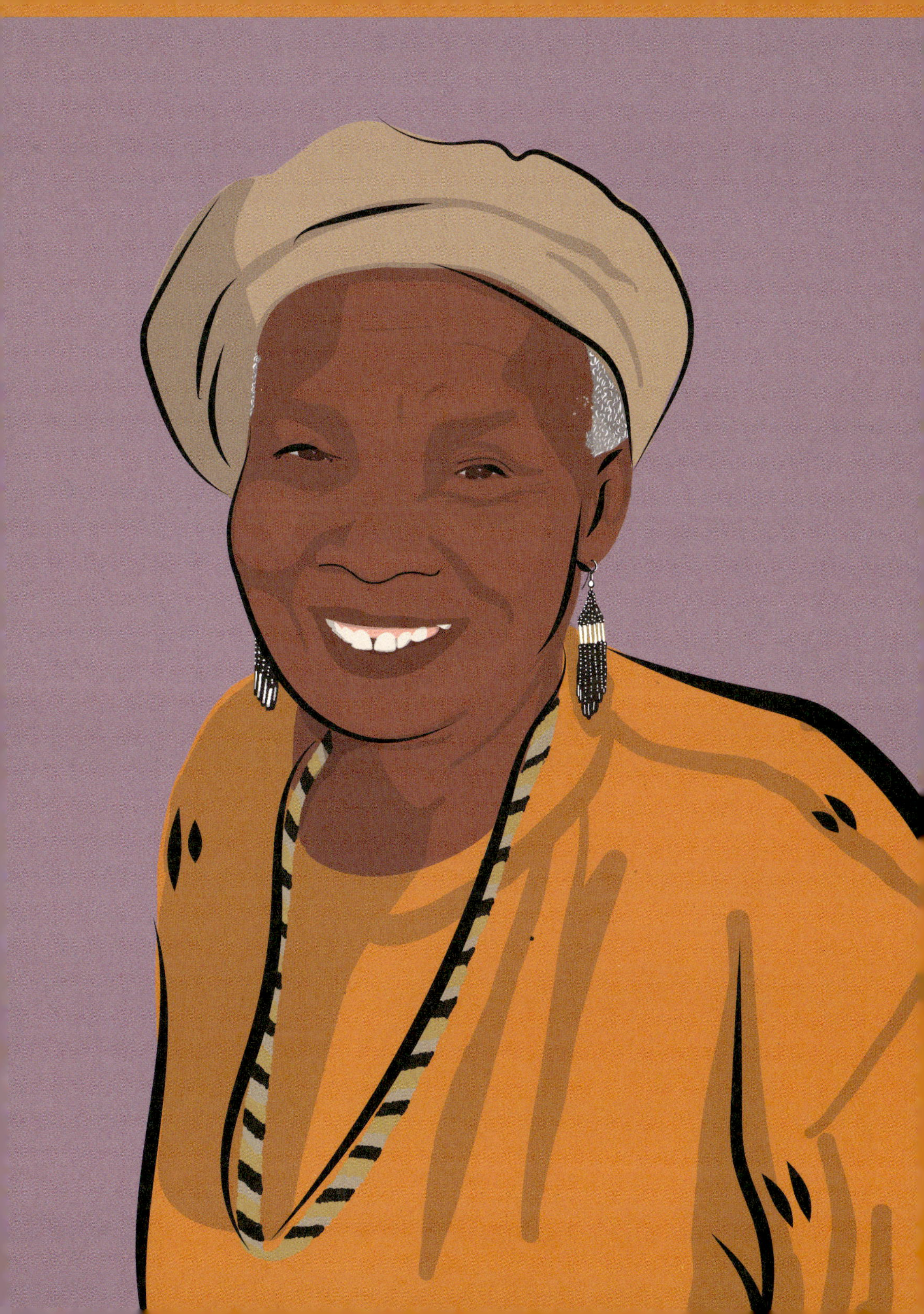

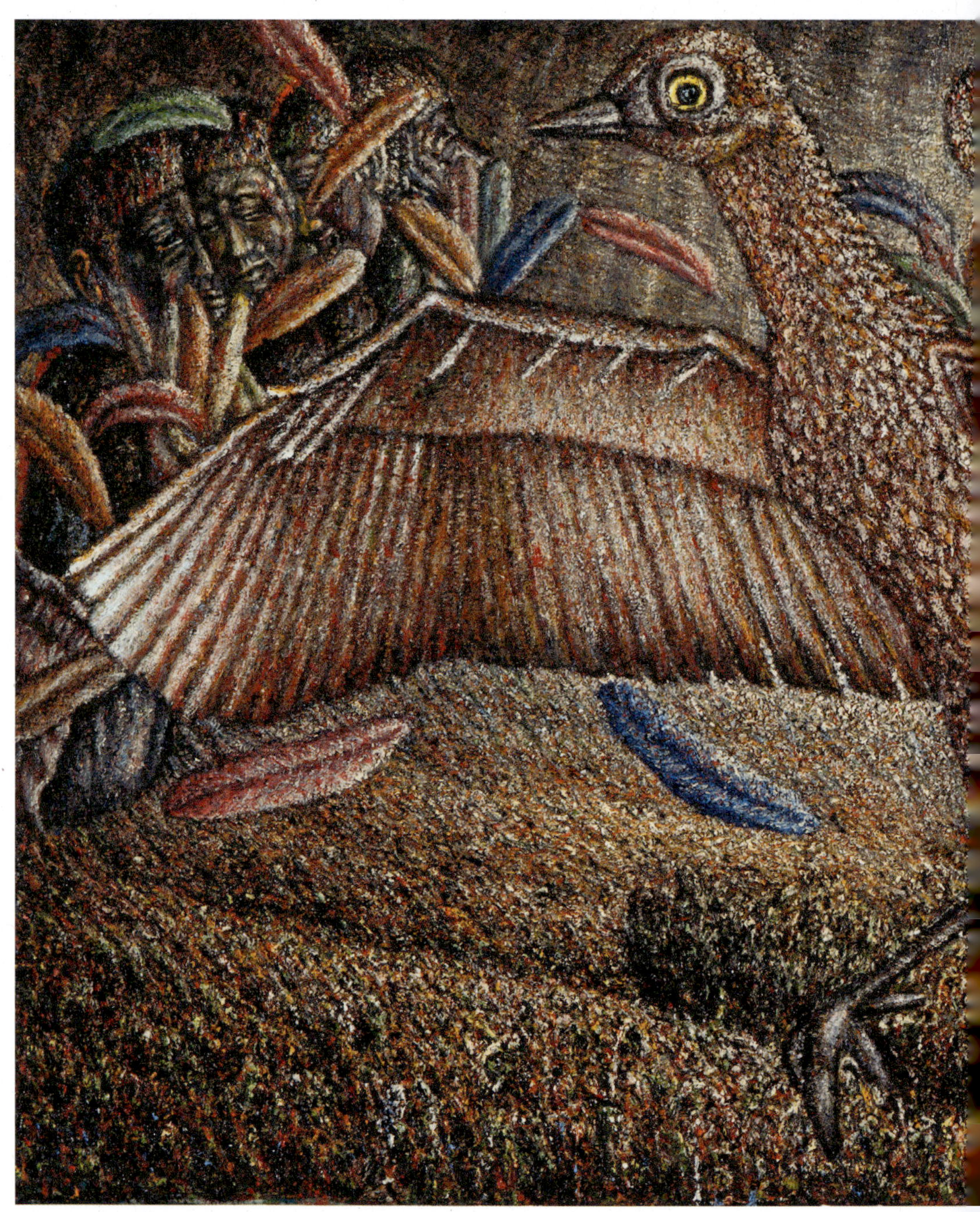

● *'The Spirit Bird Fleeing the Modern World' 2014–2016. Oil on canvas.*
  Courtesy of the artist and Everard Read Gallery.

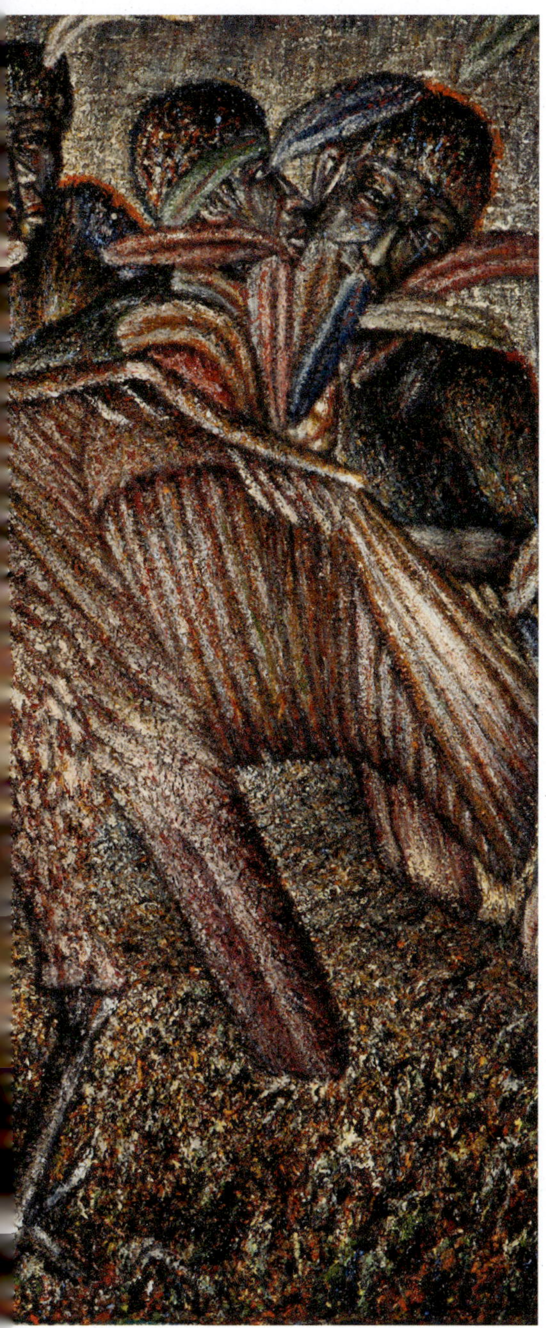

one job to another but in the evenings she started to sew and make clothes.

Helen remembered her grandmother saying, 'If our people did not have to leave and go work, where would they be now? They would be able to be themselves.' For Helen to be herself meant making art. She found a good teacher in Soweto who taught her how to paint.

But her grandmother needed her, she could no longer walk and was alone in the village. Helen had to return home. At first, she hid the paintings from her grandmother, but one day her grandmother found her painting and she was very impressed and recognised that now Helen was doing what she was meant to in this life. She gave her a room in which to paint where no one was allowed to bother her.

Helen spent time with the community elders. She cooked for them and washed them, and cut their nails, while listening to their stories. They told stories of their lives, their ancestors, their beliefs, even their dreams and this influenced her paintings. Her painting teacher said that this time with her grandmother was her research time.

Later in life she won a very prestigious award to study in America, called a Fulbright scholarship. This opened up the world for her and her art has been shown in museums worldwide. But in her work, what remains important is to give life to the stories that she was told by the elders of her community and her grandmother.

NANDIPHA MNTAMBO

If your father is a pastor, he has to go from congregation to congregation where he gets placed by the church. That means a lot of moving around. That is how Nandipha Mntambo grew up. She was always experiencing new places and new people.

Her family made sure she went to good schools wherever they lived. Sometimes people thought that she was a very confident young girl, but her big personality was a way of defining herself. She often got into trouble for wanting to do things her way.

As a little girl, Nandipha was very interested in bodies and decided to become a forensic pathologist – someone who tries to understand how people have died. But later she realised she was more interested in bodies that were still alive, and specifically understanding her own body and how it fits into the world.

As Nandipha studied art, she found she absolutely loved sculpture. Sculptures are three-dimensional and can be made in many different ways. Her student work was bought by the South African National Gallery. She used cowskins and shaped them to look like her own shape, or a woman's body. She also casted shapes of her body in bronze and made herself look like mythological figures.

Now Nandipha is a very successful artist. She has a gallery that takes care of her work and her exhibitions while she looks after her little girl, Isiuwa. Her dream is to have a big sculpture studio in her back garden where she will spend a lot of time drawing, making sculpture and, sometimes, just thinking.

For Nandipha art is a way to remind people that even though we live in a world where so much divides us, such as skin colour or how much money we have, we all have similar joys and struggles. Art can make these shared experiences visible and maybe help us to understand each other better.

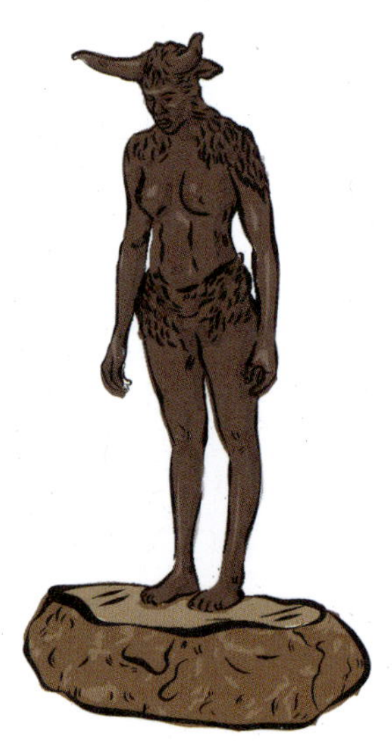

• *Illustration of 'Minotaurus', 2015. Bronze, sandstone base.*

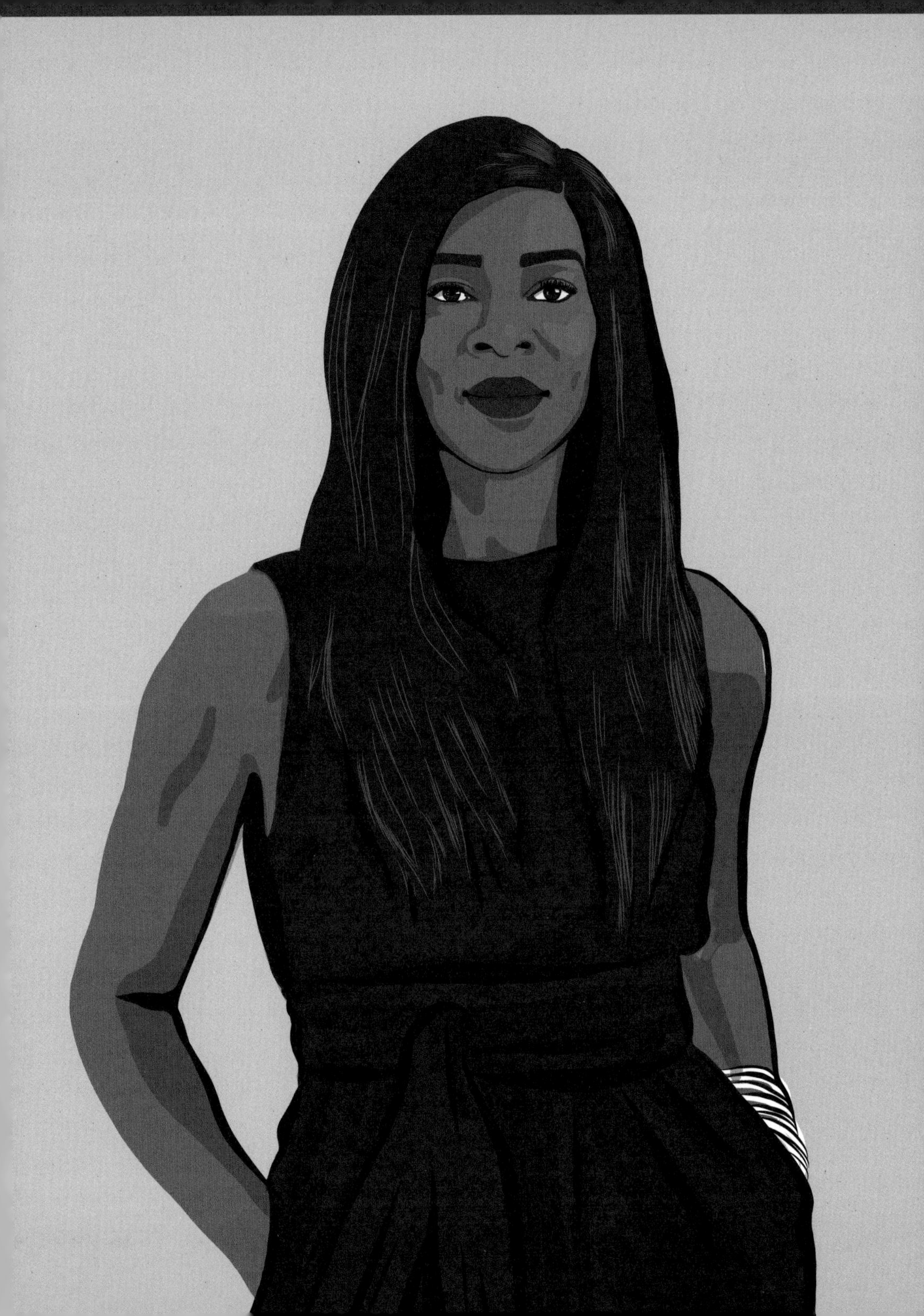

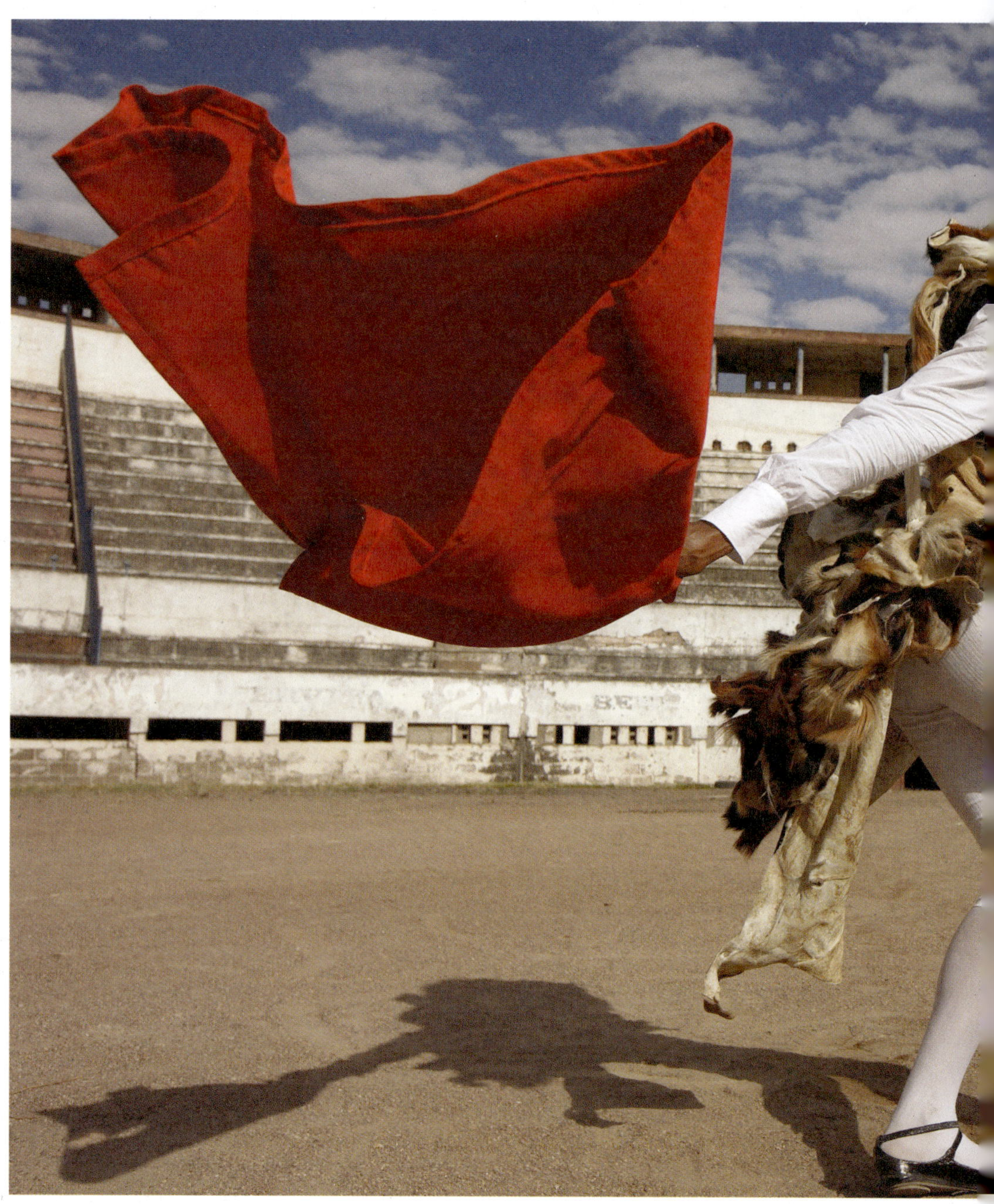

● *Praça de Touros II, 2008. Archival pigment ink on cotton rag paper. Courtesy of the artist
and Stevenson, Cape Town and Johannesburg.*

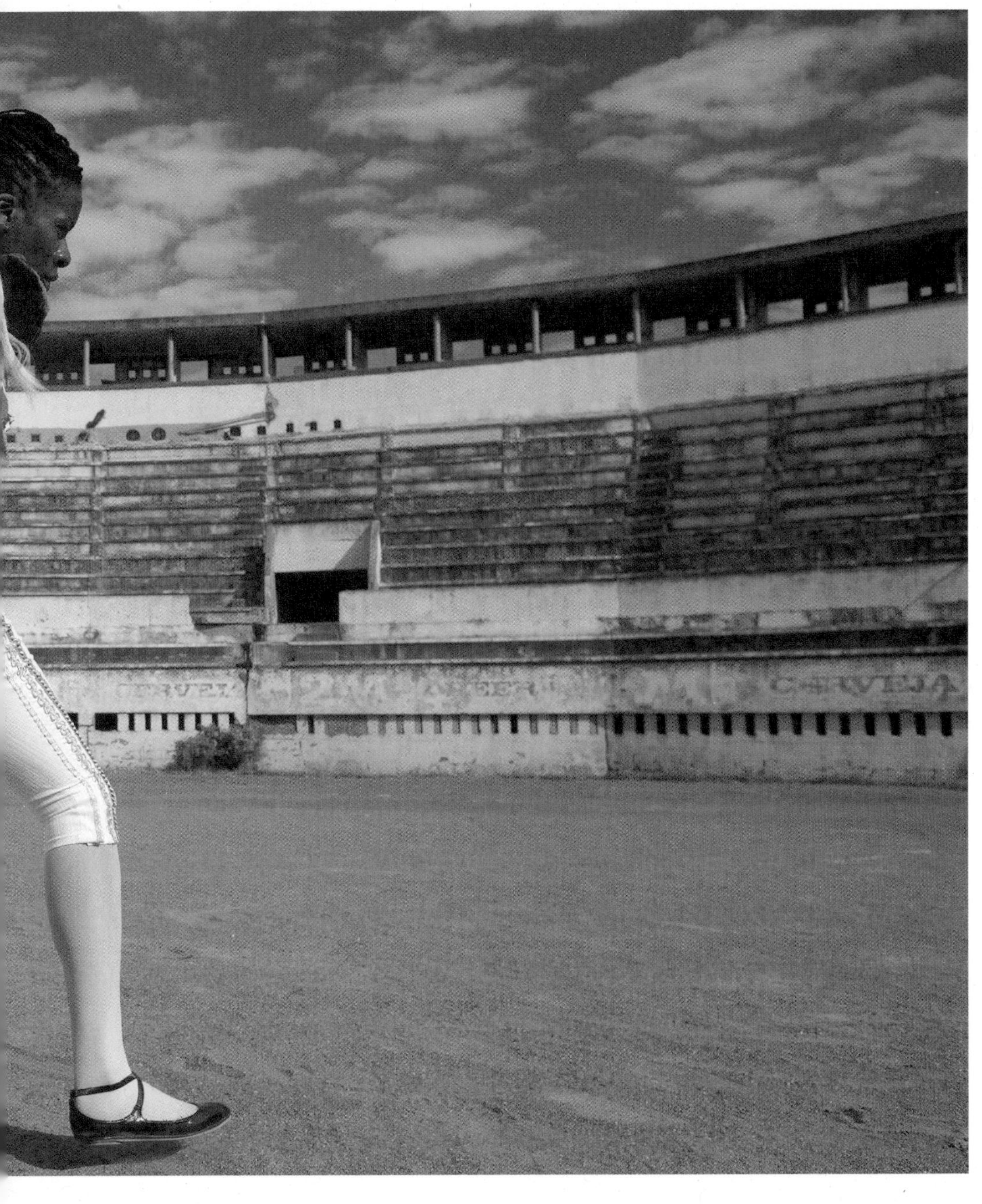

NKULE MABASO

It is strange to think that Nkule Mabaso at first struggled with schoolwork. They realised later that it was because she was left-handed and was being forced to do everything with her right hand. She grew up in KwaZulu-Natal as one of seven children and her parents were both teachers. At one point her mother had to travel many hours every day to teach at a school far away. That meant that she spent time in aftercare and in extramurals, which was the perfect opportunity for her to draw and paint.

For a long time before she decided on art, Nkule thought she would be a fashion designer. She liked that it was a type of art that people could wear and other people could see. Her father wanted her to be an engineer to make sure that she had many options in life. So there was a bit of a fight when Nkule insisted on art or nothing. But in the end she got to go to art school. She found she was dissatisfied that there was too much focus on only making art, so she took on lots of other subjects. Nkule was used to doing more than she had to because in matric she took ten subjects rather than the usual six!

Afterwards, Nkule went to study curation in Switzerland. A curator puts exhibitions together and decides which artworks to use and how they should be displayed. In this way, it is the curator's job to bring the audience and the artwork closer together.

One day, Nkule and her friend Nomusa Makhubu decided to enter a competition the government put out to be a curator of one of the biggest international exhibitions that happens in Italy every two years. This event is the Venice Biennale. They could not believe it when their entry won and they became the curators for the 58th Venice Biennale's South African Pavilion. This is a very big honour and the highlight of many curators' careers. They used this opportunity to show art that tries to tell the histories of our country that have been left out and called it 'The Stronger We Become'. The artists they chose to work with, Tracey Rose, Mawande Ka Zenzile and Dineo Seshee Bopape, all look back at where we come from in order to understand our present better. Nkule says, 'You never know if you might win, so you have to be brave. Every competition or funding application is a test and this time we got 10 out of 10!'

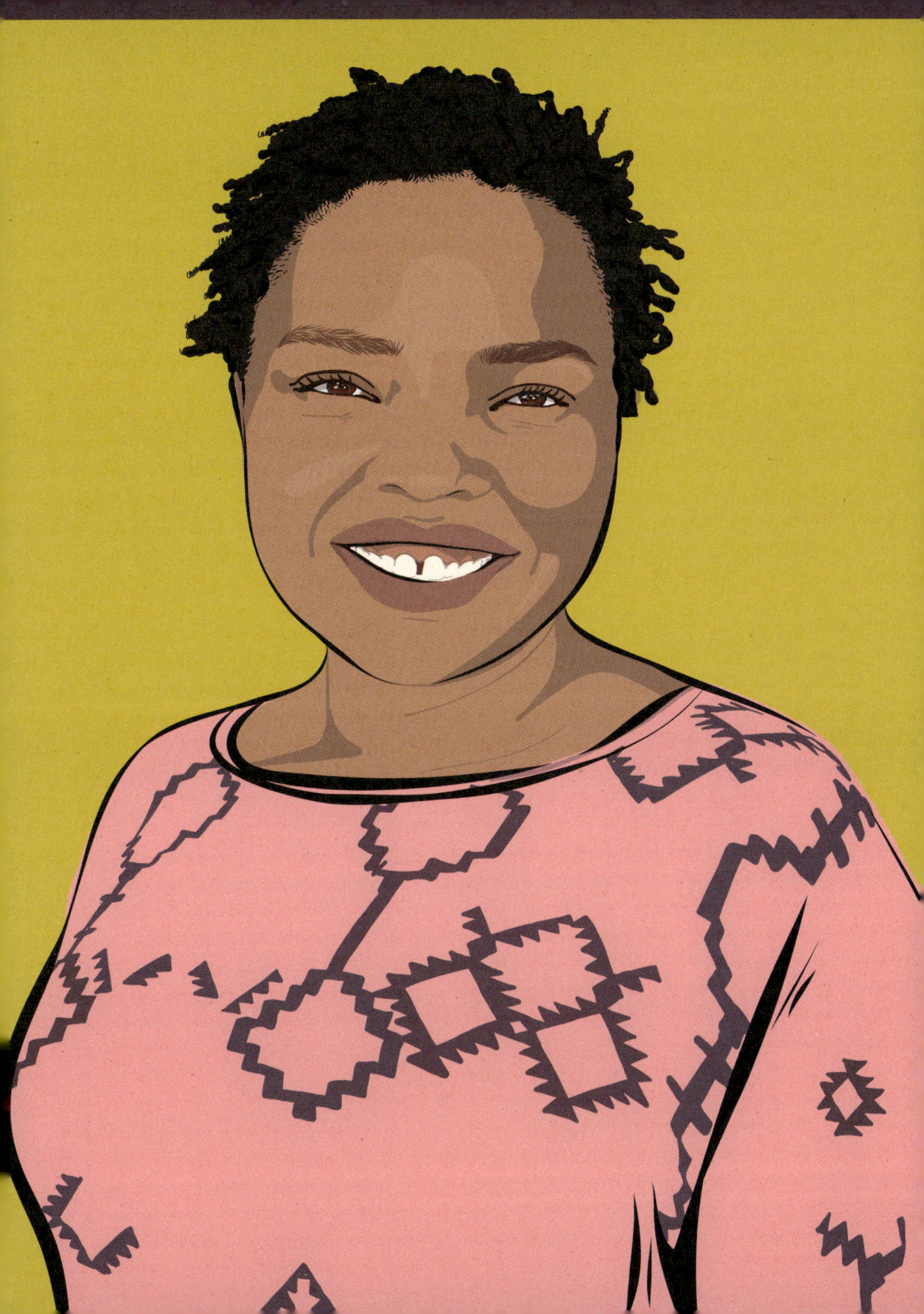

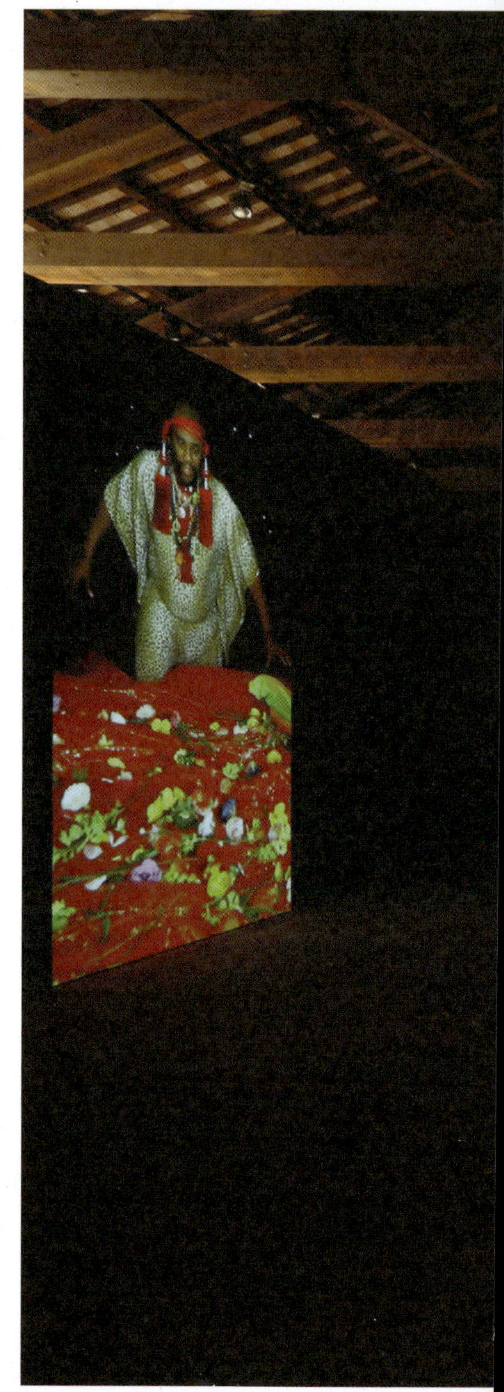

● *Installation view, 'The Stronger We Become',
2019. South African Pavilion; Arsenale, Venice.
Nkule Mabaso and Nomusa Makhubu curate the
work of Dineo Seshee Bopape, Tracey Rose and
Mawande Ka Zenzile at the 58th Biennale Arte.
Courtesy of the curator.*

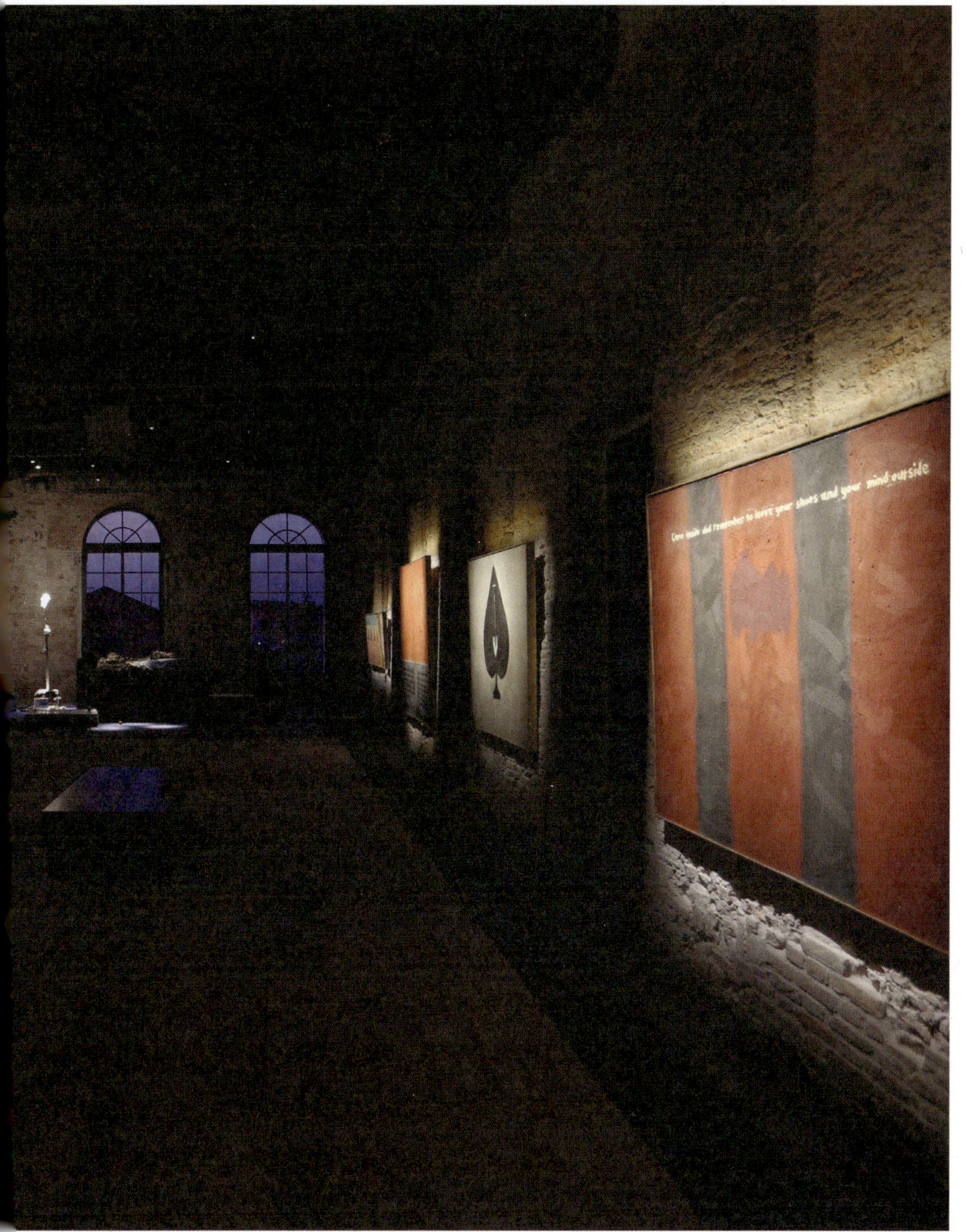

Come inside and remember to leave your shoes and your mind outside

Penny Siopis

As a child, Penny Siopis was always improvising with what was available to make things. Rummaging through her mom's dress-up box and making little worlds in the garden is how she spent her early childhood. For Penny this is a form of raw creativity that many children do automatically but that is later forgotten as adults. Her Greek parents inherited a bakery and they lived in the small town of Vryburg when Penny was young. Music also has an important place in her life, because her mother was a singing teacher and her grandmother a pianist.

Penny worked as a lecturer in Johannesburg for many years. She always made art while teaching. As a teacher she had a salary, which freed her to experiment without worrying if someone would buy her work. She was an artist, a lecturer, an activist and a mother. Many people thought it was impossible to combine all these roles, but when Penny was pregnant she made her famous painting 'Patience on a Monument', a collage of pictures from apartheid-era history schoolbooks and oil paint. The huge size of the painting and her growing pregnant belly made it impossible for her to complete the work in the small room she used as a studio – so she dragged it into the yard where she had more space. She finished it shortly after her son was born. Penny saw limitations as an opportunity to be creative.

Penny has changed the way she works many times, using different painting techniques and also objects and film. For her, to change her way of working opens new ways of thinking. This openness to the world is echoed in the process of change in her mediums. She is not interested in just making finished paintings.

In her latest paintings she puts the canvas flat on the floor and pours white wood glue on it, she then adds ink and water to the glue, making it move by tilting the canvas. As the glue dries it becomes hard and transparent – freezing the ink into interesting patterns and shapes. The image is also made by gravity and the air that dries the glue – things that are largely out of her control, but all part of the process of change she is exploring.

For Penny change is a social, political and philosophical idea that is important for how we get a long with each other, as well as how we live on the planet.

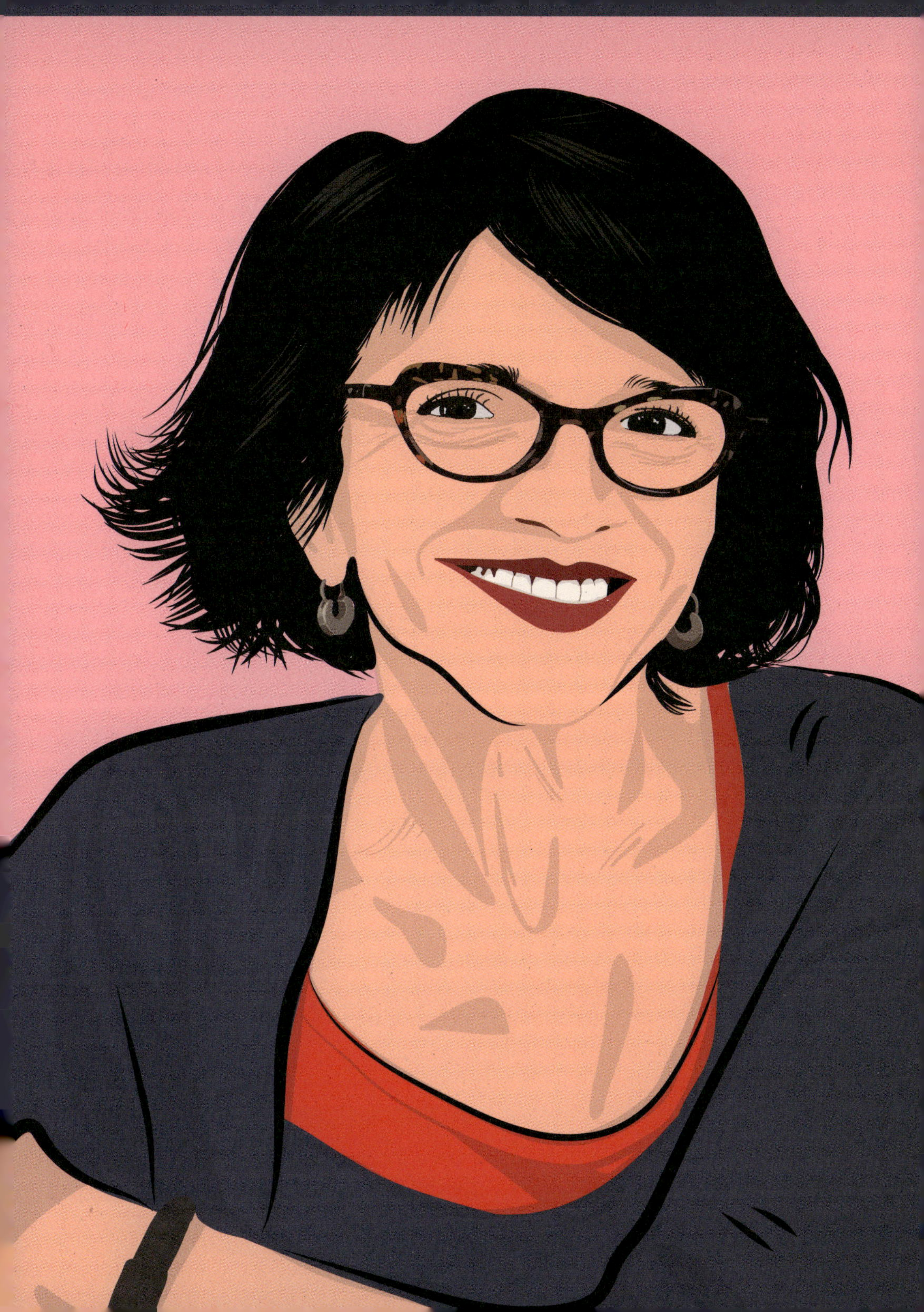

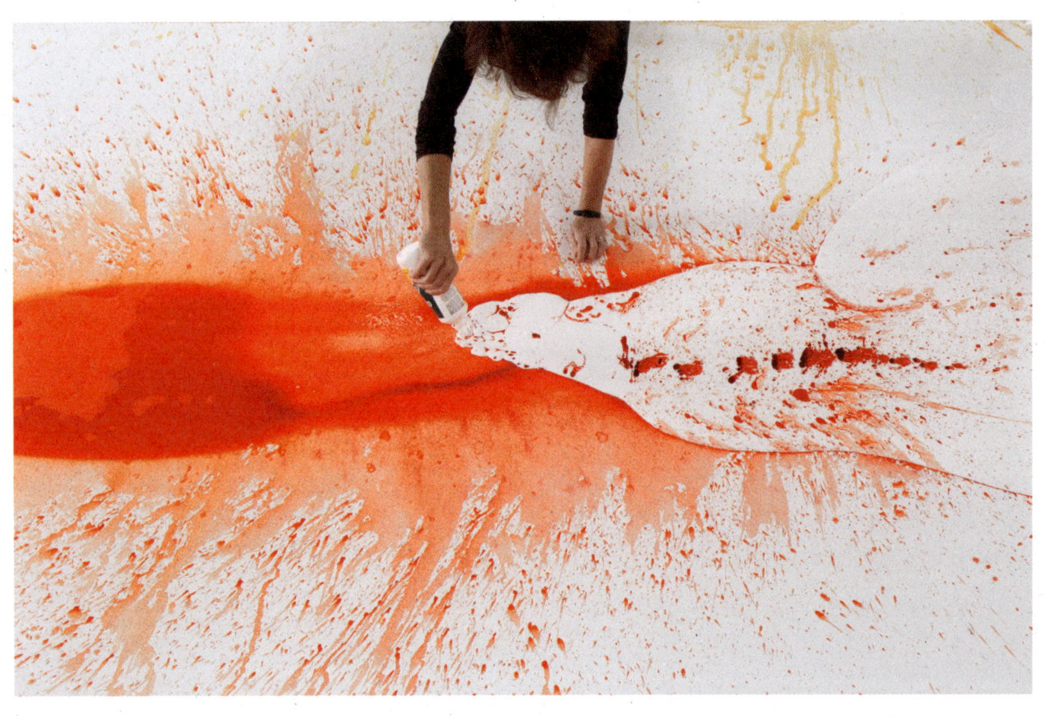

● *Photograph of the ink and glue process, Maitland Institute, 2017.*

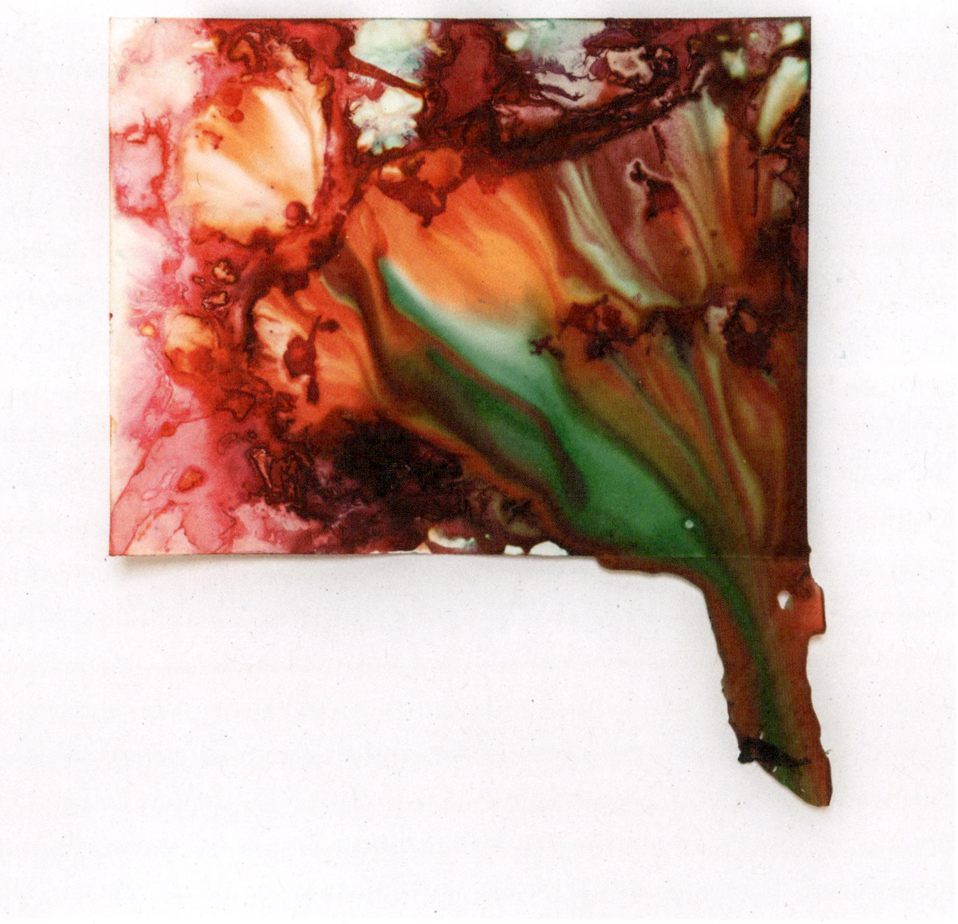

● *'She Breathes Water', 2010–2018. Glue, ink and oil stain on canvas. Courtesy of the artist and Stevenson, Cape Town and Johannesburg. Photo by Mario Todeschini.*

robin rhode

Imagine it was the beginning of the school year and you were being handed out your textbooks. You open your maths textbook and there, all around the edges, are little drawings decorating each page. You might wonder who did this, and why. Maybe someone who loved to draw so much, they couldn't stop? Maybe someone who was very, very bored? Maybe someone who didn't care so much about rules?

With Robin Rhode all of those things were true. Because he was a timid child, drawing gave him a sense of pride and it made him cool. When he had to do an art project, he was so enthusiastic, he would do three projects instead of one. But by the time Robin was in high school, he couldn't do art anymore, because it wasn't offered at his school. He started to struggle to concentrate and became a frustrated and rebellious child. He often got into big trouble for not doing what he was supposed to.

These difficulties continued when he went to study art. He just could not get himself to do what his teachers wanted from him and failed his first year. He was spending a lot of time in the library reading about what was going on in international art and paging through top art magazines like *Artforum* and *Frieze*. Can you believe that this guy, struggling to pass his first year, would have his work in one of those very same magazines just a couple of years later?

It was one day in his third year at technikon when he started to think back to his childhood experiences. He remembered drawing on walls with chalk. He was also very inspired by a famous French artist, Marcel Duchamp, who used to put objects that he had not made himself, like a bicycle wheel, in art galleries. Now Robin remembered this and he started drawing a bicycle on the wall. He then took photos and videos of himself performing with this drawn bicycle. And that was the start of him drawing or painting on walls and then getting a performer or himself to be photographed interacting with these drawings.

He has such a strong sense of style, line and colour that his work became very recognisable and before he was even 30 years old, his art had been bought by some of the top museums in the world. Robin has become one of South Africa's most successful artists and he says, while he does not know the recipe for success, what has helped him is just to keep doing what he believes in.

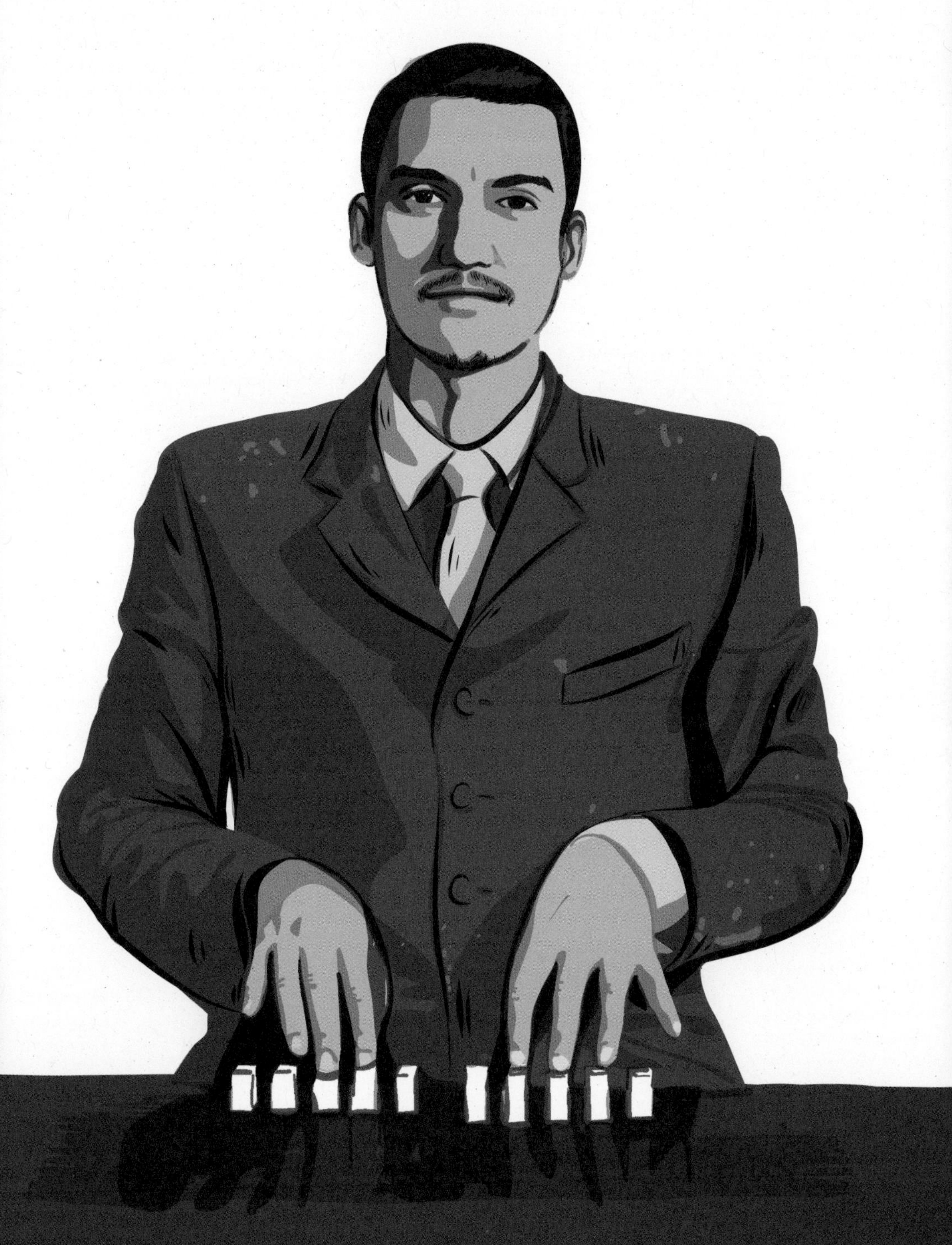

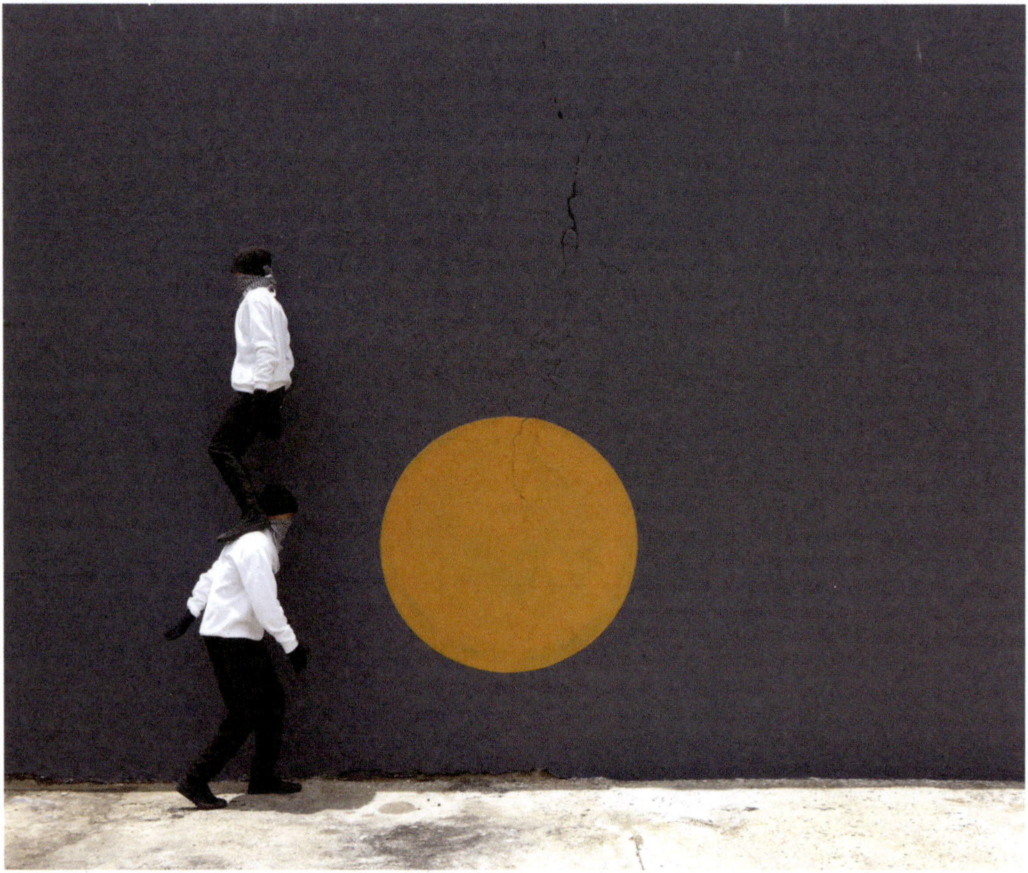

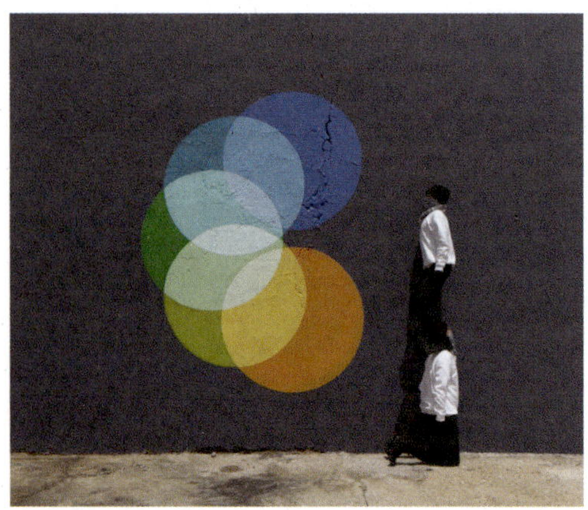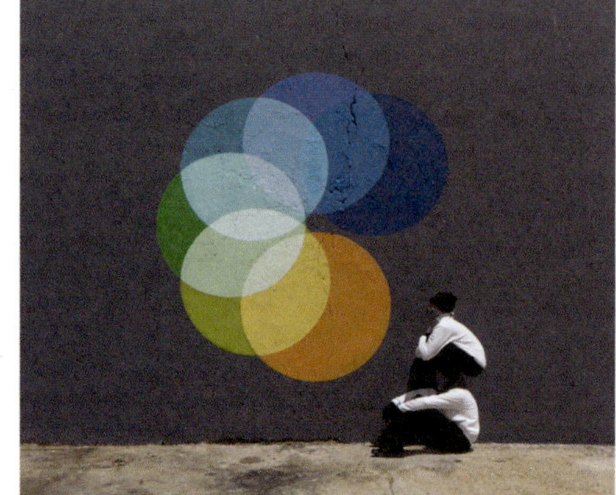

● *Inverted cycle', 2016. C-print, 8 parts. Courtesy of the artist.*

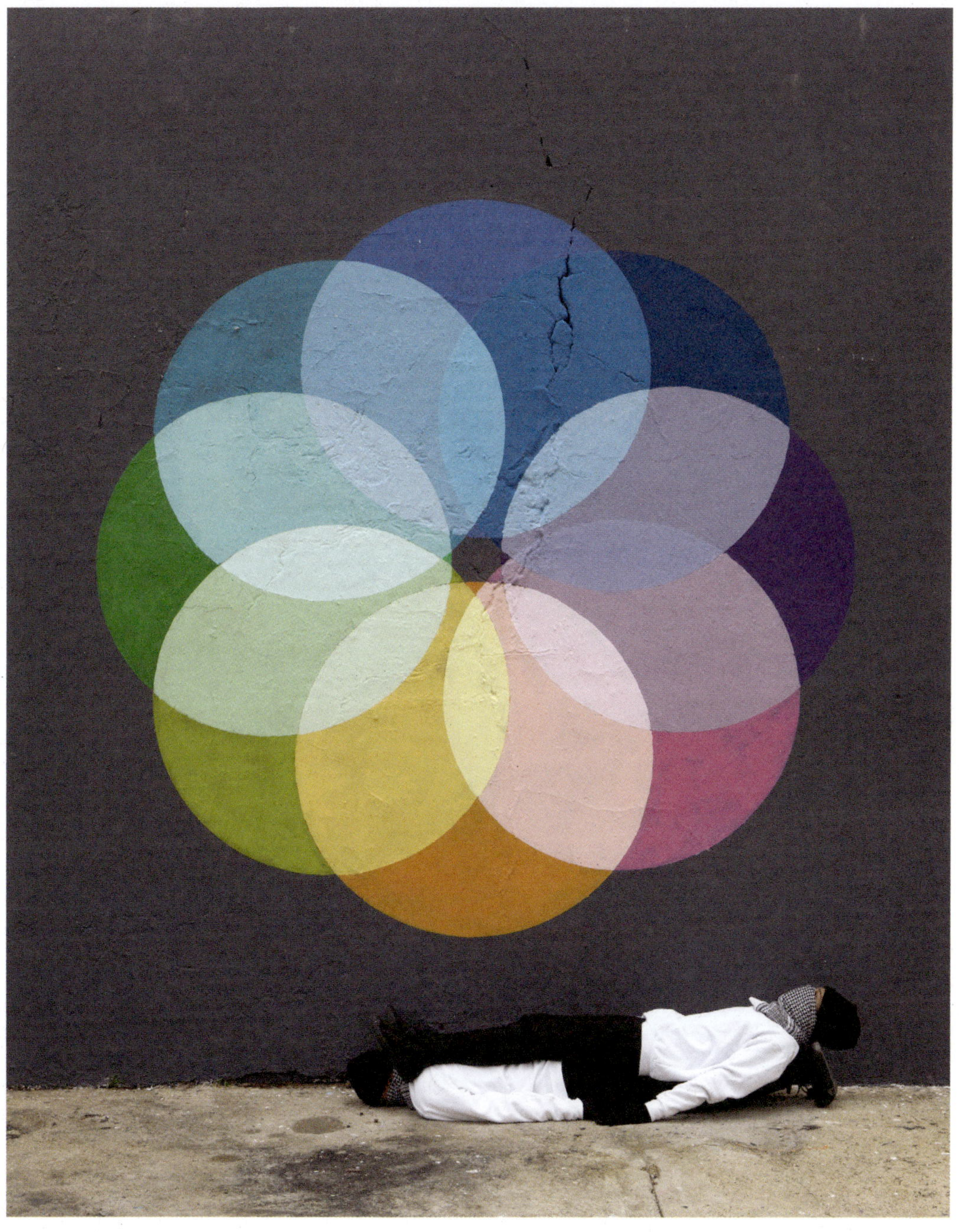

Sam Nhlengethwa

Some artists take long to start turning art into their job, but Sam Nhlengethwa started earning money for his art when he was still in primary school! His classmates used to admire his drawings and pay him little bits of money to decorate their exercise books. He also used to make collaged books of Orlando Pirates by collecting all the pictures from magazines and newspapers. These were his first 'artworks'.

When Sam was in high school in the mid-1970s in a township to the east of Johannesburg, there were riots against apartheid in the streets. During this time, there wasn't much teaching going on and they mostly just played. One day his teacher said they should draw a picture. Sam drew the garden as he saw it through the window and his teacher said: 'Wow Sam, I'll give you 10 out of 10 for that drawing! You should think about becoming an artist.'

After that there was no turning back. He told his parents he wanted to go to Rorke's Drift Art and Craft Centre. It was very far away in another province and his mother did not agree. But Sam had already bought a train ticket. His mother realised she could do nothing about him leaving so she called the neighbour to pray for him before he left. He had 12 hours on the train ahead of him and he felt bad about leaving his mother so worried. But soon he was able to send a letter back that he was doing well.

Sam learnt all he could about art and made art about whatever he liked: dancing, listening to jazz music, getting married. Some people thought this was strange because many artists

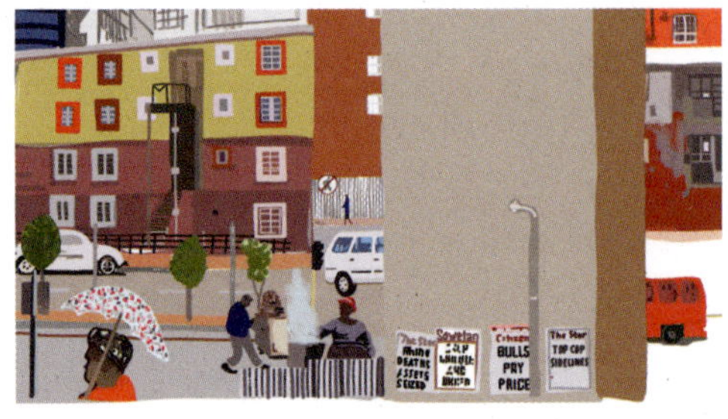

were making art that protested the politics of the time, but Sam was interested in everyday life in the township where he, and many others, grew up.

Sam makes his work by both painting and sticking pictures onto a canvas and has done some television and advertising work too. He believes artists look at the rest of the world and say 'we are your mirror.'

If he had another chance to choose a different career, he would choose to be an artist all over again. Sam is sad that his father passed away long before he started making art and that he has not been able to see him become successful as an artist, but he knows that he would have been very proud of his son.

• Illustration of 'Cyclists Mural', 2012. Oil and mixed media on canvas.

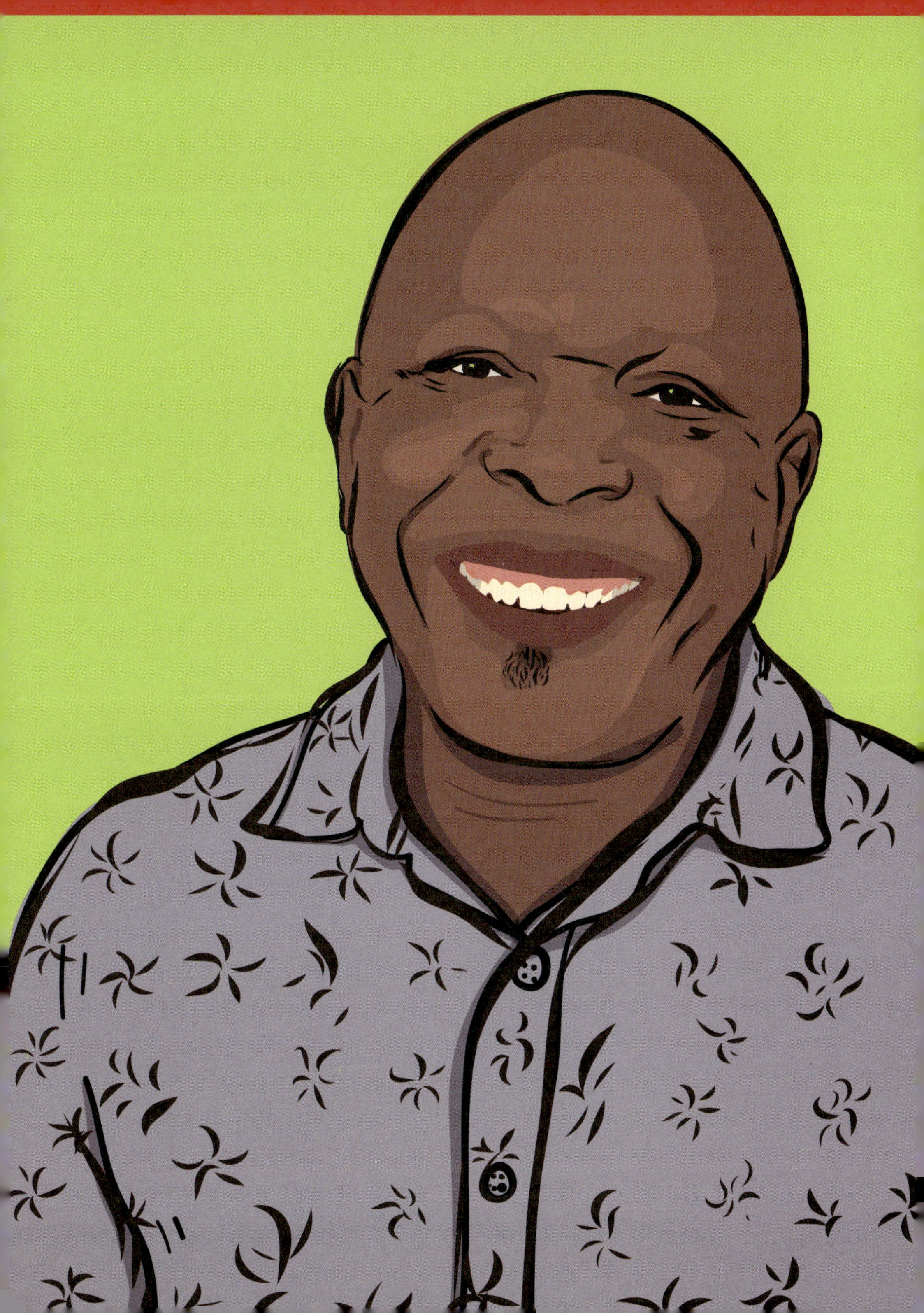

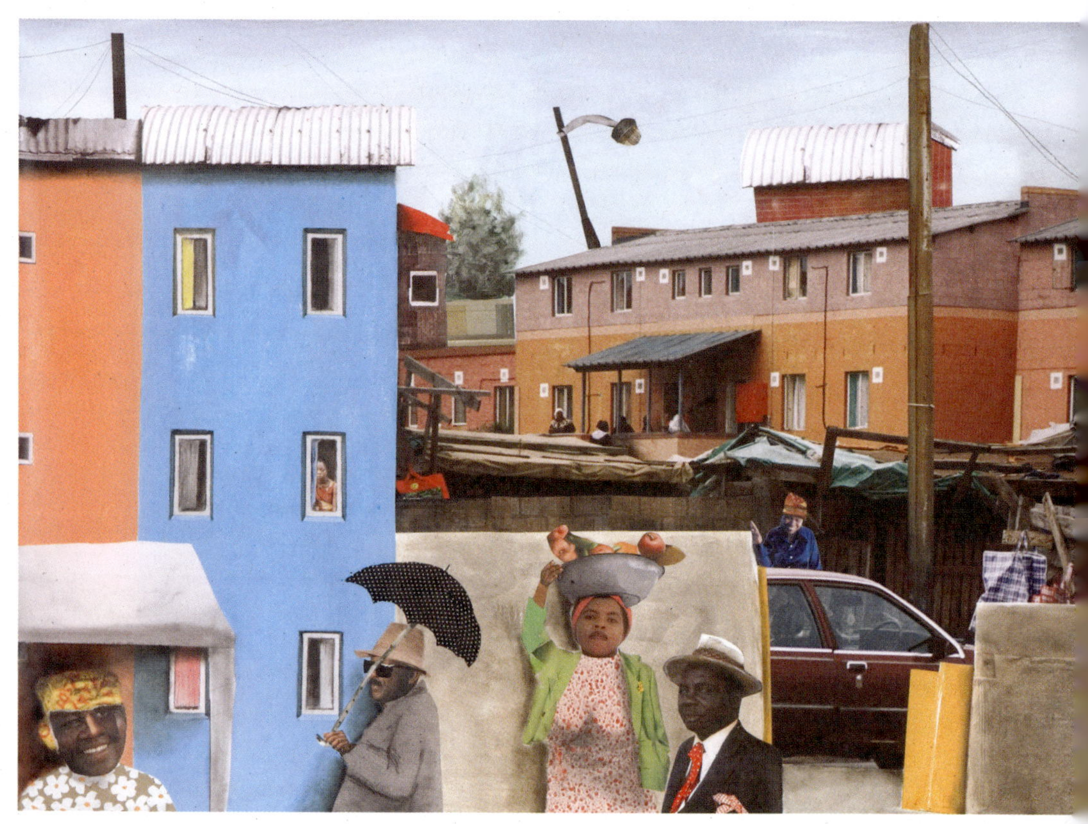

• 'Nyanga, Western Cape', 2006. Mixed media on paper. Courtesy of the artist
and Goodman Gallery.

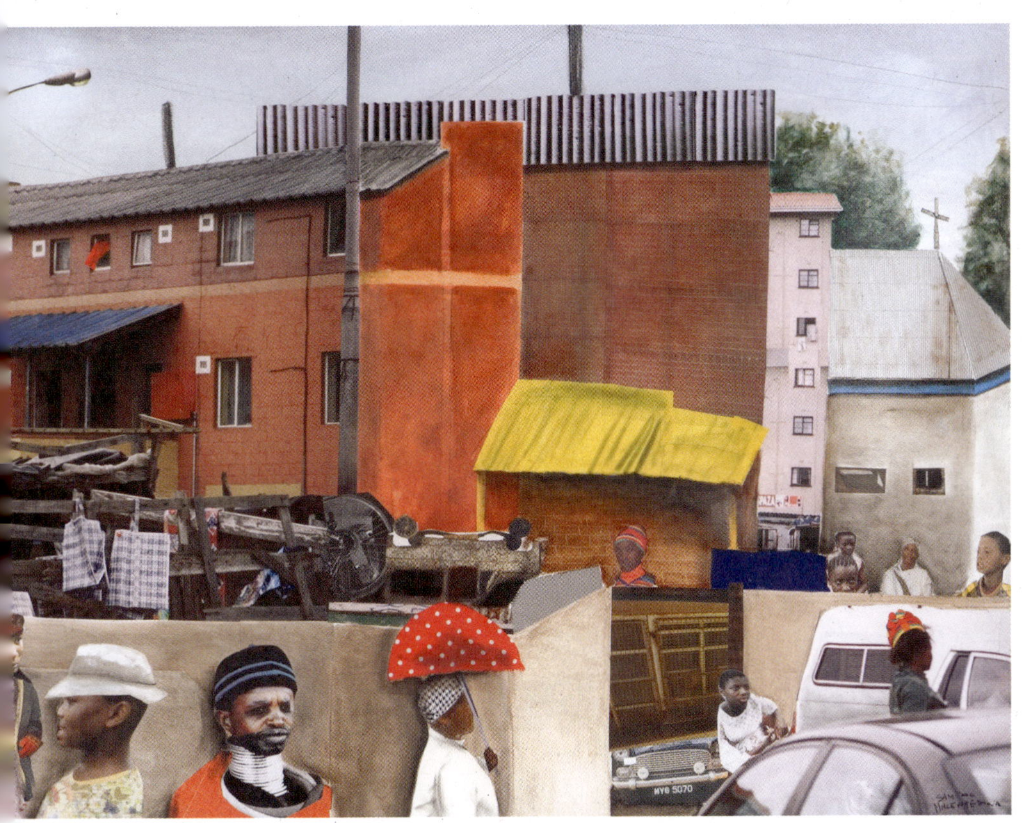

Same Mdluli

Sometimes history shapes people's understanding of the world around them in ways that inform what they eventually decide to grow up and do. In 1985 the South African Defense Force (SADF) raided Gaborone in Botswana, which led to Same Mdluli's family moving to America for political exile. Her family returned to South Africa following the first democratic elections in 1996 where she was enrolled at the National School of the Arts in Johannesburg. After matriculating she decided to do a fine arts degree instead of architecture because she felt it would offer her more freedom.

Same was appointed as the curator of one of South Africa's largest corporate galleries in 2018. A curator is someone who looks after artworks and so she introduced an exhibition highlighting the concerns she had identified during her doctoral studies in history of art at Wits University. Like other practitioners in the arts, Same thinks of her practice as a form of advocacy for being the change you want to see. After doing her master's in heritage studies she worked at one of the most prominent galleries in South Africa. She then decided to pursue a doctorate as a way of empowering herself to speak authoritatively on the subject of art in South Africa because often Black women are not taken seriously in the field.

While she still paints in her spare time, she also writes about art and artists in South Africa. Her interests include exploring music, especially jazz, and how it connects with visual art. As part of her artistic practice, Same also explores different kinds of ideas around Blackness and modernity. Blackness is an idea she says is about to her own experience of being a young Black woman and modernity is about living in a current time.

Both these ideas, she feels, reflect history back at people through the way in which Black artists have been given recognition in art history. In South Africa there has been a focus on only European art in schools and universities and on the work by white South African artists which is being written about in books and sold for millions of dollars at international auctions. To try and solve this problem, Same and other art scholars have taken it upon themselves to ensure that Black artists' artworks are exhibited for everyone to see. This will make sure that they are also recorded in important art history books for future generations.

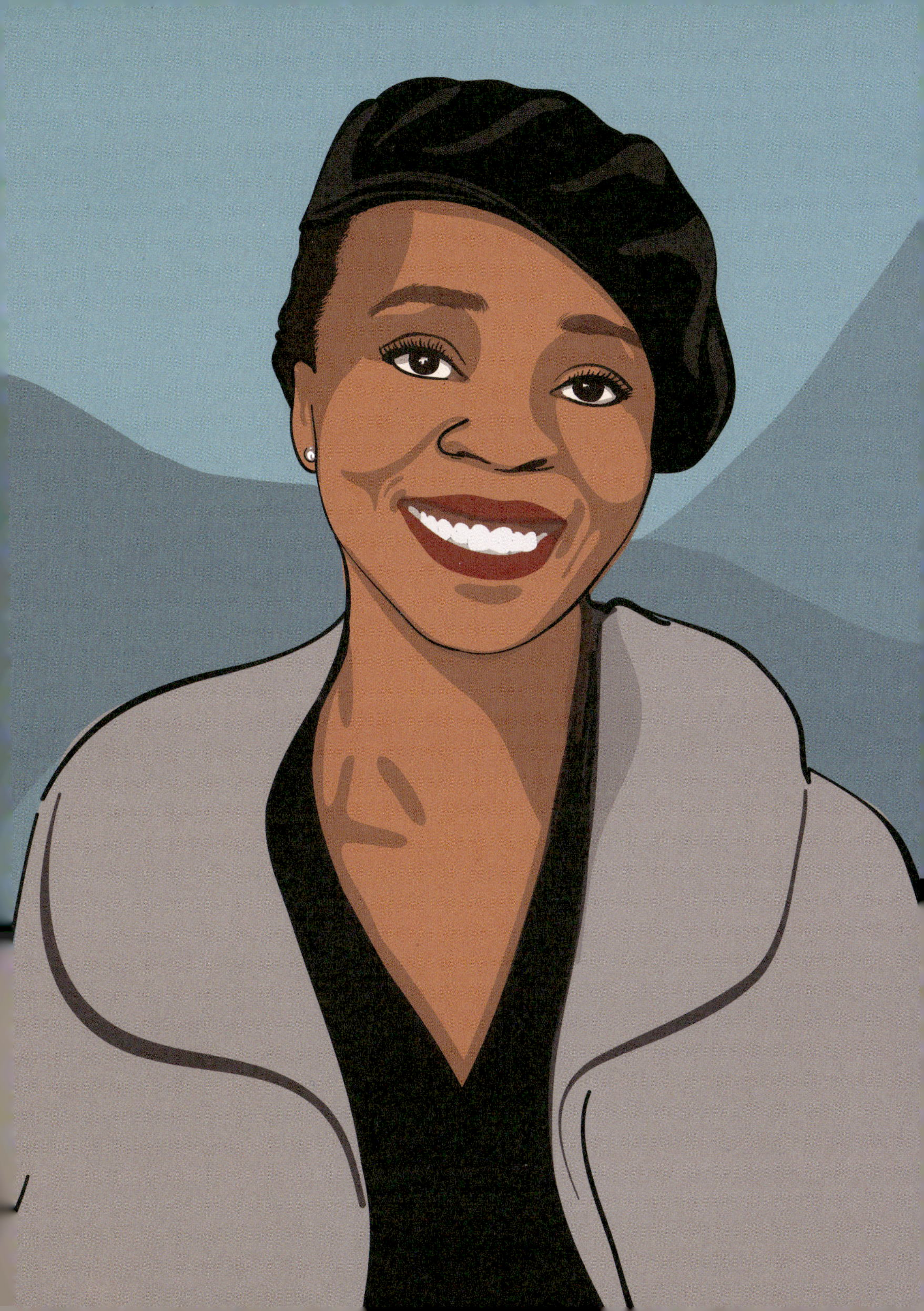

SANTU MOFOKENG

Running around Orlando East in the late afternoon was far more interesting to the young Santu Mofokeng than sitting indoors listening to the boring adult conversations. Every day the children of the neighbourhood would meet outside and play 'Black Maipatile' hiding in back gardens. Through mielies, flowerbeds and fruit trees they would try to find each other.

When he was older Santu decided to become a street photographer because it seemed to him that those with cameras were always more popular than he was. He liked how the camera made him feel important. At first he was shy and only took portraits of his family. For a long time afterwards, he had to work as a darkroom assistant for other photographers and newspapers, because black people were discouraged from being photographers during apartheid.

Later, he became part of a group of documentary photographers, called Afrapix, who were showing the terrible effects of apartheid. But Santu felt unhappy that it did not show how complicated life actually was.

When he started working at the Wits University Institute for African Studies he was able to spend more time understanding a subject. During this time Santu decided to make a story of many photographs. The first one he did was called 'Train Church' where he took photos of the long journeys black people had to take to go to work, sometimes starting at 4am.

He realised that many turned the train journeys into a religious session of singing, praying and helping each other.

One day he put up an exhibition and when he looked in the visitor book, he saw someone criticised him for taking photos of black people and selling it to white people. He was angry about this simple accusation, but it did make him think about his work differently.

He asked himself, 'What am I doing and why am I doing it?'

Santu started noticing that many people had photographs in their houses of their families from long ago. He set out on a research project to collect the stories of the people in the photographs along with documenting the photographs themselves. Many of the photographs were prized possessions while others were hidden in the backs of cupboards and the bottoms of drawers. It was important for Santu to name and date each photo to counter the way black people are often left nameless in stories of art and history. He made it into a book so that it could be seen by anyone.

● Right background: Illustration of photo by Steve Tanchel.

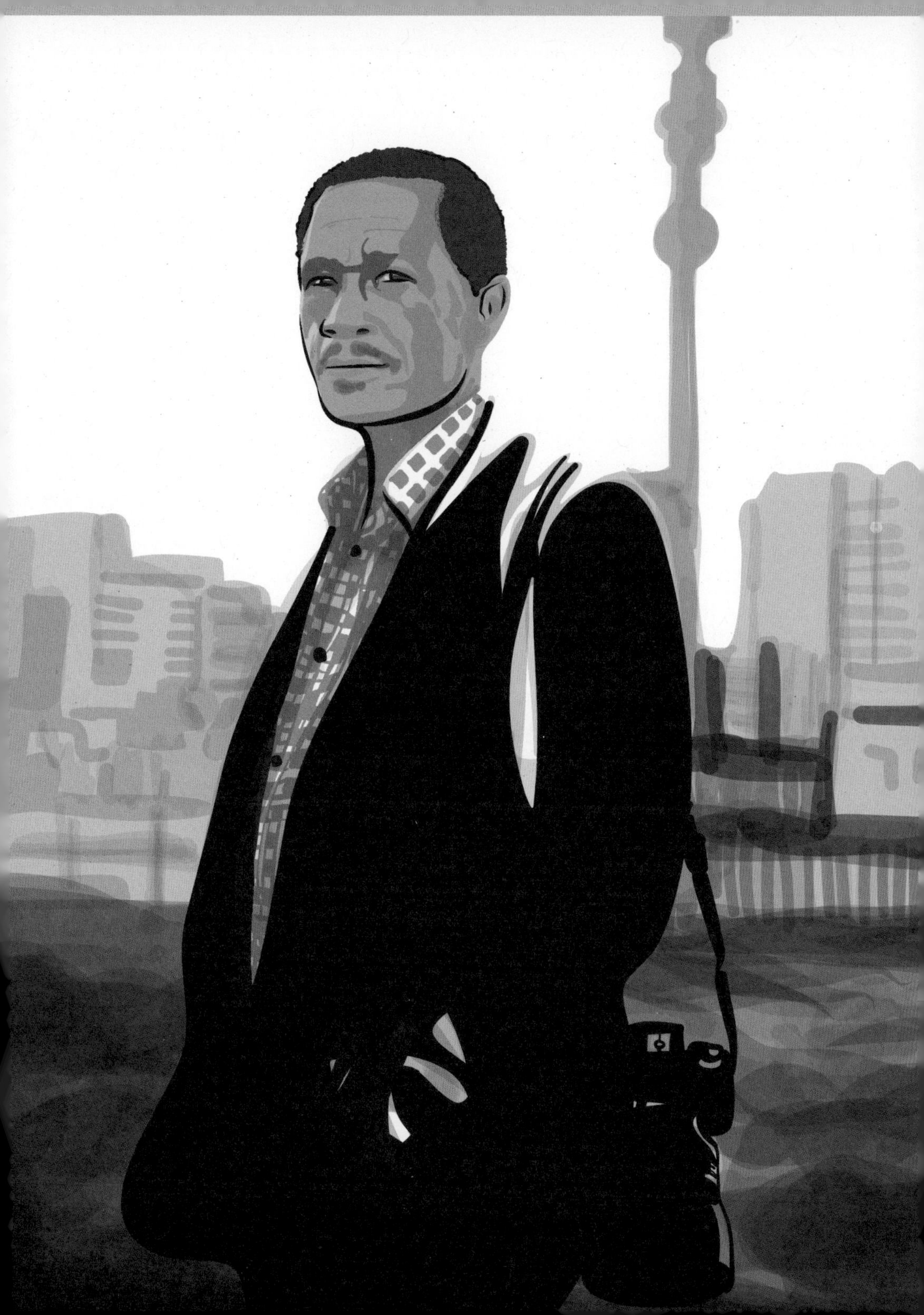

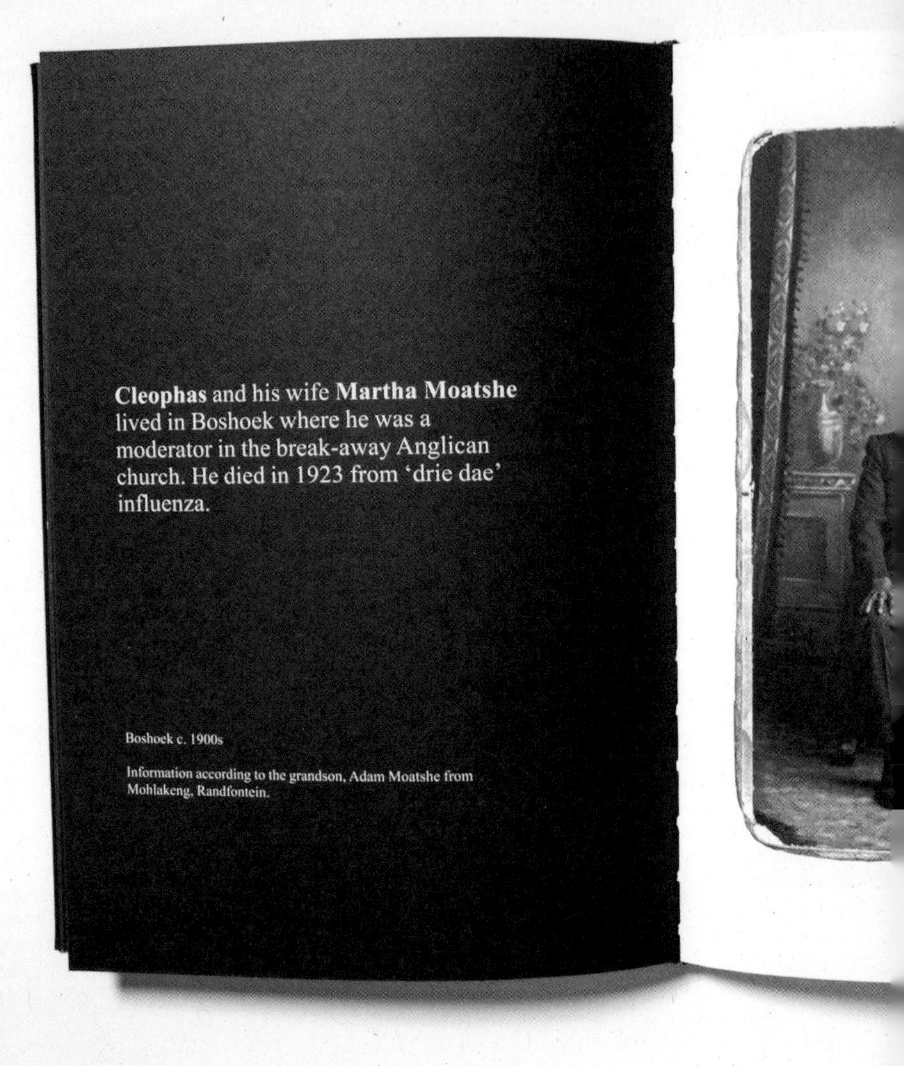

● *'The Black Photo Album / Look At Me: 1890–1950'. Steidl, 2013. Courtesy of Lunetta Bartz.*

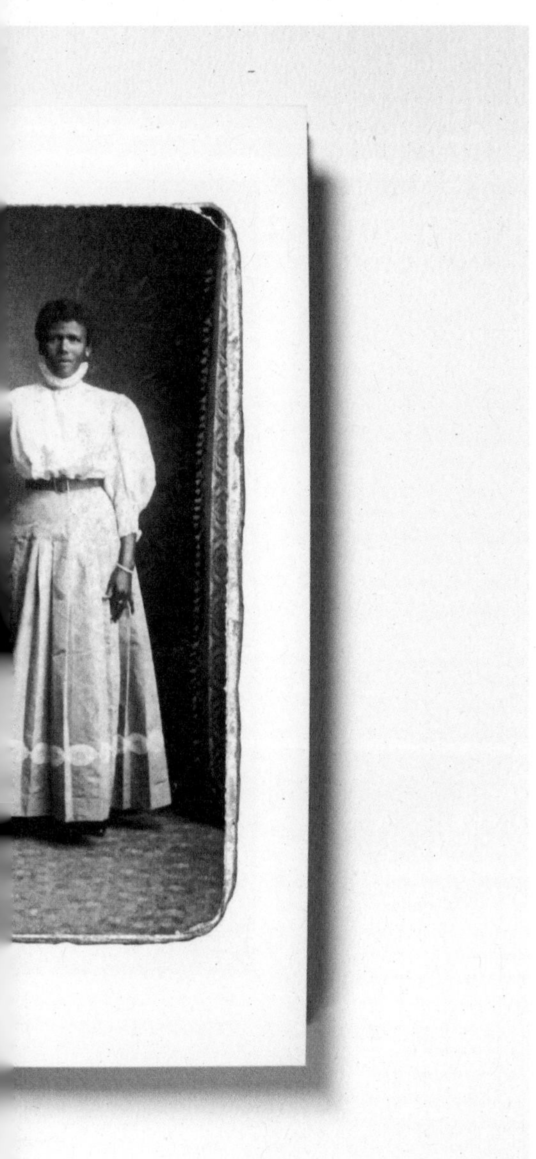

Santu won a couple of international awards for his work, which took him to America and Europe and he became more famous abroad than in South Africa. Throughout his life Santu was interested in the idea of a photo trying to copy reality. He used writing to wrestle with this and he wrote a lot about his own work. He decided that even if the photo is fixed, never to move again, the meaning of the photograph might change every time a different person looks at it.

STEPHANÉ CONRADIE

Not so long ago in South Africa there was a law that said white people could only marry white people and black people could only marry black people. It was a racist and unjust system. So people broke the law when they fell in love, but they had to find ways to not end up in jail! Stephané Conradie's parents did not have the same skin colour and her mother was from Namibia. They decided to live in Namibia until the laws changed. That was how Stephané came to live the first seven years of her life in a different country.

When they moved to Cape Town, it was strange for her to be called a brown person and she started getting really interested in how people decide what group it is that they belong to. Stephané was very musical when she was growing up. It was clear that she was talented and everyone thought she should definitely become a musician. But Stephané wanted to do something that she had to work harder at and so she decided to study art instead.

One day an opportunity came to show her work at one of South Africa's top galleries because they happened to have some space available. She told the gallery that she didn't have any work, but they said, 'Well, you have a month to make some!' She worked really hard and managed to finish. Since then she has had many other exhibitions.

If you look at her work now, there is some painting and lots of decoration with objects other people used to own that she has found in second-hand shops. She is interested in how people surround themselves with things that tell us about their lives and their culture.

Stephané believes that art is a way to work through things and to show people what is going on at this moment in time that we live in. But she also believes that art is not just in galleries, it is everywhere: in designing buildings, in making decorative objects, in decorating your home or your room. Once you start really looking at the world, Stephané believes, you will see art everywhere.

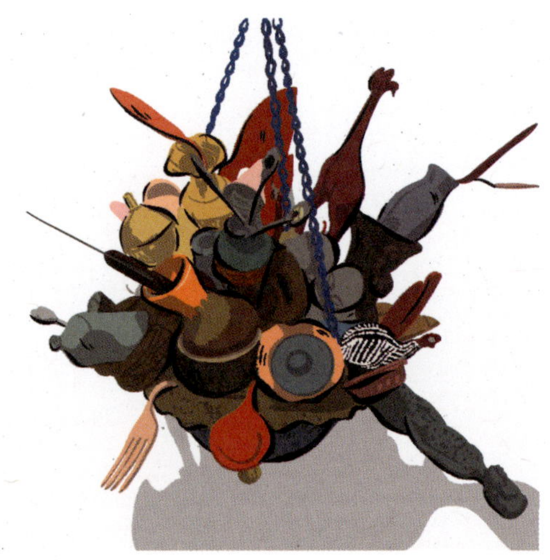

• *Illustration of 'geraniums and petunias', 2019. Mixed media.*

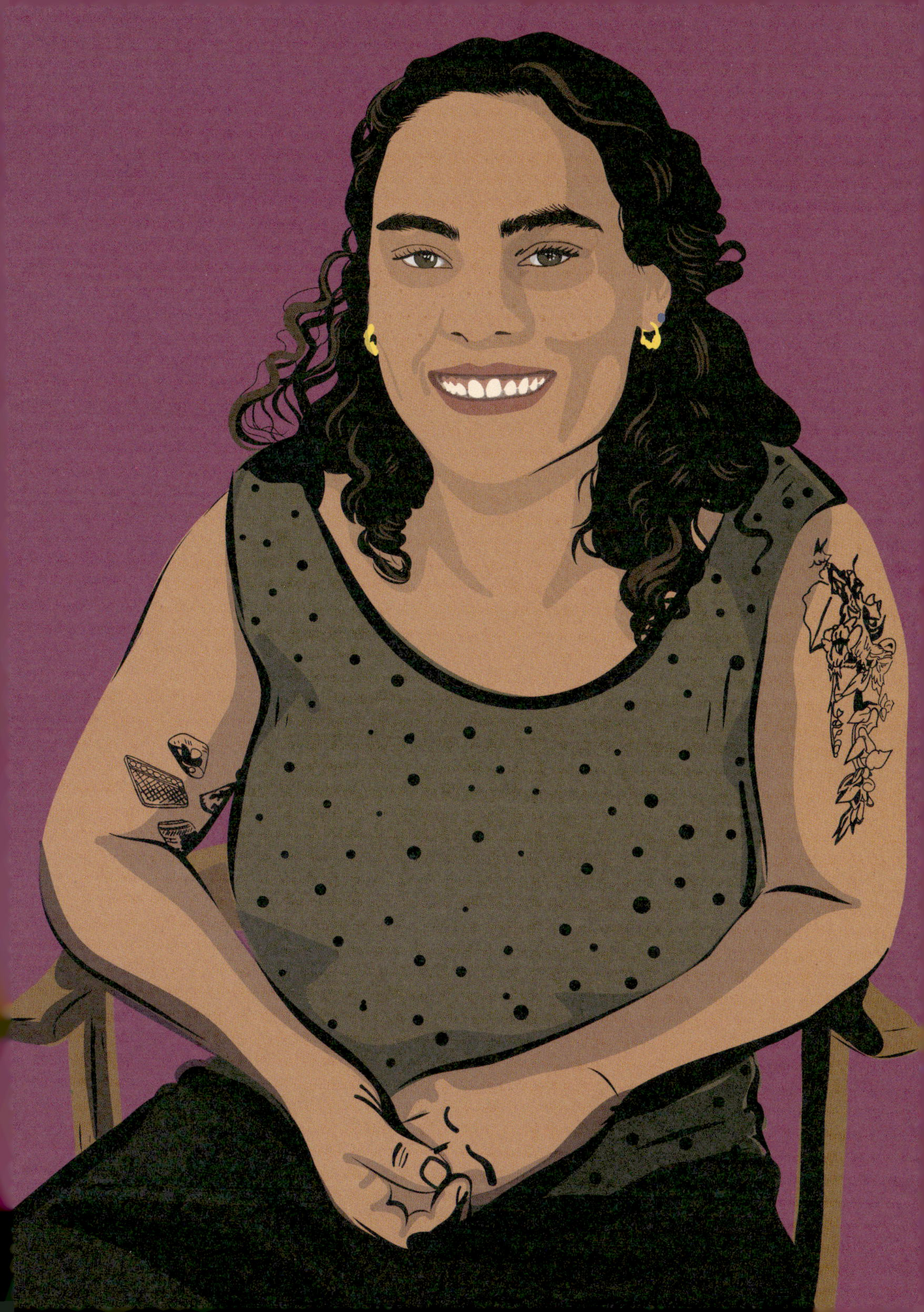

STEPHEN HOBBS

If you want to understand how Stephen Hobbs sees the world, you have to imagine paging through a giant pop-up book. Every time you turn the page, you walk around inside the page and crawl through the openings to see it from all sides and different angles.

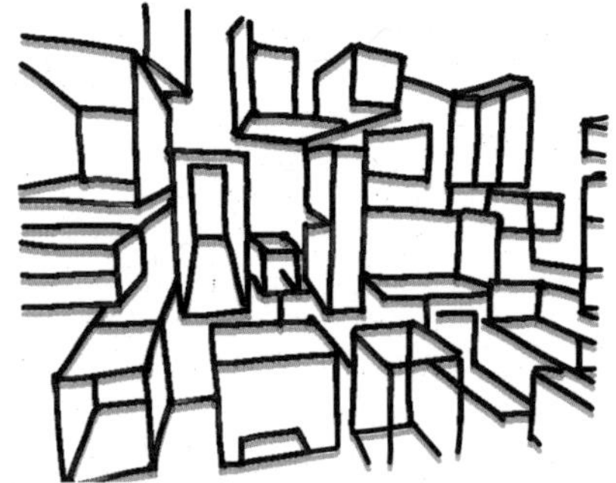

Stephen can't really remember a time when he was not making some sort of art. His mother was a ceramist, his father was a painter and his grandparents were also artists. When he was a teenager, he would come home in the afternoon after school and use an airbrush to make all kinds of pictures. After that he changed his parents' basement into a print-making space.

He went to art school and did very well – even selling the work he made in his final year at university to a big art collector. This work was just a block of ice that the buyer has to keep freezing every time they want to exhibit it. It is a conceptual work of art. Conceptual artists work with ideas. They then find a way to show you what that idea is.

Stephen likes to ask questions when he makes art, like: How does your body feel when it is in a room? How do you feel and respond to the objects that are in the room with you? He has created an art company with a friend, Marcus Neustetter, called The Trinity Session, which also asks questions but often about cities. For example, how does your body feel in the city? Does it feel safe? Is your body comfortable? How do you create better spaces? How do we make these spaces beautiful using art, and how do we make them safe by using good design?

The Trinity Session has commissioned many public sculptures in Johannesburg. You might have seen cut-out trees in the Braamfontein Precinct. For this project they worked with an arts and crafts organisation (Imbali Visual Literacy Project). They asked the crafters to imagine fantasy plants with cut-out shapes and colours.

Nowadays Stephen draws, he takes photographs, he can build a garden, he can design a building, he can shoot and edit a film, he can create an installation and has even made a pop-up book that has been bought by international museums! Because, for him, art is not one thing, it is about knowing that your idea can become a reality. And in this way, you can change the way the world looks and the way you look at the world around you.

● *Illustration of 'Flat City', 2019. Mild steel. Work in progress.*

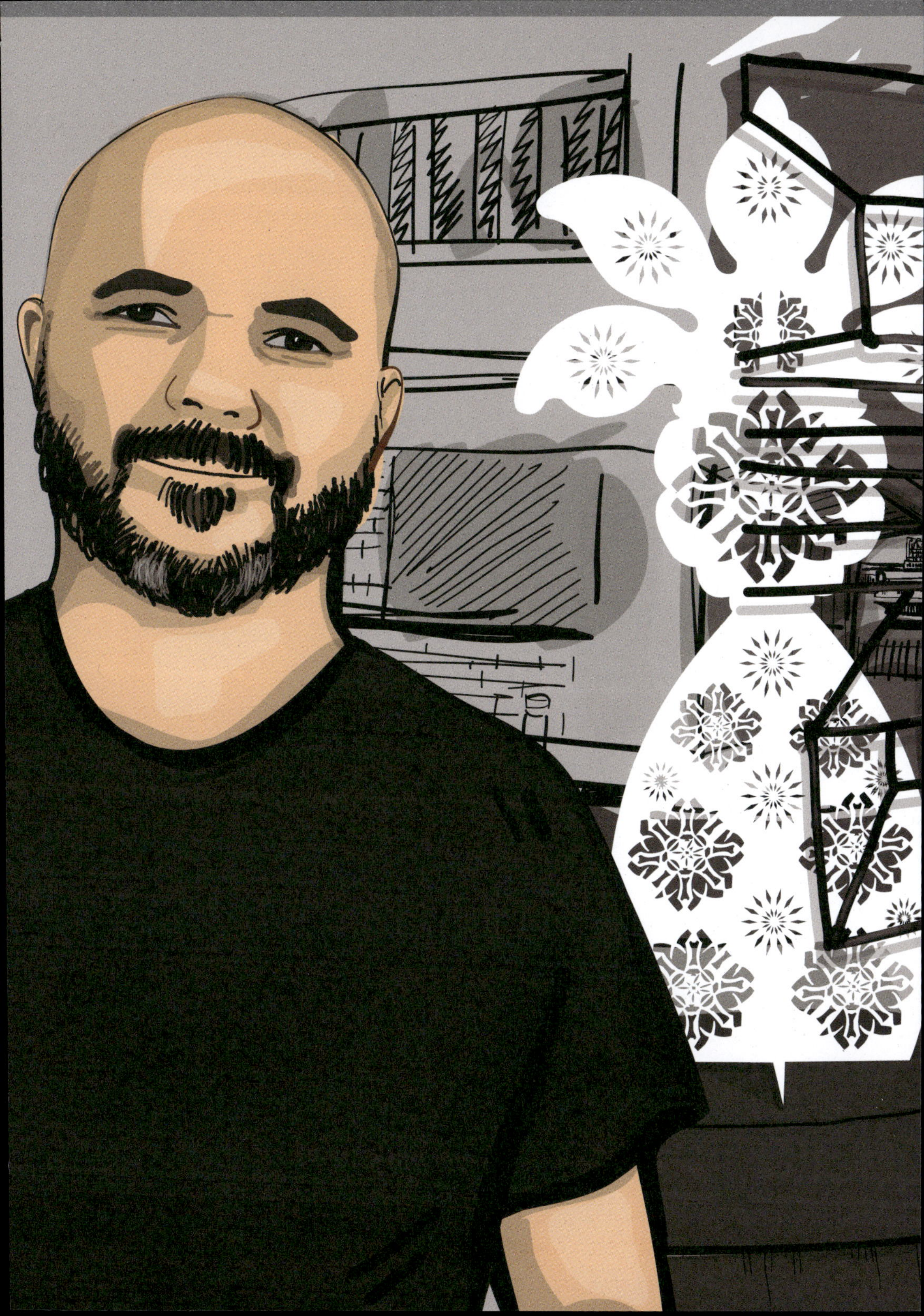

SUE WILLIAMSON

In the house where Sue Williamson grew up, there was a big roll of paper and every now and then her father would cut a piece off and stick it on a drawing board for her to draw on. Drawing was something that she often did, but once a teacher told her that she would never be good at art, so she turned her attention to writing instead. She studied journalism.

When she was an adult a friend told her that she could do some evening classes in painting. Sue loved these classes and realised that her teacher was wrong! She was good at drawing. She was offered an opportunity to do a diploma in fine art so that she could move on to do a master's degree. It was when she was still doing this diploma that she made one of her most famous works of art: 'A Few South Africans.'

For this first work, she wanted to show some of the heroes who were fighting to bring down the apartheid regime in South Africa. Sue remembers that at the time one hardly ever saw the faces of black people on television. It was as if that whole side of the country did not exist. So she created postcards with the faces of female political activists of the time. These went all over the world and became very well known. She even gave Winnie Madikizela-Mandela a set to give to Nelson Mandela in prison.

During this time she was also a journalist and had a column in a newspaper. She decided that it was necessary to write about the work that artists were doing to speak about the difficult situation in South Africa. Her book *Resistance Art in South Africa* sold 5000 copies just in America and more all over the world.

Shortly after that, she started the online magazine Artthrob. This was back when almost no one had email addresses and the page took so long to load you could go and make a cup of tea while waiting for it! Artthrob has made it possible for people from anywhere to learn about South African art and know what our artists are creating.

Sue believes artists are curious about the world and they follow their curiosity to show and explore difficult things in society. For this reason Sue has always tried to make art that anyone can understand if they are interested in trying to find out.

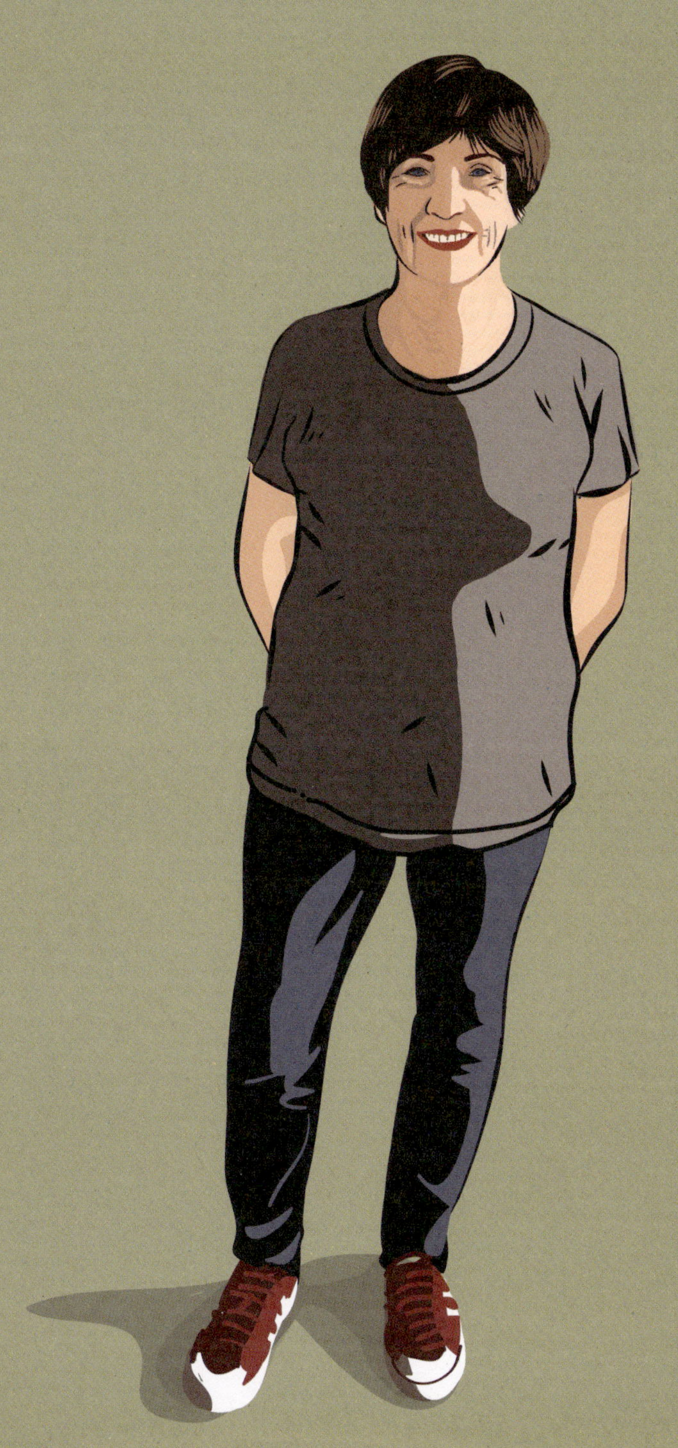

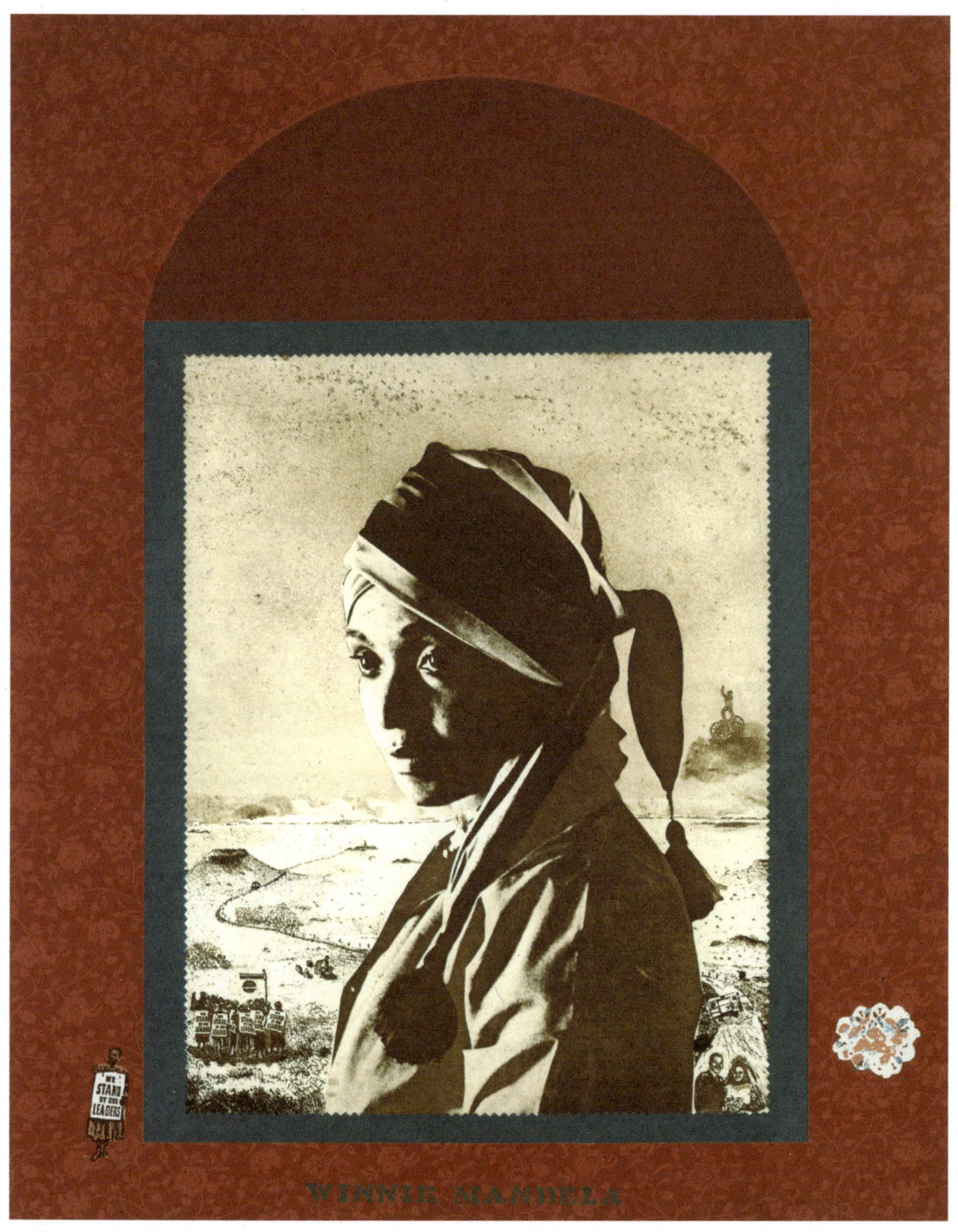

● 'Winnie Mandela', 1983. 'A few South Africans' series. Photo etching/screenprint collage.
Courtesy of the artist and Goodman Gallery.

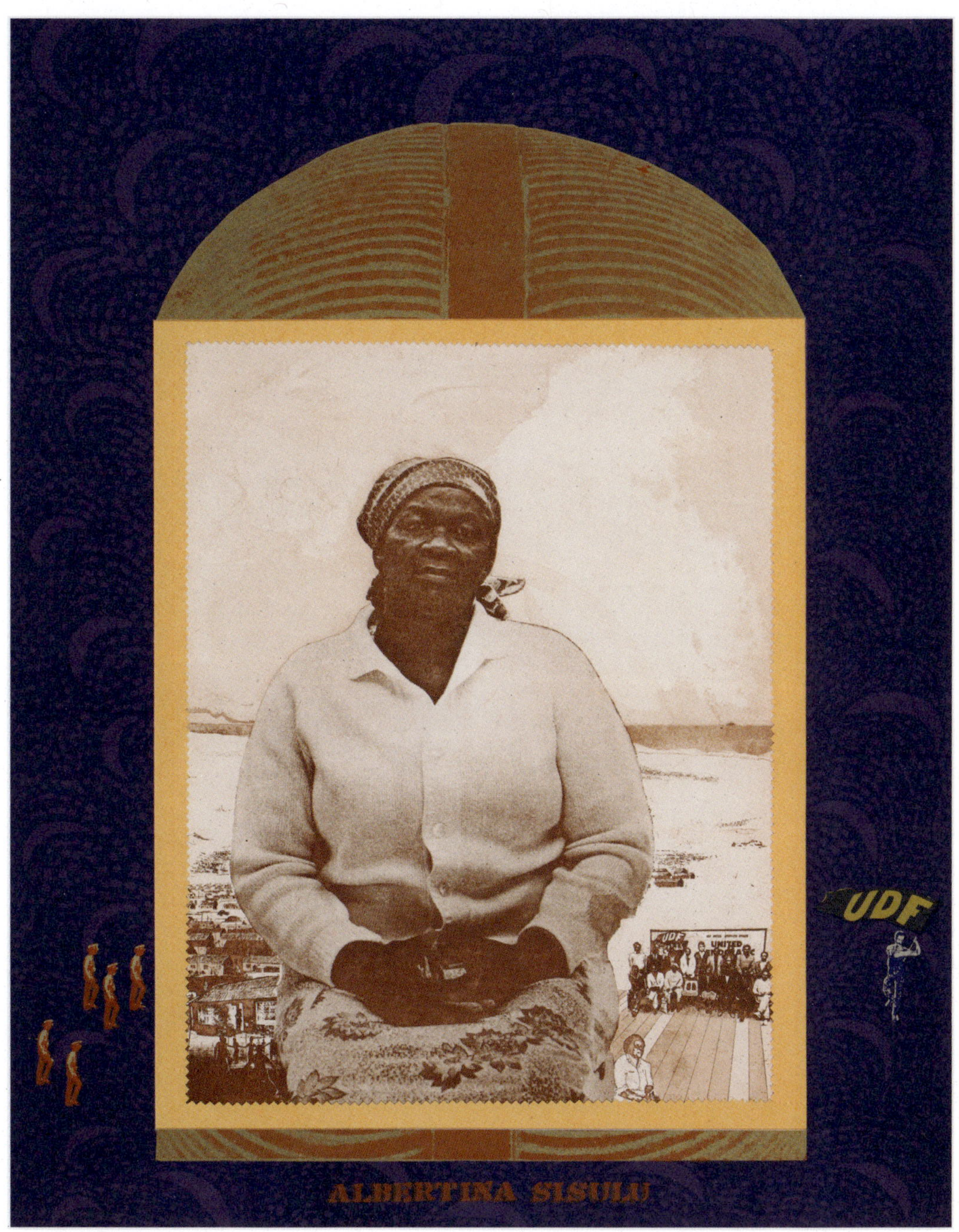

● *'Albertine Sisulu', 1983, 'A few South Africans' series. Photo etching/screenprint collage. Courtesy of the artist and Goodman Gallery.*

THENJIWE NIKI NKOSI

Imagine your parents are always talking about a special place that they remember. All the music they listen to, the plays, the films, all has to do with this faraway place. Sometimes people visit from there and you hear more stories. You might create an image in your mind of this magical place. This was how Thenjiwe Niki Nkosi came to know South Africa for the first 12 years of her life. She grew up in New York because her father was a political exile and could not return to South Africa.

When she did finally go to this place, South Africa, in high school, it was both familiar from all the stories and unfamiliar at the same time. Her new life was different from the stories she'd heard, and she struggled to find belonging in this new place. She thought she might find that sense of belonging back in America again. What she would later realise was that belonging is something you can find inside yourself. She started studying art but had no idea what a real artist was. It was only when she returned to South Africa to work in one of the most famous printing studios, Artist Proof Studio, that she met a lot of inspiring professional artists. Then she started making her own art.

Looking back on all the years before she started selling her work regularly, she remembers it being really hard. What do you do when no one is buying your work and no one is interested? She says you should keep going. Slowly you grow more confident, which for Thenjiwe means giving yourself more time to do what you believe in.

One day she was looking through the money in her wallet and saw faces of people on them. She wondered what it was that made some people more memorable than others and why some people end up in history books and others don't. She started a series of portraits of people who are heroes. Some portraits were of famous people like Francis Baard and Winnie Madikizela-Mandela, but others were people who were only heroes to her, like her great-grandmother and her best friend. Whenever she feels that she wants to always remember someone, she paints a portrait to go into her growing series.

Thenjiwe uses her art as a way to face big questions in her life, like the feeling of needing to belong. She believes everybody should have the opportunity to use art to try to understand themselves and the world a bit better.

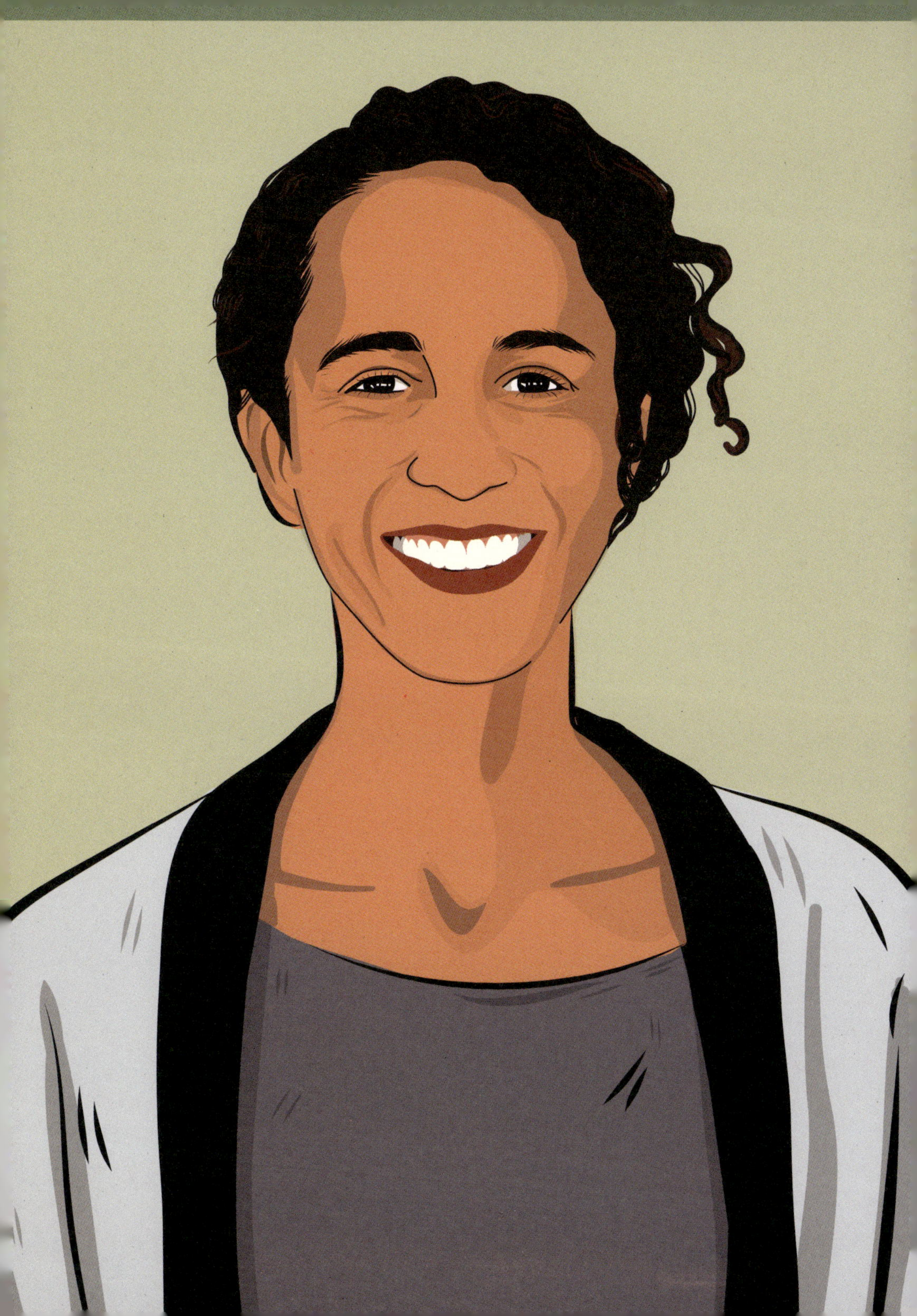

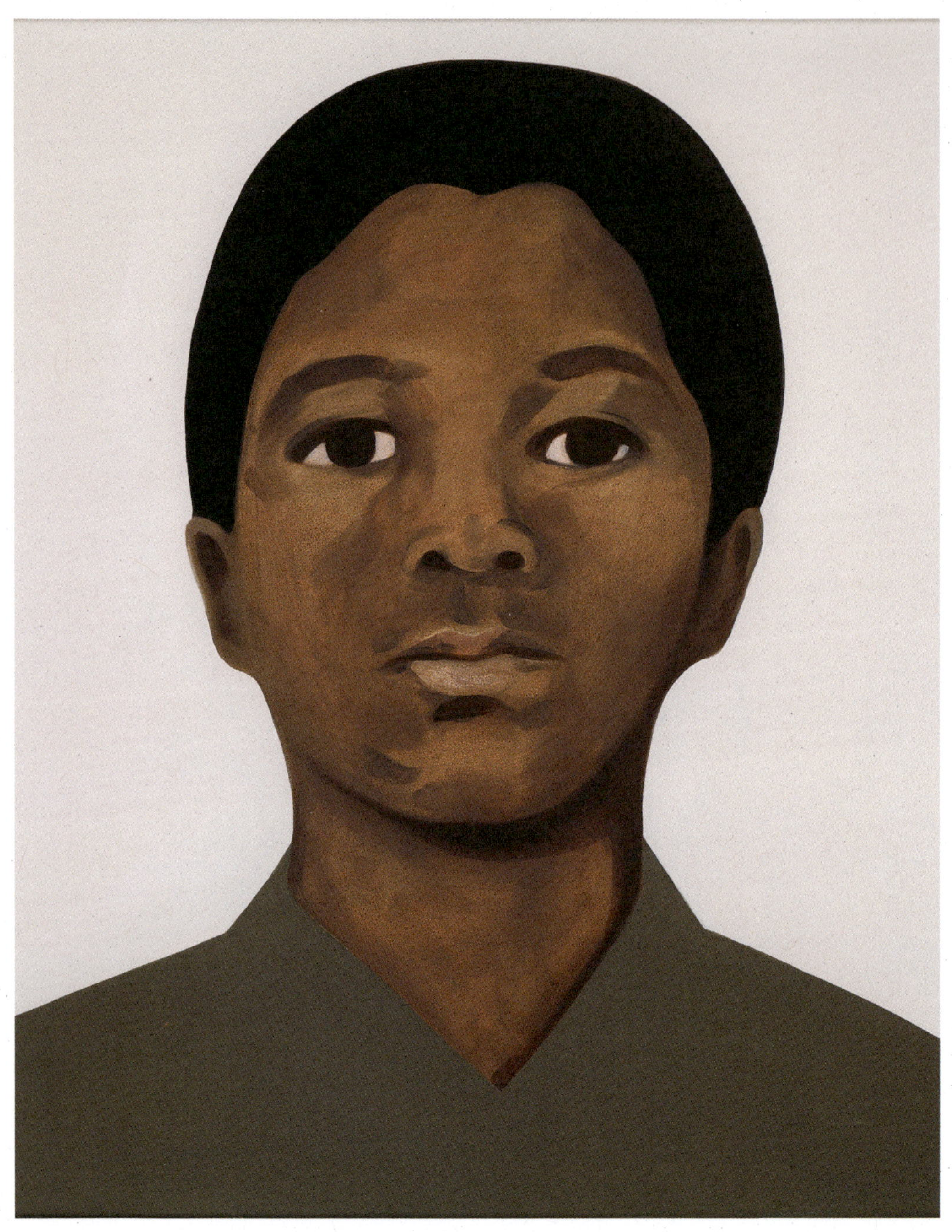
• '9609: *Nana (After Gladys Nana Nkosi) (my aunt)*', 2018. *Oil on canvas. Courtesy of the artist.*

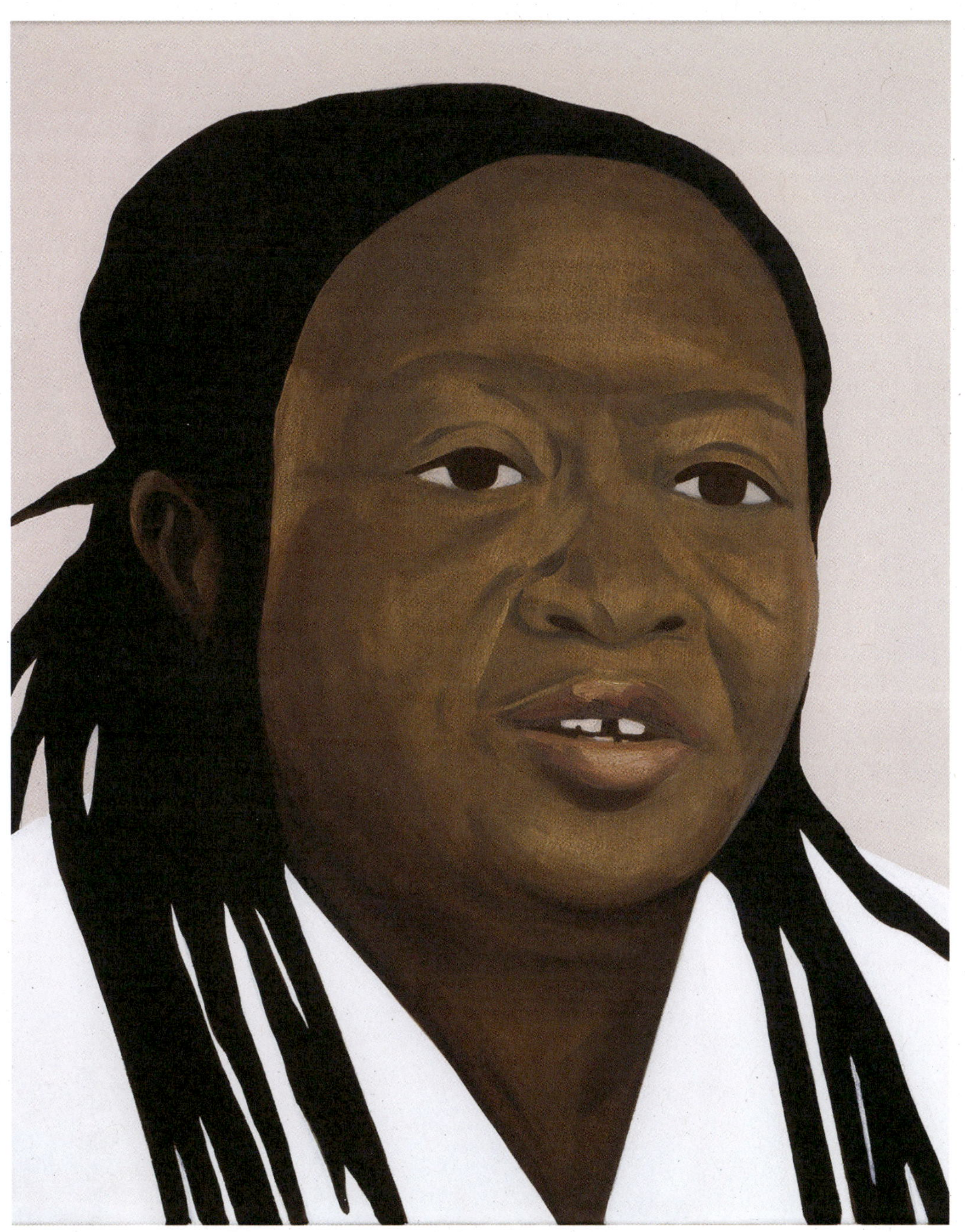

● '9604: *Creuza (After Creuza Maria Oliveira) (activist)*', 2018. Oil on canvas. *Courtesy of the artist.*

THANIA PETERSEN

Once Thania Petersen watched a TV series about a lawyer and for about two weeks she thought that she wanted to be one when she grew up. But for every other moment of her life before and after that, she knew she was going to be an artist. Art, music and theatre were all important parts of her family and her childhood.

Thania grew up between England and South Africa because her father went into political exile when she was still young. Every time she came back to South Africa she struggled to find where she could belong. She couldn't understand why people who looked like her, mixed race people, sometimes called Cape Malay people, were never in TV programmes or adverts.

She decided to make a video artwork as a gift to her children to show them some of their own heritage. She didn't want them to feel like she did, that they had no historical relevance in their own country. She also wanted to show them how wrong many history textbooks are about the group of people that they descend from. This artwork is called 'I AM ROYAL' and it totally changed her life, because everyone wanted to see it.

It has travelled to almost every continent and even to an island in Malaysia where people had to get to the exhibition by boat. She filmed some scenes with her children so that they could be part of the artwork.

'I AM ROYAL' is about how people have moved all over the world throughout history and settled in different parts that are new to them. Sometimes, like her family, they moved because they were forced to. Thania wanted to show her children that you should always search for your own truth.

For Thania, making art is a bit like putting out a call to others, to ask them 'Has anyone felt this way before? How did you deal with it? Can we learn from each other?' In this way it is a kind of therapy for her. And mostly, when she shows her work, there are many, many people who respond to her questions and feel less alone in their experiences. Thania has found that art is a language that creates new conversations. She believes that if you are passionate about something you are doing, art automatically enters, whether it is cooking or dressing or science. If you love what you do, art will be there.

● *Right: Illustration of 'Musallah', 2018. Embroidery thread, glass beads, fringing, cotton cloth.*

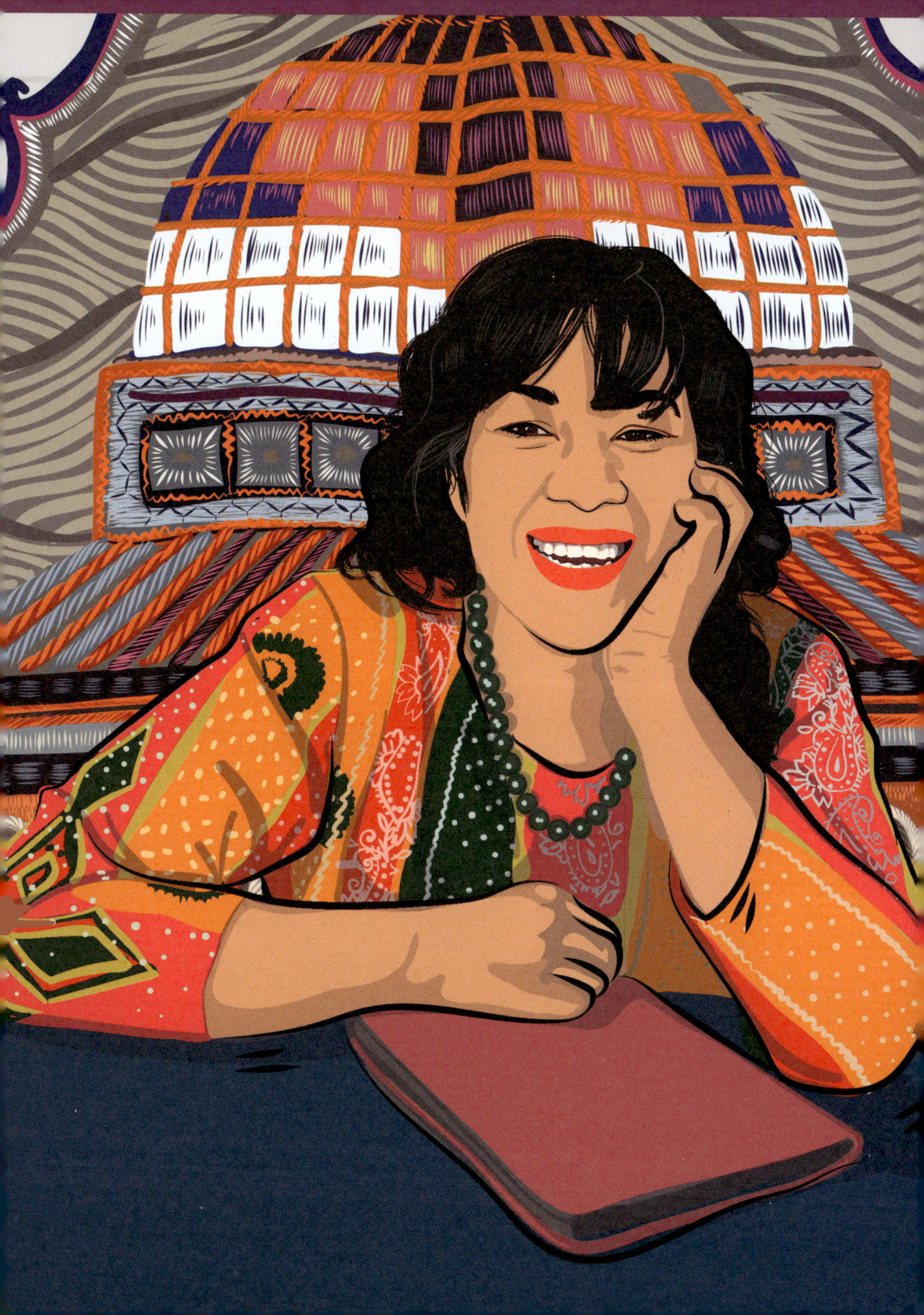

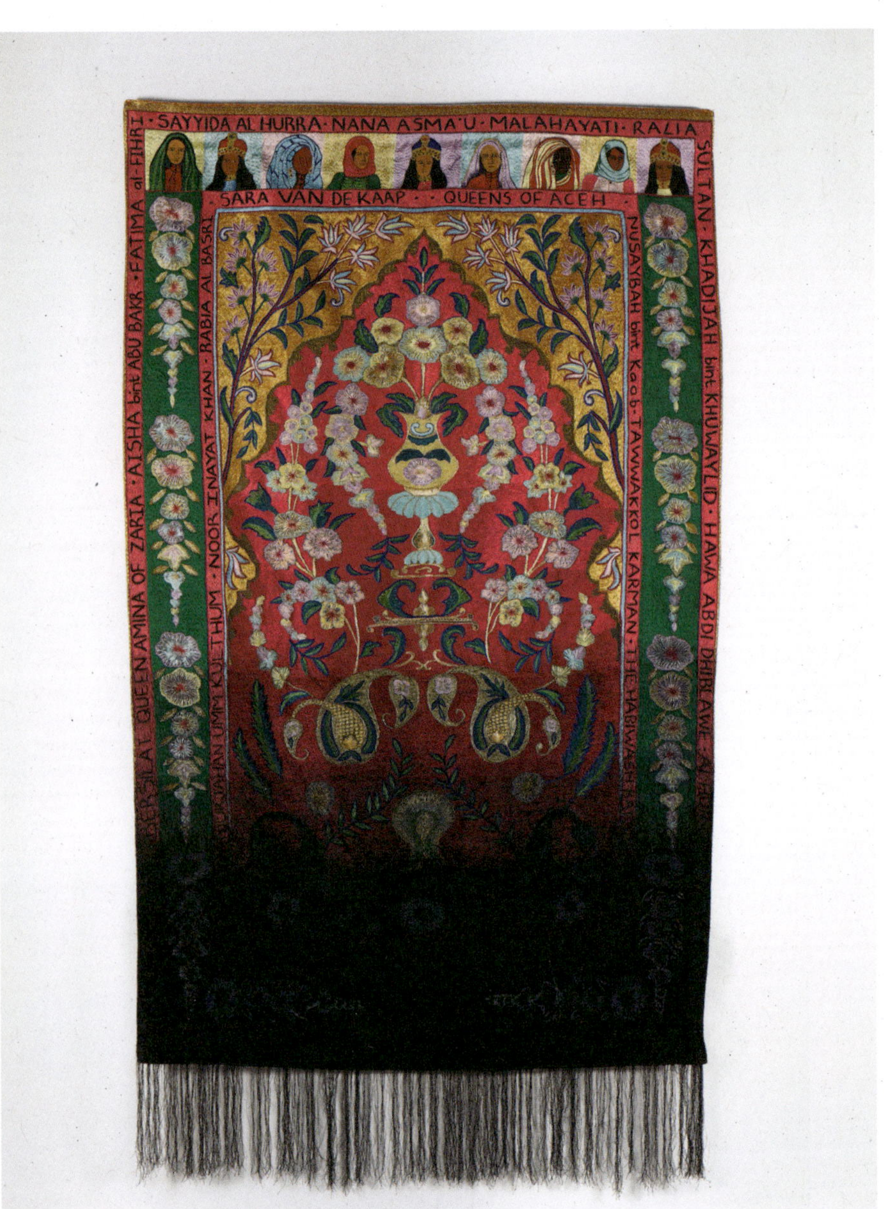

● 'Al Hurra', 2018. Embroidery thread, glass beads, fringing, cotton cloth. Courtesy of the artist and WHATIFTHEWORLD.

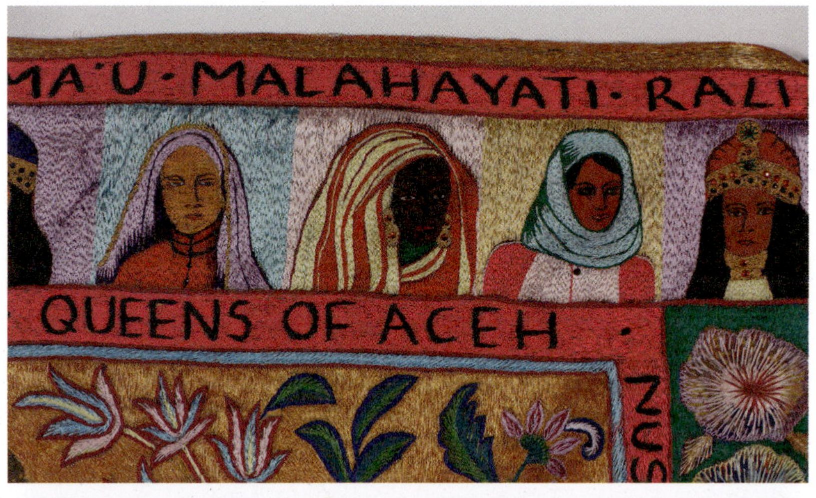

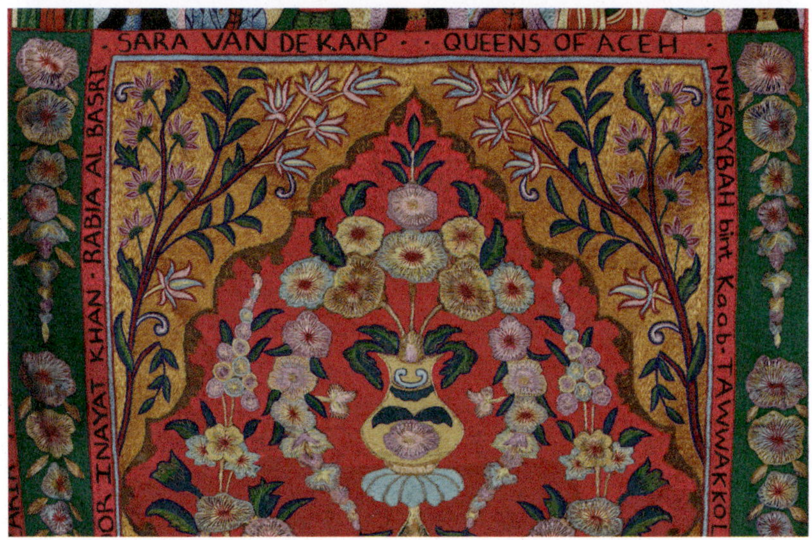

● *Detail of the same artwork.*

THULI MLAMBO-JAMES

Thuli Mlambo-James grew up in Soweto until the passing of her mother when she was a teenager. She then went to live with her aunt and uncle in eSwatini. The walls of their house had artworks of some very famous South African artists, such as Dumile Feni and Thami Myeni. Her mother had been an artist herself but she lived in South Africa at a time when there were no opportunities for black people to study art. This influenced Thuli, who knew art had to be part of her life somehow.

While Thuli was working in TV she saw an advert for a job as the director of the Bag Factory Artists' Studios, which is a very important art space in South Africa. She applied for the job, although she was very doubtful that they would take her seriously if she applied. Even while waiting her turn to be interviewed, she looked at the other applicants and thought, 'I will never be chosen'. But she got the job!

Becoming the first black director of the Bag Factory Artists' Studios was a very scary thing, because she had a lot of learning and work to do! But it was also a place where she could offer artists some studio space and the chance to meet other artists from around the globe. She was able to invite creative people to exhibit different artworks, including photography, drawing and painting.

But Thuli wanted to do more in the arts, so she left the Bag Factory and started her own arts business, which focuses on projects with artists from townships around the country. One of the big projects she did was bringing graffiti artists together to paint murals on the walls of the houses in townships. Figures of people and important social messages made up the graffiti created. Children in the community would come and watch as the artists painted the murals. They found it fun and very interesting to talk to the artists and also help spray paint small parts of the murals.

Thuli uses art to make a difference in people's lives. She says she will never give up working with local communities and giving them opportunities to make a living through art.

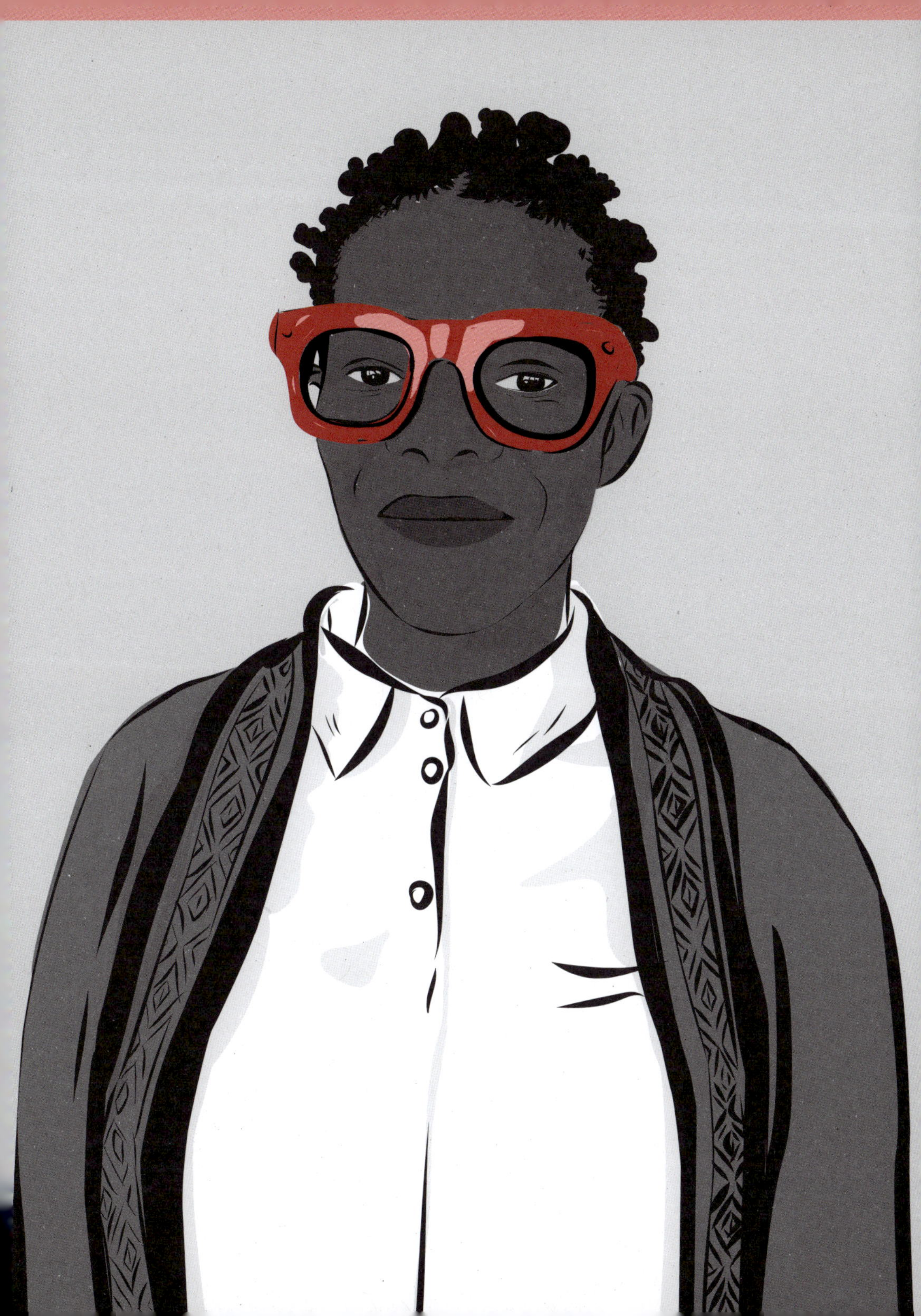

USHA SEEJARIM

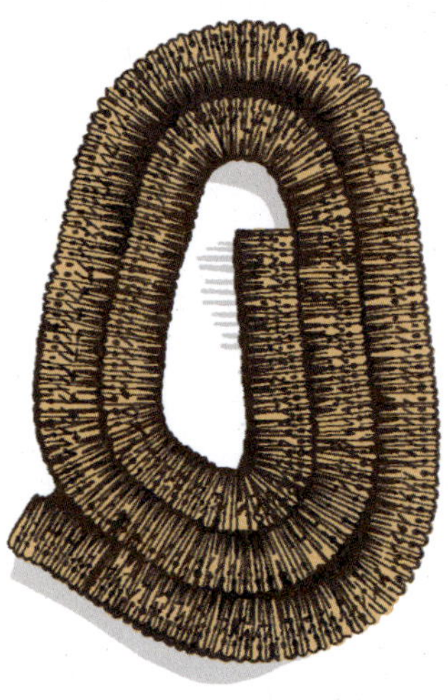

Usha never did art at school, because it wasn't offered, but when it was time to study she knew she wanted to try it. She found herself at a disadvantage because she had no art training and she failed her first year. When she repeated the year, she got terribly bored and despondent. For the first month she just sat in the canteen and played card games! Until one day, she decided that she would have to get herself out of this rut. She asked the life drawing teacher if she could join his classes. He said: 'You're welcome any time you want.' Usha spent most of that year in the life drawing class and in the library. She started doing so well that she got a bursary to do her master's degree and very soon after that she started exhibiting all over the world.

Usha is a conceptual artist and nowadays she finds it hard to explain exactly what kind of art she makes to people who are not used to contemporary art. They always assume she makes paintings or sculptures. But when she shows them a picture of her work, it becomes more clear, because she uses objects in her work that we all see and use every day. One of her first successful works was a life-size bathtub shaped out of bread tags. She also makes works out of broomsticks and by putting hundreds and hundreds of clothes pegs together. Usha likes the ordinary-ness of these objects and how your imagination can turn them into other things.

Usha believes art makes us see things in different ways. This is important because, unlike words, an artwork can have many different meanings for different people.

● Illustration of 'Kundalini in the Kitchen', 2019. Pegs and wire.

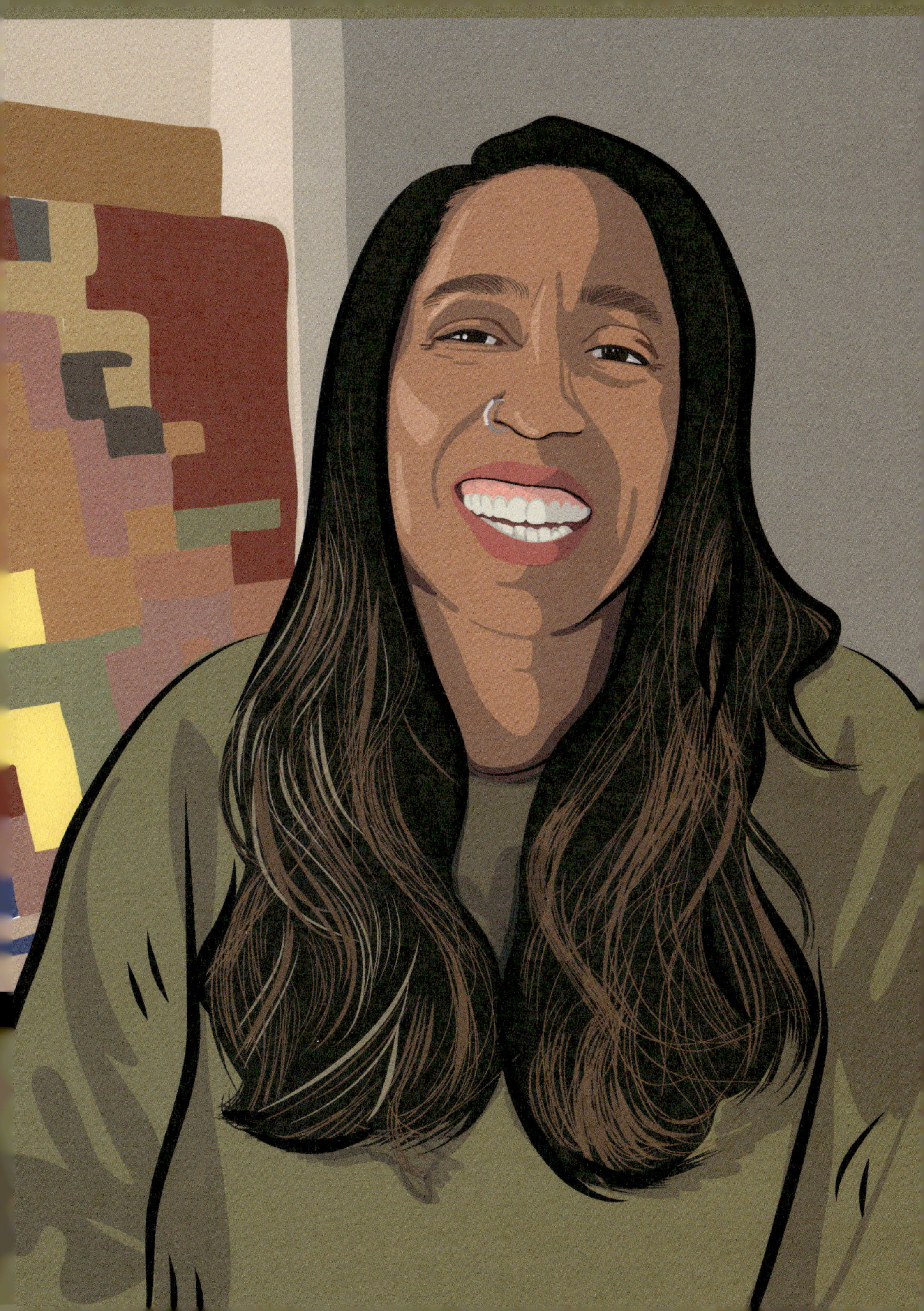

WAYNE BARKER

As a child running around in the veld of Pretoria, Wayne Barker was most interested in being the captain of the soccer team. His childhood was free and full of adventure. He thinks that spirit of adventure is what pushed him into the art world and he became a professional artist when he was still young. Wayne has spent his whole life making art and he doesn't mind if he has lots of money, or just enough to buy food, as long as he can make the art he wants to make.

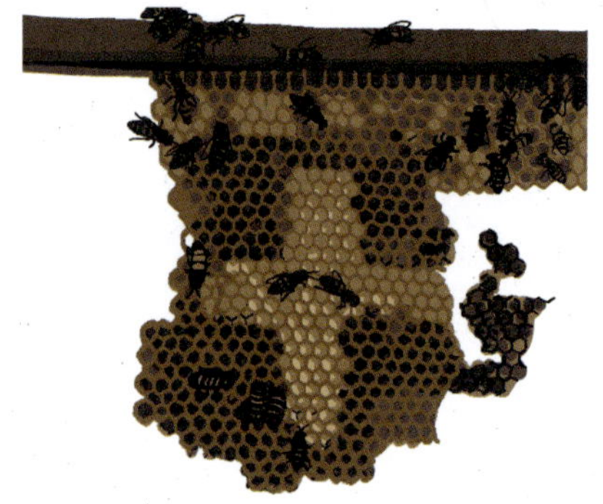

One day Wayne was invited to enter a competition where you had to use wax to make an art piece. It felt like a new adventure, so he wanted to give it a try. He got frustrated trying to paint with wax and, while he was working late one night, he threw the hot wax onto the canvas and then went to bed. When he opened his eyes the next morning, he couldn't believe it, his canvas was covered in bees!

That day he decided to make an artwork with the bees. He learnt a lot about how bees work and asked an expert beekeeper to teach him. He learnt that beehives in apiaries are made from a tiny mesh in a frame and inserted into a box. There are many frames side by side in one box. He thought it would be fun to ask the little children who lived in the same block of flats as he did to trace their hands on paper, cut them out and stick them onto the mesh. Then Wayne used the handprints to cut hand shapes out of the mesh so that there was a hand-shaped hole in the middle. He also made crosses into some of the mesh. He put the frames back into the box and left them for a couple of weeks. When they came back, no one could believe what had happened.

The bees had created wax strands over the hand-shaped holes that were cut into the mesh and when you held it up to the light there was a lighter shade of wax that made the picture of a child's hand, or a cross. Wayne said that the bees 'healed' the hands that were cut out of the mesh.

Healing is an important theme in Wayne's artworks because he believes that South Africa's violent history has created a lot of pain and misunderstanding and there is a need for people to heal.

● *Illustration of 'The Bees, the Beekeeper, the Children and the Artist', 2007–2008. Bees wax.*

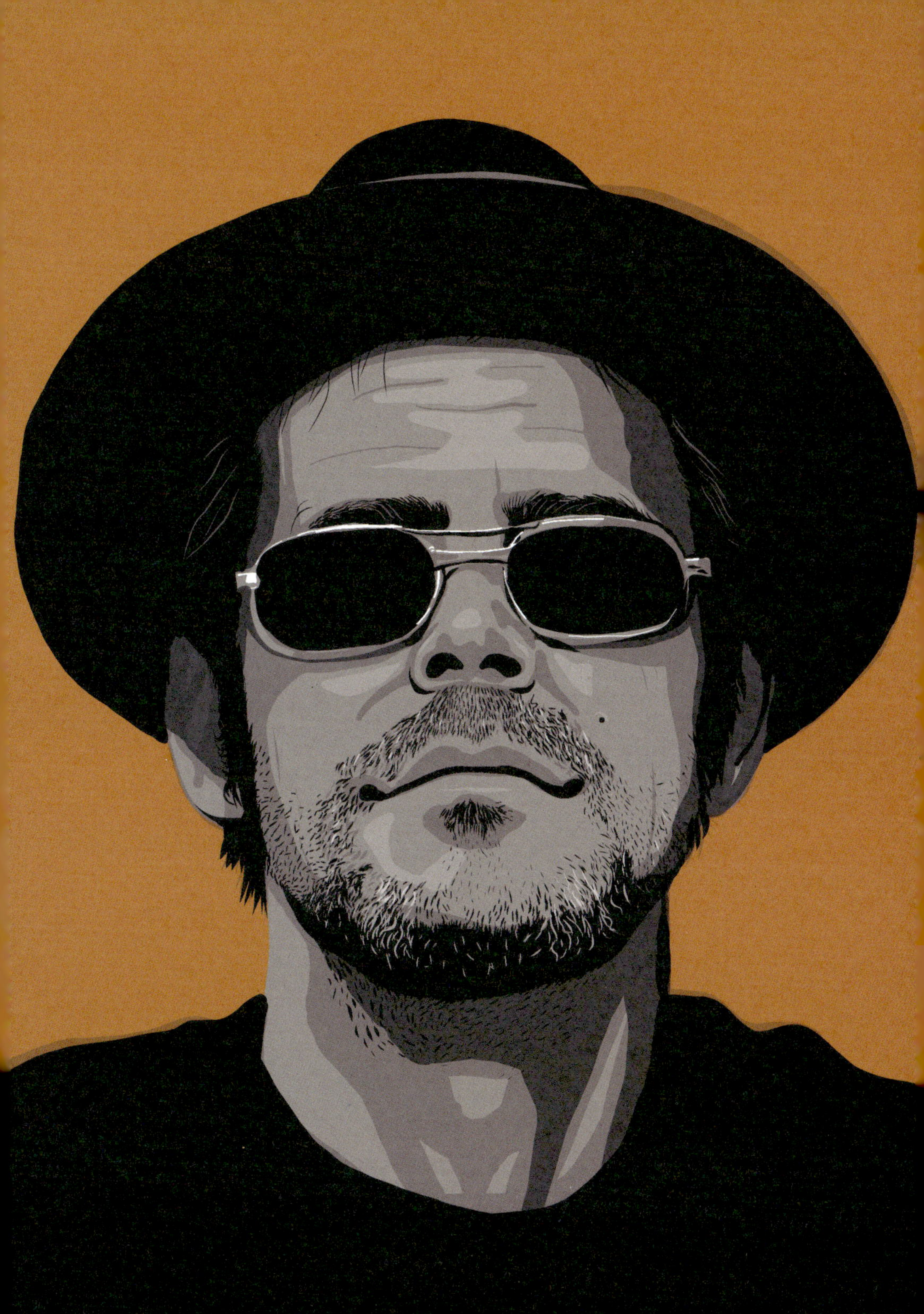

William Kentridge

Some areas of Johannesburg are beautifully green, and some areas are dry and dusty. William Kentridge grew up in the green parts where hundreds of trees were planted when the city was first formed. At the bottom of William's garden was a group of fir trees and the veranda had a mosaic table. He loved looking at those mosaic tiles and he spent a lot of time with the trees. But as his family drove out of the suburbs on trips, he would notice how other parts of the city had been left to show the real dryness of Johannesburg. That meant that some people had comfortable lives, and others didn't.

William's family was politically involved in fighting apartheid, but it took some time for William to understand it all. His father was a defense lawyer for the famous Treason Trials, where 156 people, including Helen Joseph, were accused by the government. He thought when his father went to the Treason Trials, he went to the bottom of the garden to be with the trees and tiles!

When William finished university he didn't know if he should draw, or act, or make films. People told him 'If you try do too many things you'll never get good at any of it.' He stopped drawing and went to Paris to study acting, but it didn't feel right. He then came back to South Africa to try to make films, but that didn't quite work either. It took him many years to throw away that bit of advice and create artworks using drawing and film and acting and music. That's the kind of work that William became famous for all over the world and in many of his works he tries to understand the different landscapes in South Africa that he noticed as a child.

Another idea that has been important to William is what he calls 'peripheral thinking'. You know the way you can see things out of the corner of your eye without really looking there? That means your eye is busy looking at things without you knowing it. Peripheral thinking is a similar concept, where the brain thinks about things without you concentrating on them. Drawing is a way to allow peripheral thinking to come out. While you are concentrating on the drawing, thoughts form without you directing them.

In this way, William sees his studio as a place where the world around him can be taken apart and put back together by thinking and making art. Although he has worked and travelled all around the globe, it is still in his studio that he learns most about the world.

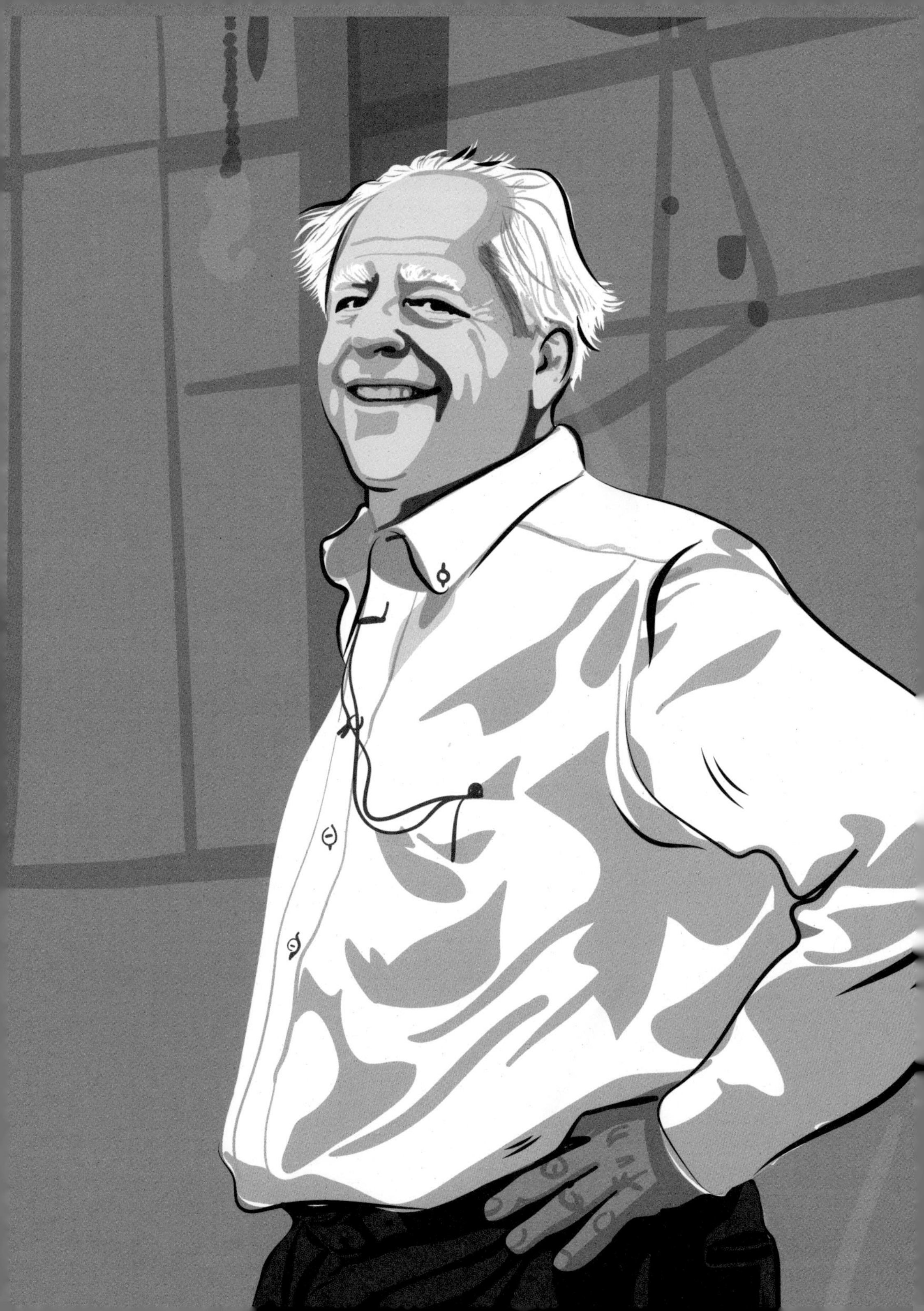

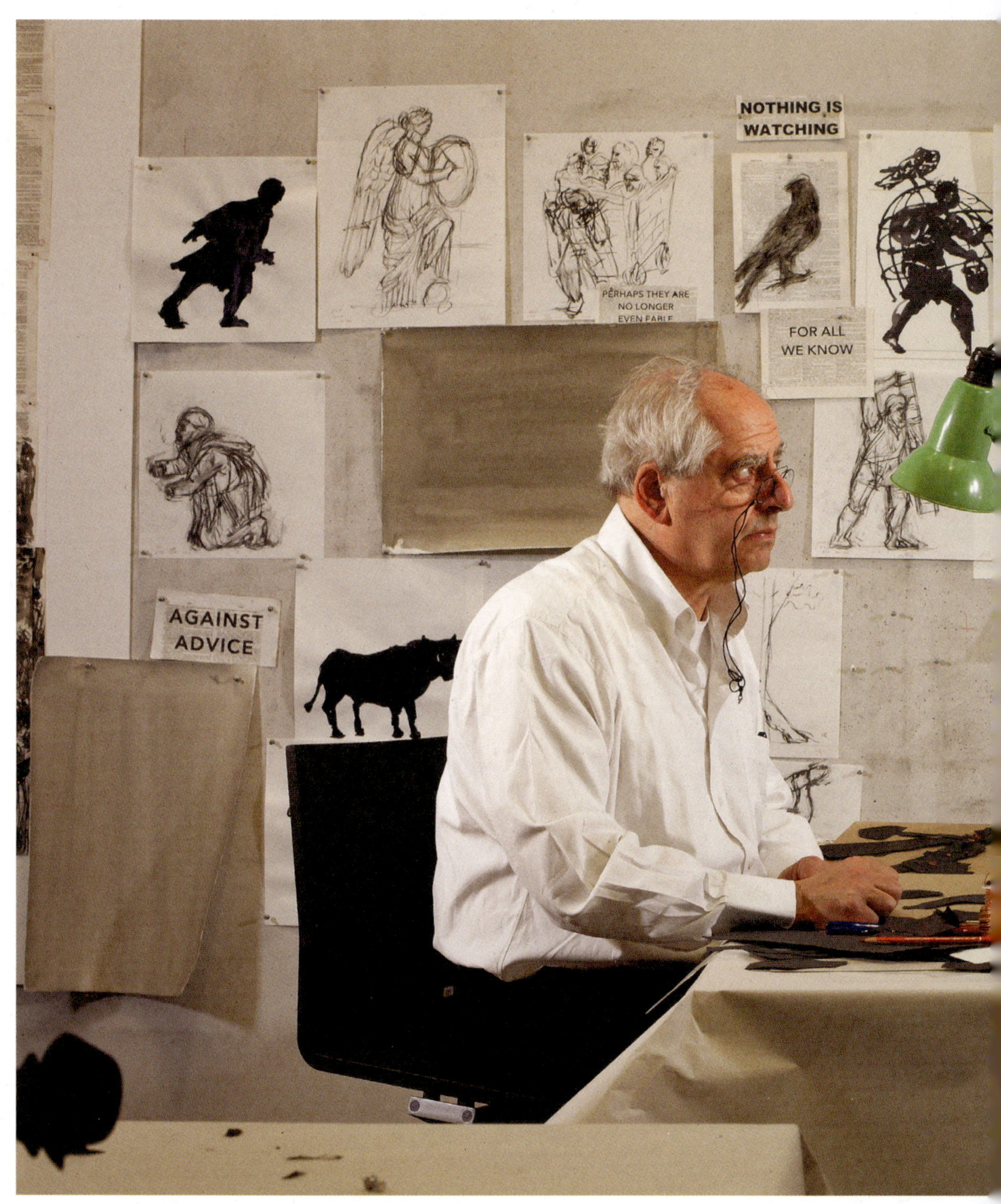

● *'Triumphs and Laments', 2013. Photograph. Courtesy of the artist.*

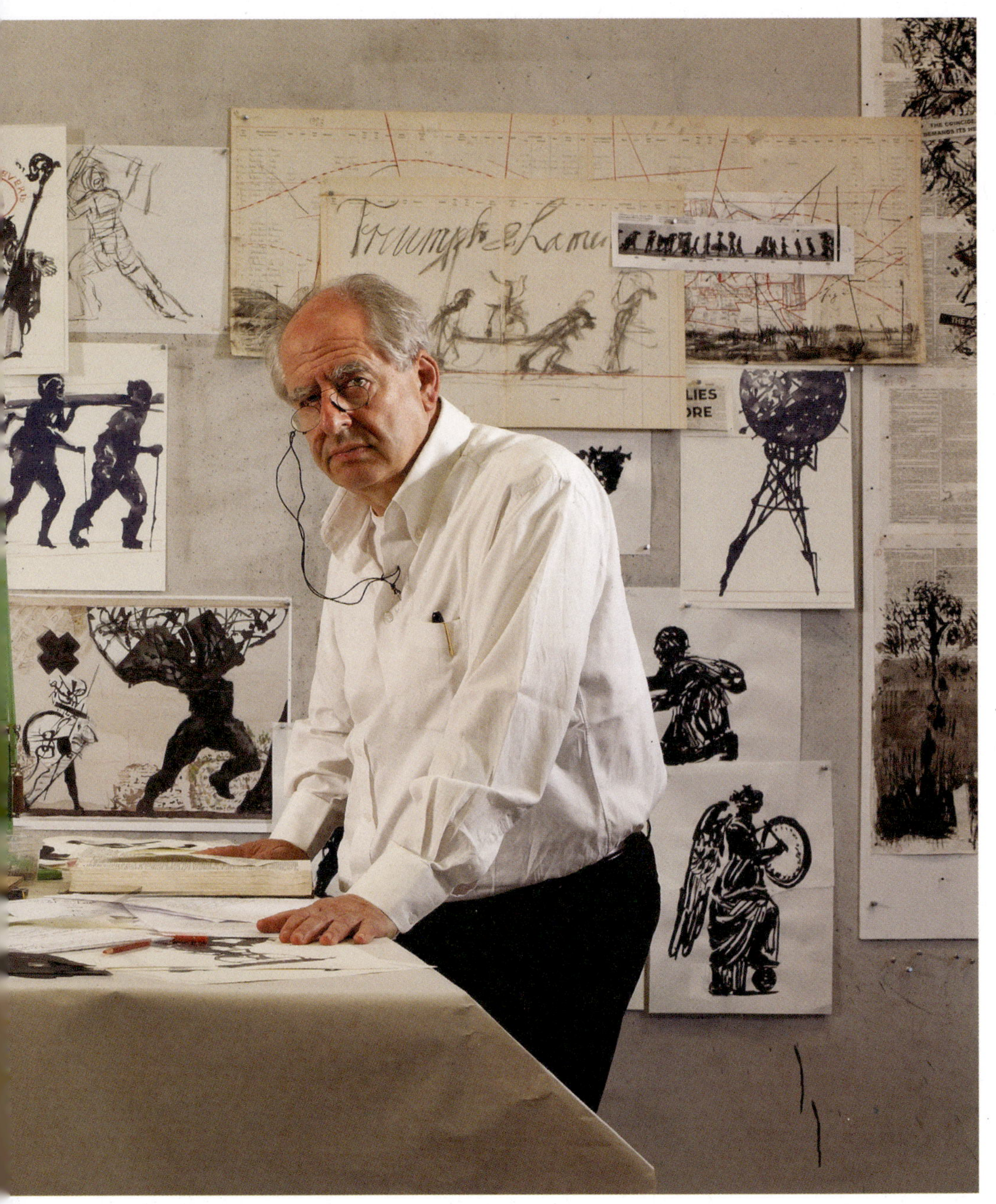

ZANDER BLOM

If you happen to drive through the small holiday town of Strand in the Western Cape, you might notice one house that stands out from the rest. The front of this house is covered with paintings of animals and birds in a forest. On the other side is a giant underwater scene with fish and seaweed. This was Zander Blom's family holiday home, which they all painted together. And the reason it looks so different from the houses around it is probably because the life they lived in that house and in their house in Pretoria was so different from their neighbours'. Zander's mother was always busy making jewellery, pottery and painting and getting the three children involved.

So it might not come as a surprise that the only thing Zander ever really wanted to do was be an artist. But his parents were worried that he might not be able to support himself, so he went to study graphic design. Although Zander tried it out for a while, he realised that if he was honest with himself, he didn't want to give up his time for anything that anyone else wanted him to do. 'Because,' he says, 'if you do something that makes you happy you have way more chances of doing it well.'

When he started to make his own art, he mostly took photographs and it wasn't that long before a big South African gallery wanted to show his work. Since then, many books have been published on his work, and his paintings and photographs have been exhibited all over the world. These exhibitions and people buying his work has made it possible to do what his father never thought possible: to live as an artist without having to do other jobs for other people.

An important part of his life and his personality is that he understood from an early age that if you want to make something happen, you have to do it for yourself. When he was still in high school and university he organised little group exhibitions with his friends in someone's garage, printing hundreds of flyers and dropping them off all over Pretoria. Zander makes the comparison with someone who wants to be a musician. 'You get musicians sitting around waiting for someone to sell their music for them, and then you get those who go out and perform as much as they can to find an audience.' Zander believes you have to create your own audience.

• *Right background: Illustration of 'Untitled or The Boulevard, Bedroom 1, Corner 2, 5.11 p.m., Friday, 1 June 2007'. Photograph.*

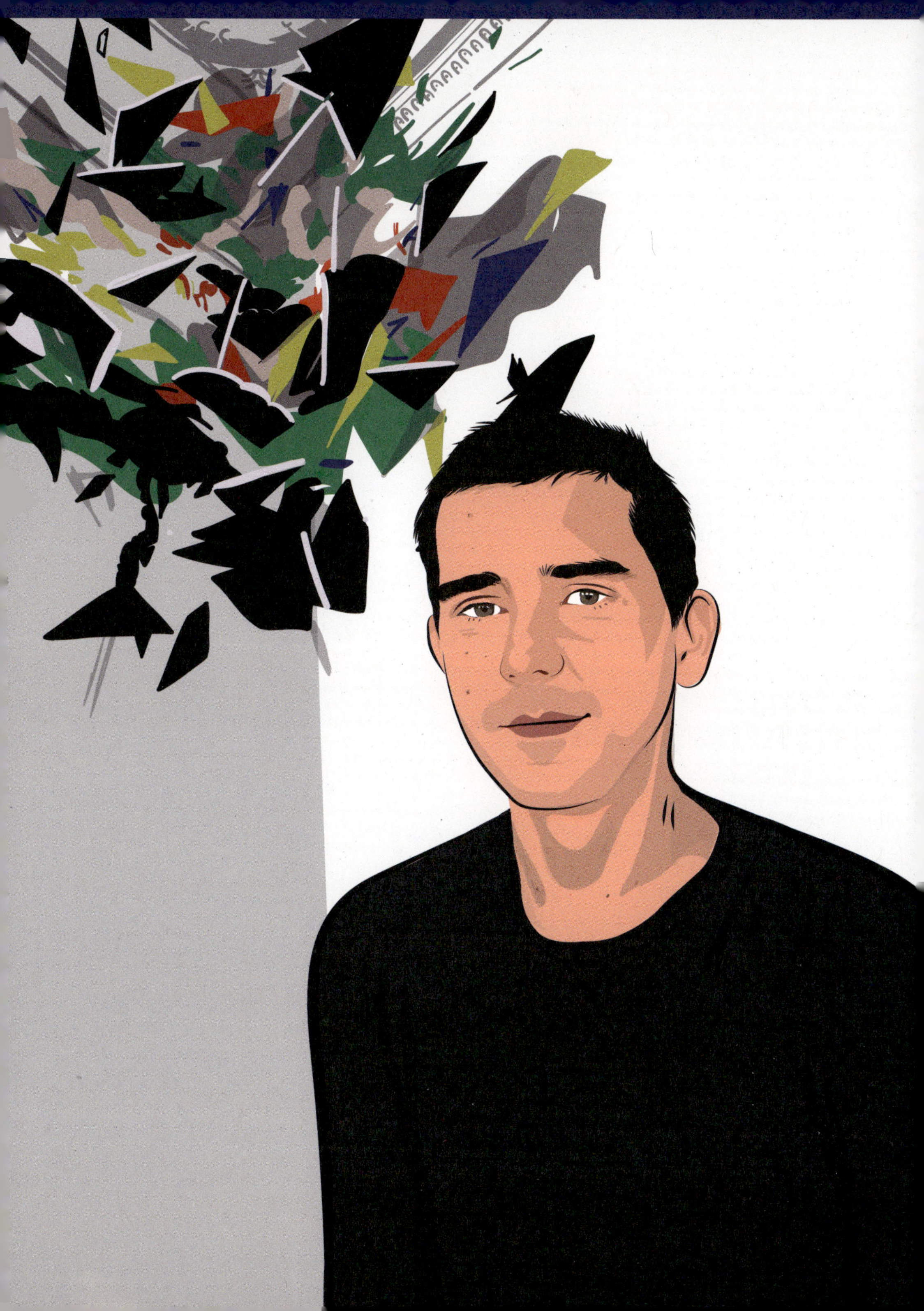

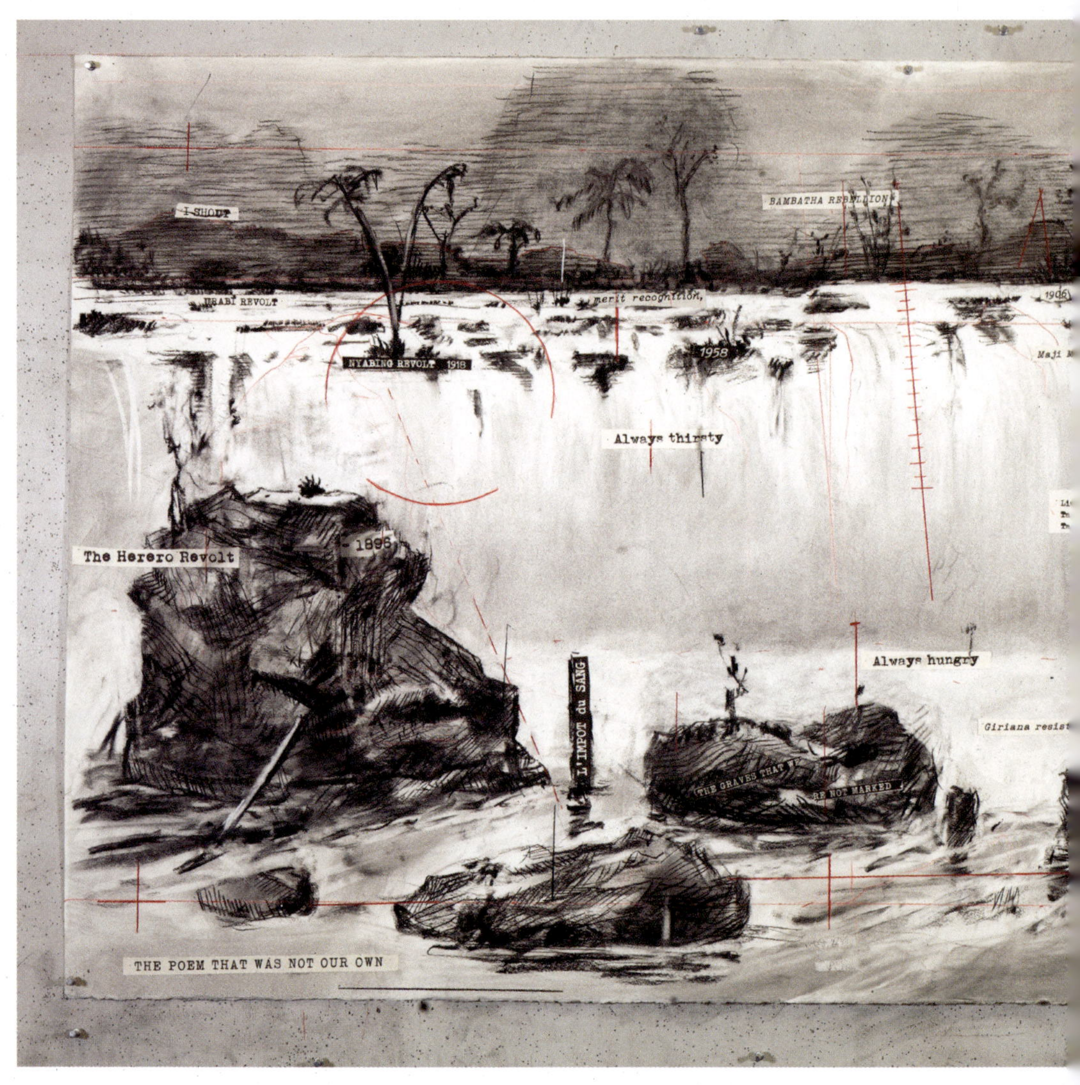

● *William Kentridge. Drawing for 'The Head & the Load', 2018. Charcoal and computer printed texts on paper. Courtesy of the artist.*

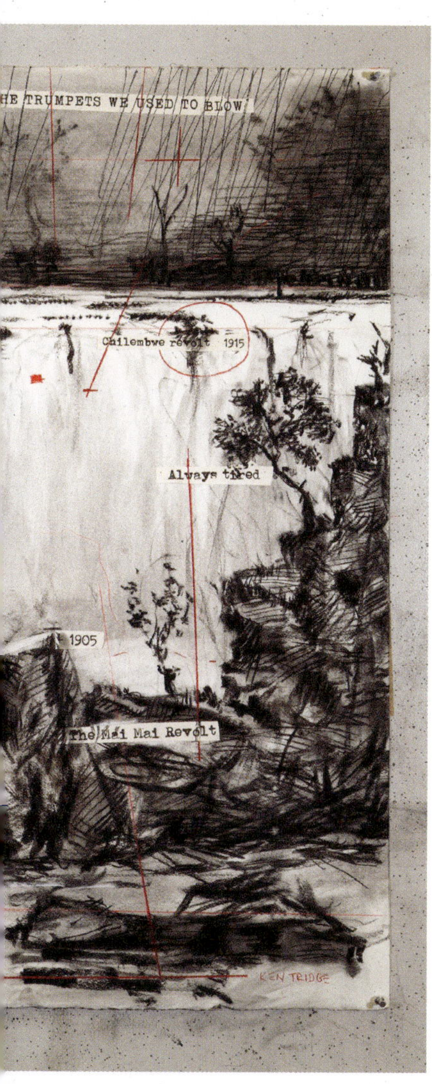

ARTLOGIC

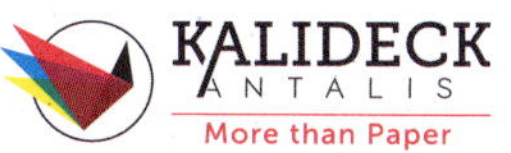

Acknowledgements

A project with so many elements and moving parts needs someone that is always there to bring perspective and advice. For that I thank my husband, Nduka Mntambo. Ellen and Lunga also offered wonderful ideas throughout. I would like to thank Nicole Siegenthaler for her astute project management, without which the project might have taken several years longer. Thank you, too, to my father, Jan Labuscagne, for being supportive and enthusiastic. Efemia Chela has been indispensable not only as an editor, but also to help it take shape, thank you! Thanks to all the galleries who represent these artists for continually assisting and sending all the information we needed. A special thanks goes to Eben and the team at Breinstorm for bringing so much magic to the pages with their design work. Thanks to Artlogic for supporting this project and for all these years of immersing me in the world of contemporary African art and placing me at the very forefront of trends and ideas. Thanks to Carol Broomhall at Jacana Media for believing in it when it was just an idea and for advice and guidance throughout. I shared the book with Lauren as the illustrator from the very beginning and am very grateful for her generosity in time and creativity.

Explore! printed on Lenza Green

Kalidek Antalis is proud to introduce Lenza Green, a high-quality recycled paper produced from 100% recovered fibre. Manufactured without chlorine bleaching, Lenza Green's high whiteness is thanks to a special converting process for recovered fibre. It boasts high opacity, good sheet information and good ageing resistance, as well as excellent usability on all types of processing machinery. Lenza Green is suitable for laser and inkjet. Because great paper loves great art, Lenza Green brilliantly brings to life the work of SA's top contemporary artists in *Explore! Awesome South African Artists*.

Buhlebezwe Siwani

JYOTI MISTRY

CAMERON PLATTER

KAREL NEL

DAVID KOLOANE

KELEKETLA! LIBRARY

Frances Goodman

KEMANG WA LEHULERE

GaBrieLle gOliAtH

LADY SKOLLIE

Igshaan Adams

makgati molebatsi

Jo Ractliffe

MarK AtTwood

JULIA CHARLTON

MIKHAEL SUBOTZKY

JUSTIN DINGWALL

MMAKGABO MAPULA HELEN SEBIDI